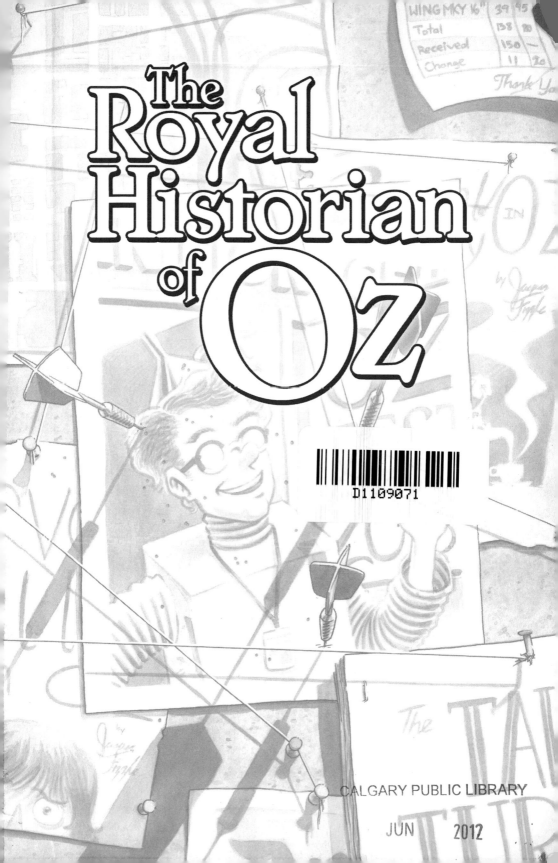

The Royal Historian of Oz

The Royal Historian of Oz

Written by
Tommy Kovac

Drawn by
Andy Hirsch

Logo Design by
Bryan Dobrow

ISBN-13: 978-1-59362-216-9
First Printing: September 2011

Published by SLG Publishing
P.O. Box 26427
San Jose, CA 95159
www.slgcomic.com

Table of Contents

"More Royal Historians than You Can Shake a Stick At"

By Eric Shanower

The Wonderful Wizard of Oz by L. Frank Baum was published in 1900. The book and the subsequent Broadway musical based on it were hits and made Baum rich, prompting him to write thirteen full-length Oz sequels, an Oz picture book, and more than thirty Oz short stories during the remainder of his life. He called himself the Royal Historian of Oz.

Upon Baum's death in 1919, the publishers of the Oz series, Reilly & Lee, didn't want to let their cash cow die. They contracted with Baum's widow for the Oz series to continue and hired a succession of Royal Historians of Oz. Ruth Plumly Thompson wrote nineteen Oz books until she finally got tired of it in 1939. Then John R. Neill, illustrator of all the Oz books up to that point except the first, wrote three. After Neill died in 1943 the series slowed down. Jack Snow wrote two Oz books later in the 1940s. In 1951 the publishers tried to inject some life back into the series with a new Oz book by Rachel R. Cosgrove (Payes), but sales didn't warrant continuing. The publishers tried another reboot in 1963 with the fortieth and final "official" Oz book by Newbery Honor author Eloise Jarvis McGraw and her co-author daughter Lauren Lynn McGraw—to little avail. The Oz series seemed to have petered out.

The Oz series, however, refused to die. Before the 1950s, there was only a bare trickle of "unofficial" Oz books. Invisible Inzi of Oz was dictated by Ouija board to Virginia and Robert Wauchope and serialized in the magazine A Child's Garden in 1925-26, fully sanctioned by Baum's widow, Maud. In 1936 Whitman Publishing brought out The Laughing Dragon of Oz as a Big Little Book. This wasn't sanctioned by Maud Baum and she fought an embittering legal battle with the book's author, her eldest son Frank.

Then three events occurred in the late 1950s that helped turn Oz around, laying the groundwork for the many continuations of Oz that surround us today.

First, in 1956 The Wonderful Wizard of Oz entered the public domain. From that time on Baum's heirs were no longer sole owners of the story. Every single person in the world could now do whatever he or she liked with The Wonderful Wizard of Oz. Many have.

Second, also in 1956, the 1939 M-G-M motion picture adaptation of The Wizard of Oz starring Judy Garland was first broadcast on network television. It proved so popular that it became an annual tradition for decades, cementing the story and characters as icons of American culture and spawning nearly its own industry of toys, collectibles, and other ephemera.

Third, in 1957 a thirteen-year-old Brooklyn boy named Justin Schiller brought together fifteen other Oz enthusiasts and chartered The International Wizard of Oz Club, where Oz lovers of all stripes have since united to share their enthusiasm for Oz in all its multiple forms.

As the "official" Oz series slowed in the 1950s and began to go out of print in the 1960s, Oz fans composed their own Oz stories. Some published their efforts privately for distribution to other Oz lovers, while in the Soviet Union, Alexander Volkov was busy writing a whole new series of Oz books in which Oz is instead known as Magic Land. The trickle was growing.

By the early 1970s the trickle was becoming a stream. The International Wizard of Oz Club inaugurated Oziana, its annual magazine of new Oz fiction written by Oz fans, and the Oz Club began a series of new Oz books by writers associated with the "official" Oz series, including Ruth Plumly Thompson, Eloise Jarvis McGraw and Lauren Lynn McGraw, and Rachel Cosgrove Payes.

In the 1980s, when most of L. Frank Baum's works entered the public domain, the stream grew into a major river. New Oz books appeared from publishers large and small. Oz comics—whose sporadic appearances until then had consisted mainly of Oz parodies, adaptations of the Oz books, and adaptations of adaptations—burst onto the scene with brand new Oz stories, equivalents of the "unofficial" Oz books already appearing. Walt Disney Pictures released a new feature film, Return to Oz. It wasn't a financial success, but it helped prompt the "official" Oz series back into print and spawned even more "unofficial" Oz books.

In the 1990s with the advent of easy desktop publishing, the river turned into a flood. Every time an Oz lover turned around there was a new Oz book or comic to read—from those written by classes of elementary school children to Gregory Maguire's best-selling Wicked.

Today, the flood has yet to abate. Large companies, small companies, do-it-yourselfers—they're all squeezing out Oz books, Oz comics, Oz movies. If anyone who writes an Oz story can be considered a Royal Historian of Oz, then the number of Royal Historians has become legion. And there doesn't seem to be an end in sight.

Of course, their works vary in quality. Which brings me to Jasper Fizzle, a man you're about to meet in the Oz comic you're reading right now—The Royal Historian of Oz by Tommy Kovac and Andy Hirsch. Jasper Fizzle writes Oz books with titles such as Muffin McClane, the Manliest Munchkin in Oz and Percival T. Cozy in Oz. These don't sound so awful when compared with actual published "unofficial" Oz titles like Radioactive Teddy Bear from H*** Destroys Oz and Three-Headed Elvis Clone Found in Flying Saucer Over Oz. (At least, they don't sound as awful to me. Tastes differ.) But the actual texts of Jasper's works are bad. Very bad. Officially bad—as officially judged by the Official Oz Society. Not even Jasper's nearest and dearest, his son Frank, can manage to completely hide his distaste for Jasper's Oz books.

I have to laugh at the idea of an Official Oz Society that can decide what a "true" Oz book is. While there are certainly similarities between Royal Historian's Official Oz Society and the real life International Wizard of Oz Club (which I've belonged to since I was nine, and, no, none of my dogs have ever been named Toto, thank you very much), imagining a group of Oz fans reaching a consensus of what constitutes a "real" Oz story is almost impossible. It's sort of like religion. No one agrees with anyone else one hundred per cent.

But I understand Jasper Fizzle's needs and motivations. I sympathize with him completely. As he says near the beginning of the story:

> I remember how much the original Oz stories meant to me when I was younger. How I clung to them for dear life. Those characters were my friends, and they rescued me from reality. I want to do that for other people.

I, myself, remember how much I loved the Oz books when I was a child, how I dreamed of finding my way to Oz somehow or other, how I cajoled my playmates into pretending we were Oz characters, how I wrote and illustrated my own Oz book manuscripts and even persuaded my third grade teacher to read one aloud to the whole class. I know where Jasper's coming from. And I, like him, continue to produce Oz stories into adulthood.

But although I have much in common with Jasper Fizzle, his son, Frank, is the character I'd like to be—even though Frank has the onerous task of trying to keep his dad centered. Frank's the one who gets to visit the Emerald City, who gets to meet all the traditional Oz characters, who gets to have a real Oz adventure.

Well, I better stop before I reveal too much. You should really go ahead and read the story. I'll just mention one thing more. When Jasper Fizzle says, "L. Frank Baum only got things half-right," he seems to be correct. You've been warned.

1
"A Lapse in Judgement"

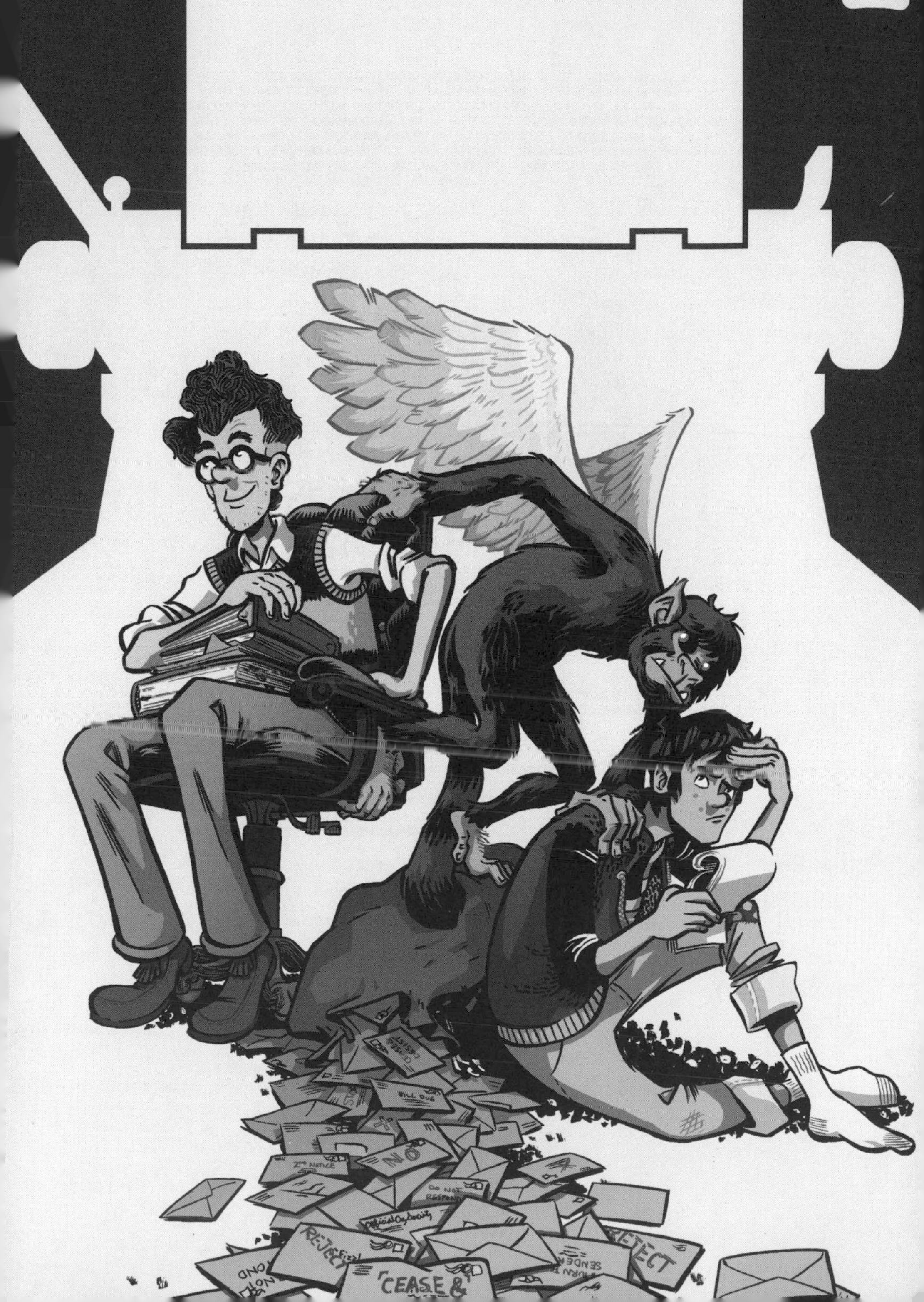
NO
REJECT
CEASE &

MY NAME IS FRANK FIZZLE, AND I DO PLAN TO CHANGE IT SOMEDAY.
IT WAS MY DAD'S DOING. HE NAMED ME AFTER L. FRANK BAUM, THE AUTHOR OF
THE WONDERFUL WIZARD OF OZ. MOST PEOPLE (WHO AREN'T MY DAD) DON'T KNOW THAT BAUM
WROTE **FOURTEEN** BOOKS ABOUT THE LAND OF OZ. HE CALLED HIMSELF "THE ROYAL HISTORIAN
OF OZ," AND PRETENDED THAT OZ REALLY EXISTED, AND HE WAS JUST REPORTING THE EVENTS
THAT WENT ON IN THAT "FAIRYLAND." THAT WAS OVER A HUNDRED YEARS AGO, THOUGH, SO I
FIGURE KIDS MUST HAVE BEEN EVEN STUPIDER THEN THAN THEY ARE NOW.

ANYWAY, AFTER BAUM DIED ANOTHER AUTHOR TOOK OVER, CONTINUING BAUM'S WORK.
THEN WHEN THAT PERSON WAS SICK OF IT, OR DEAD OR WHATEVER, **ANOTHER** WRITER TOOK
OVER, BANGING OUT MORE STORIES ABOUT OZ.

LOTS OF WRITERS HAVE TRIED TO CARRY ON LIKE BAUM, PRETENDING THAT
THEY'RE RELATING **REAL** EVENTS GOING ON THERE. SOME WERE FAIRLY SUCCESSFUL, AND
OTHERS TOTALLY FAILED. COMMERCIALLY AND ARTISTICALLY. YOU COULD FILL A BUNCH OF
WAREHOUSES WITH ALL THE BOOKS, MOVIES, TOYS, COMICS, GAMES, AND OTHER OZ CRAP
THAT'S BEEN PRODUCED. MOST OF IT SUCKS. BUT PEOPLE JUST CAN'T STOP PLAYING AROUND
WITH OZ.

THE LAST "OFFICIAL" OZ WRITER DIED OF BLOCKED BOWELS OR SOMETHING, AROUND 2050.
THEY HAVEN'T SELECTED A REPLACEMENT YET. THAT'S WHERE MY FATHER COMES IN. HE'S
DETERMINED TO BE RECOGNIZED AS THE NEW **"ROYAL HISTORIAN OF OZ."**

THE PROBLEM IS MY FATHER'S WRITING. IT'S, UM... WELL, YOU HAVE TO REALIZE HIS HEART'S
IN THE RIGHT PLACE, BUT... I MEAN... WELL...

⇒SIGH⇐

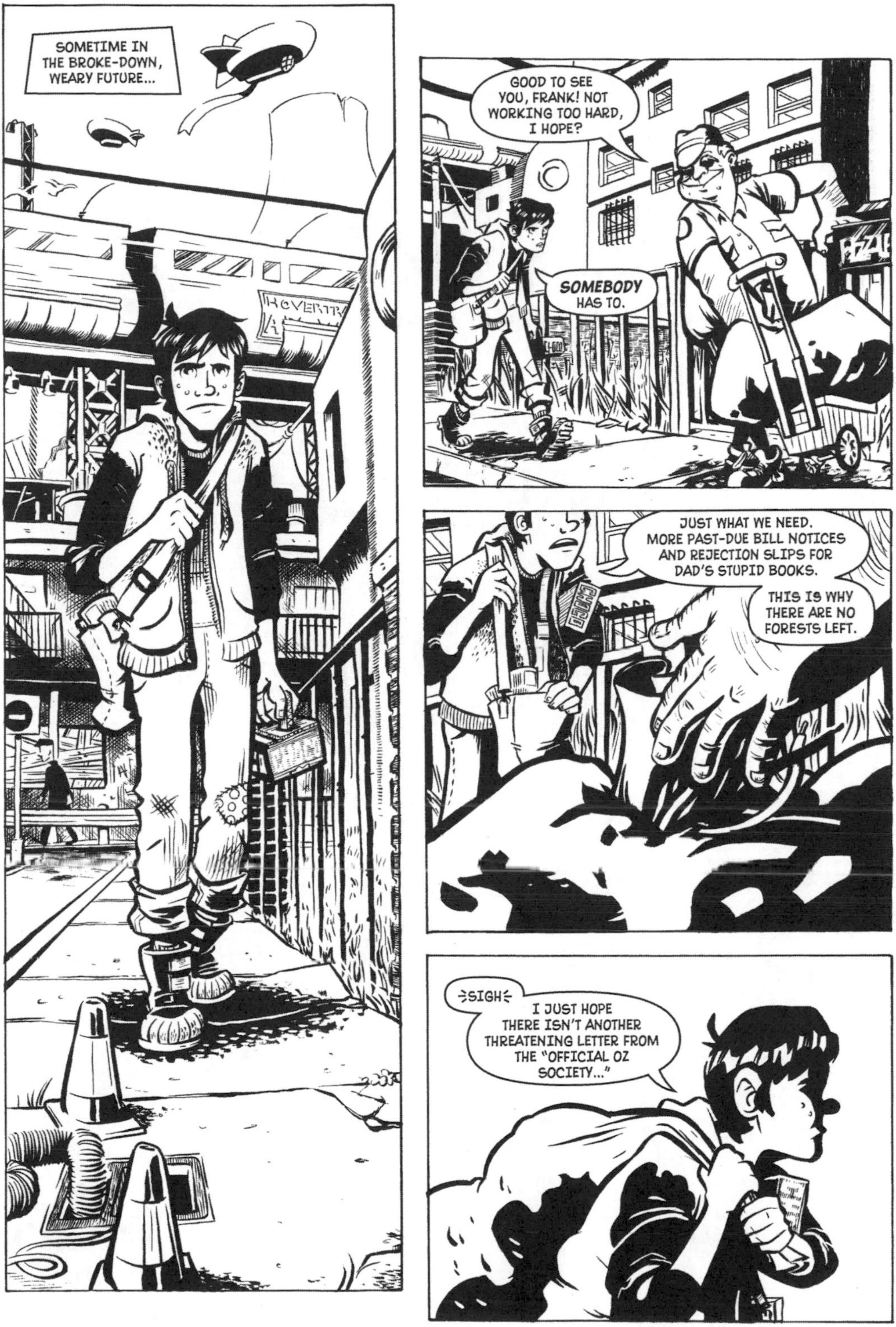
SOMETIME IN THE BROKE-DOWN, WEARY FUTURE...
GOOD TO SEE YOU, FRANK! NOT WORKING TOO HARD, I HOPE?
SOMEBODY HAS TO.
JUST WHAT WE NEED. MORE PAST-DUE BILL NOTICES AND REJECTION SLIPS FOR DAD'S STUPID BOOKS.
THIS IS WHY THERE ARE NO FORESTS LEFT.
SIGH
I JUST HOPE THERE ISN'T ANOTHER THREATENING LETTER FROM THE "OFFICIAL OZ SOCIETY..."

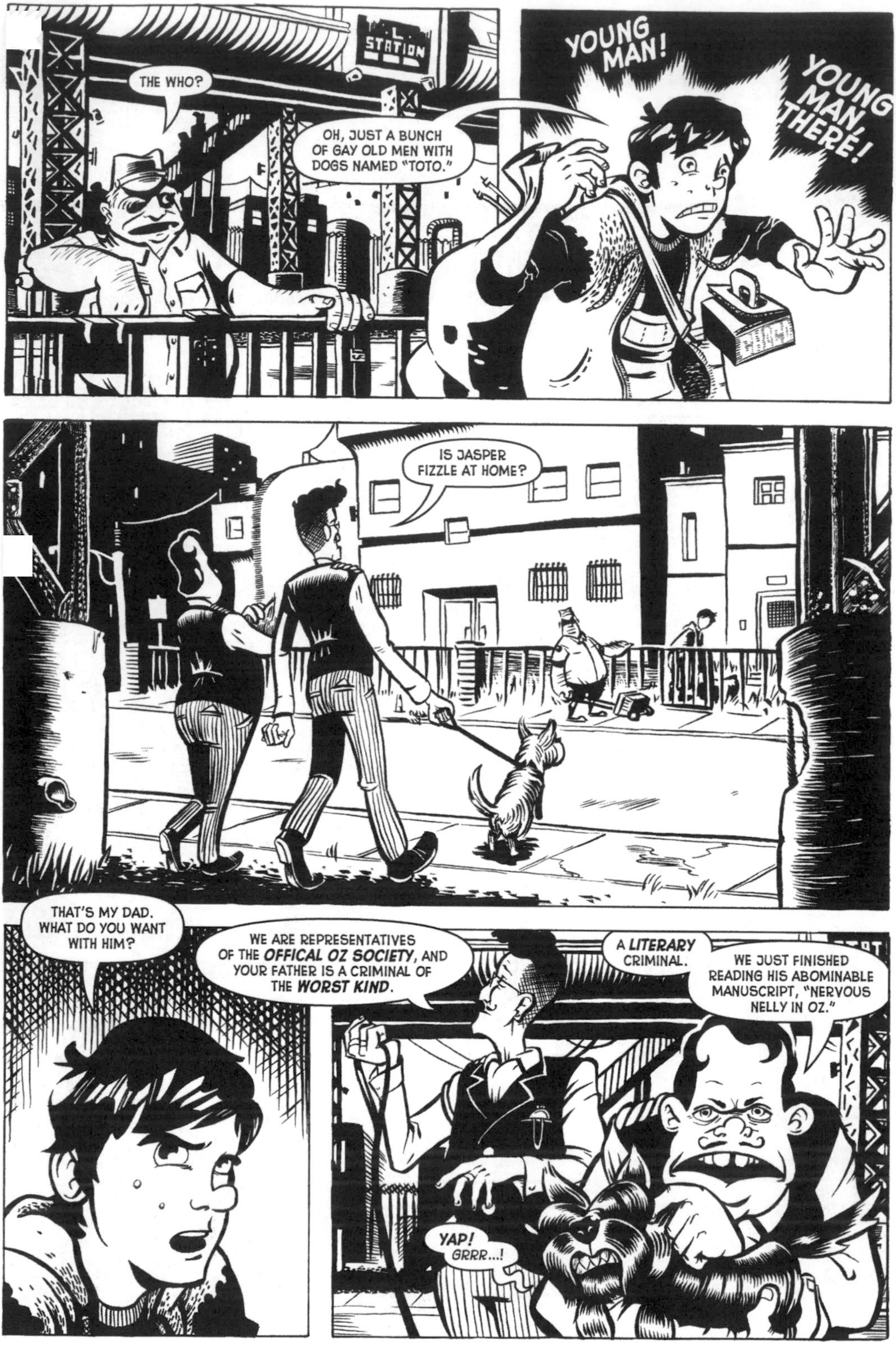
L STATION
THE WHO?
OH, JUST A BUNCH OF GAY OLD MEN WITH DOGS NAMED "TOTO."
YOUNG MAN!
YOUNG MAN, THERE!
IS JASPER FIZZLE AT HOME?
THAT'S MY DAD. WHAT DO YOU WANT WITH HIM?
WE ARE REPRESENTATIVES OF THE OFFICAL OZ SOCIETY, AND YOUR FATHER IS A CRIMINAL OF THE WORST KIND.
A LITERARY CRIMINAL.
WE JUST FINISHED READING HIS ABOMINABLE MANUSCRIPT, "NERVOUS NELLY IN OZ."
YAP! GRRR...!

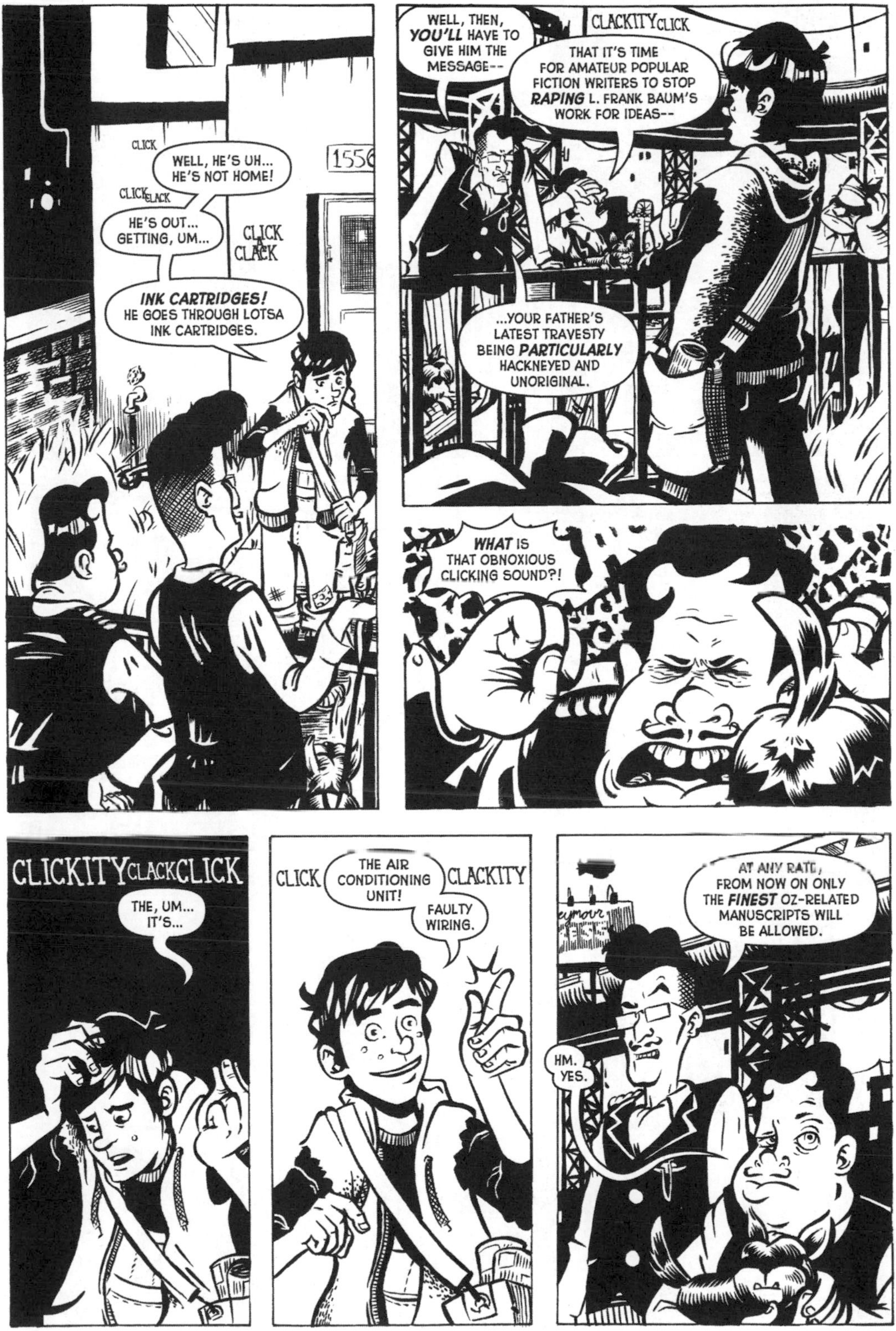
CLICK
WELL, HE'S UH... HE'S NOT HOME!
1556
CLICK CLACK
HE'S OUT... GETTING, UM...
CLICK CLACK
INK CARTRIDGES! HE GOES THROUGH LOTSA INK CARTRIDGES.
WELL, THEN, YOU'LL HAVE TO GIVE HIM THE MESSAGE--
CLACKITY CLICK
THAT IT'S TIME FOR AMATEUR POPULAR FICTION WRITERS TO STOP RAPING L. FRANK BAUM'S WORK FOR IDEAS--
...YOUR FATHER'S LATEST TRAVESTY BEING PARTICULARLY HACKNEYED AND UNORIGINAL.
WHAT IS THAT OBNOXIOUS CLICKING SOUND?!
CLICKITY CLACK CLICK
THE, UM... IT'S...
CLICK
THE AIR CONDITIONING UNIT!
CLACKITY
FAULTY WIRING.
AT ANY RATE, FROM NOW ON ONLY THE FINEST OZ-RELATED MANUSCRIPTS WILL BE ALLOWED.
HM. YES.

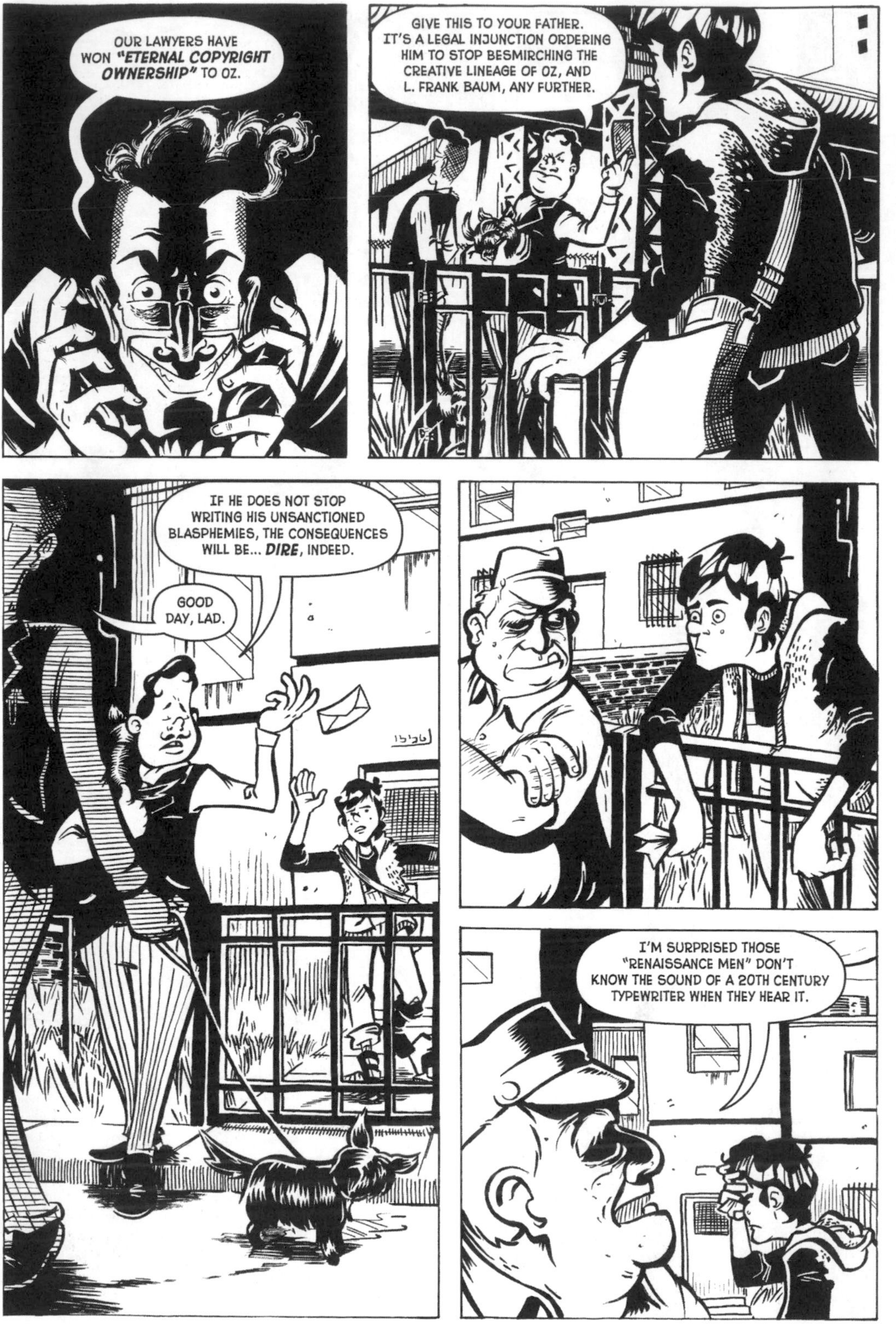
OUR LAWYERS HAVE WON **"ETERNAL COPYRIGHT OWNERSHIP"** TO OZ.
GIVE THIS TO YOUR FATHER. IT'S A LEGAL INJUNCTION ORDERING HIM TO STOP BESMIRCHING THE CREATIVE LINEAGE OF OZ, AND L. FRANK BAUM, ANY FURTHER.
IF HE DOES NOT STOP WRITING HIS UNSANCTIONED BLASPHEMIES, THE CONSEQUENCES WILL BE... ***DIRE***, INDEED.
GOOD DAY, LAD.
I'M SURPRISED THOSE "RENAISSANCE MEN" DON'T KNOW THE SOUND OF A 20TH CENTURY TYPEWRITER WHEN THEY HEAR IT.

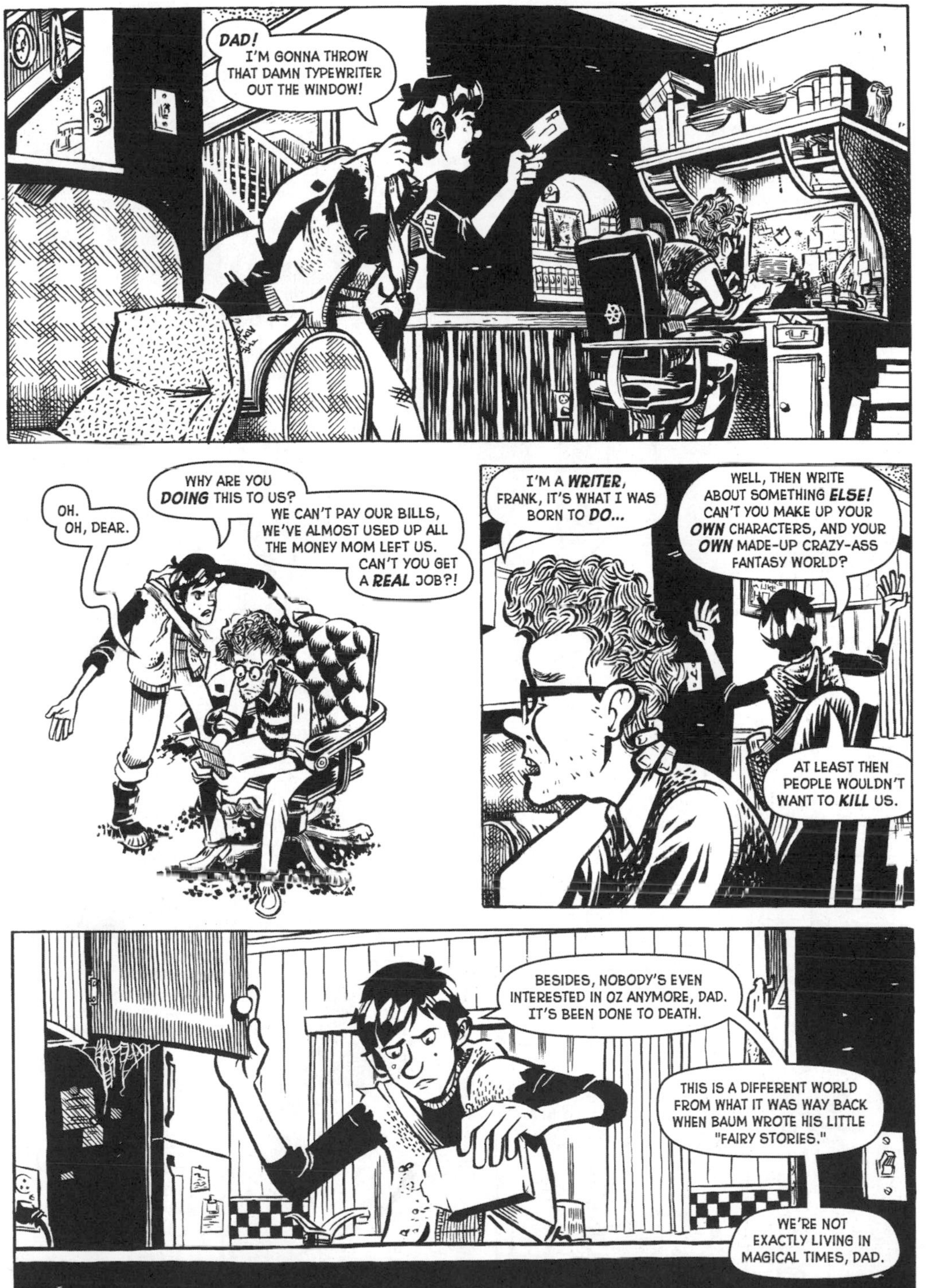
DAD!
I'M GONNA THROW THAT DAMN TYPEWRITER OUT THE WINDOW!
WHY ARE YOU **DOING** THIS TO US? WE CAN'T PAY OUR BILLS, WE'VE ALMOST USED UP ALL THE MONEY MOM LEFT US. CAN'T YOU GET A **REAL** JOB?!
OH. OH, DEAR.
I'M A **WRITER**, FRANK, IT'S WHAT I WAS BORN TO **DO...**
WELL, THEN WRITE ABOUT SOMETHING **ELSE!** CAN'T YOU MAKE UP YOUR **OWN** CHARACTERS, AND YOUR **OWN** MADE-UP CRAZY-ASS FANTASY WORLD?
AT LEAST THEN PEOPLE WOULDN'T WANT TO **KILL** US.
BESIDES, NOBODY'S EVEN INTERESTED IN OZ ANYMORE, DAD. IT'S BEEN DONE TO DEATH.
THIS IS A DIFFERENT WORLD FROM WHAT IT WAS WAY BACK WHEN BAUM WROTE HIS LITTLE "FAIRY STORIES."
WE'RE NOT EXACTLY LIVING IN MAGICAL TIMES, DAD.

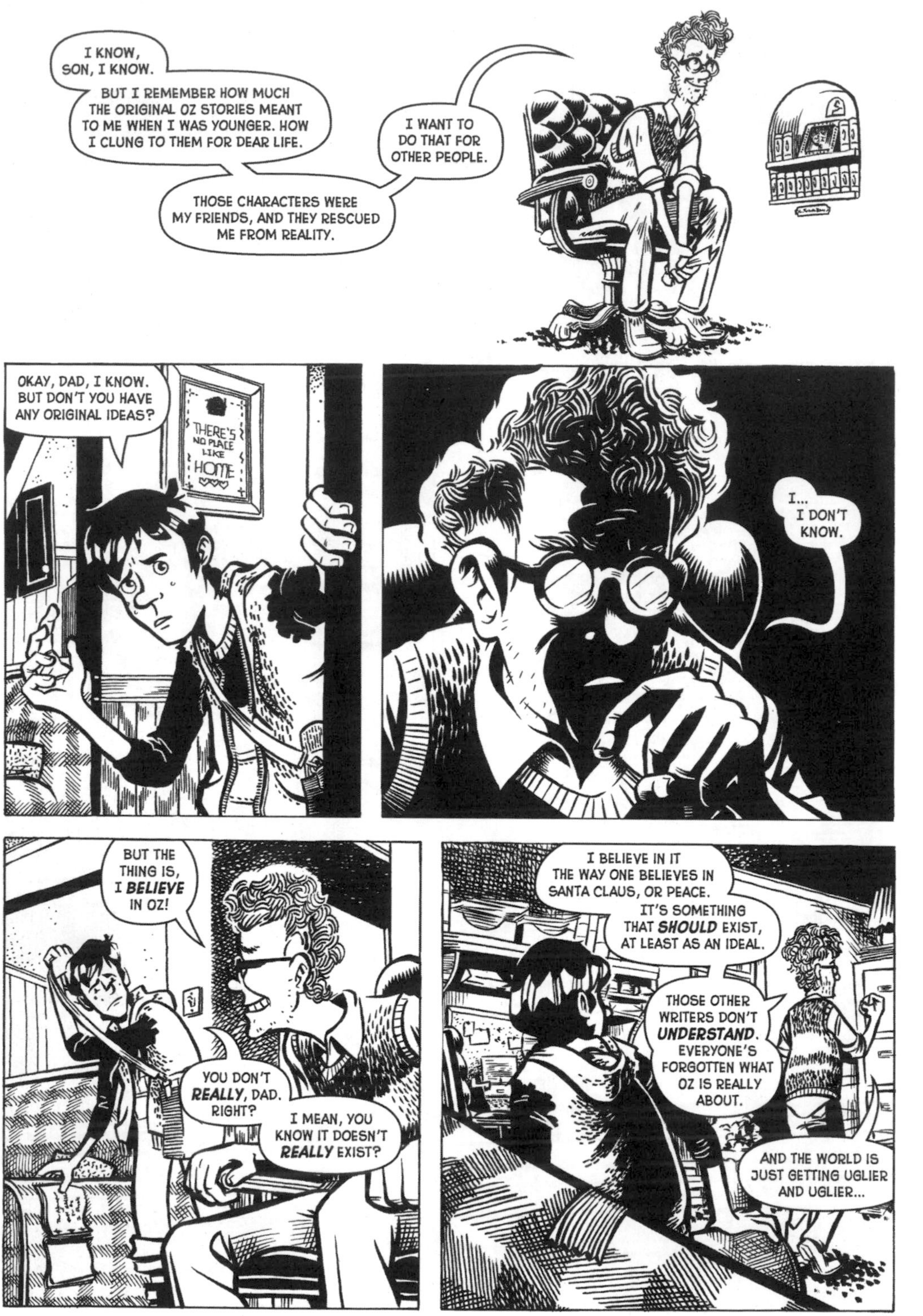
I KNOW, SON, I KNOW.
BUT I REMEMBER HOW MUCH THE ORIGINAL OZ STORIES MEANT TO ME WHEN I WAS YOUNGER. HOW I CLUNG TO THEM FOR DEAR LIFE.
THOSE CHARACTERS WERE MY FRIENDS, AND THEY RESCUED ME FROM REALITY.
I WANT TO DO THAT FOR OTHER PEOPLE.
OKAY, DAD, I KNOW. BUT DON'T YOU HAVE ANY ORIGINAL IDEAS?
THERE'S NO PLACE LIKE HOME
I... I DON'T KNOW.
BUT THE THING IS, I **BELIEVE** IN OZ!
YOU DON'T **REALLY**, DAD. RIGHT?
I MEAN, YOU KNOW IT DOESN'T **REALLY** EXIST?
I BELIEVE IN IT THE WAY ONE BELIEVES IN SANTA CLAUS, OR PEACE.
IT'S SOMETHING THAT **SHOULD** EXIST, AT LEAST AS AN IDEAL.
THOSE OTHER WRITERS DON'T **UNDERSTAND**. EVERYONE'S FORGOTTEN WHAT OZ IS REALLY ABOUT.
AND THE WORLD IS JUST GETTING UGLIER AND UGLIER...

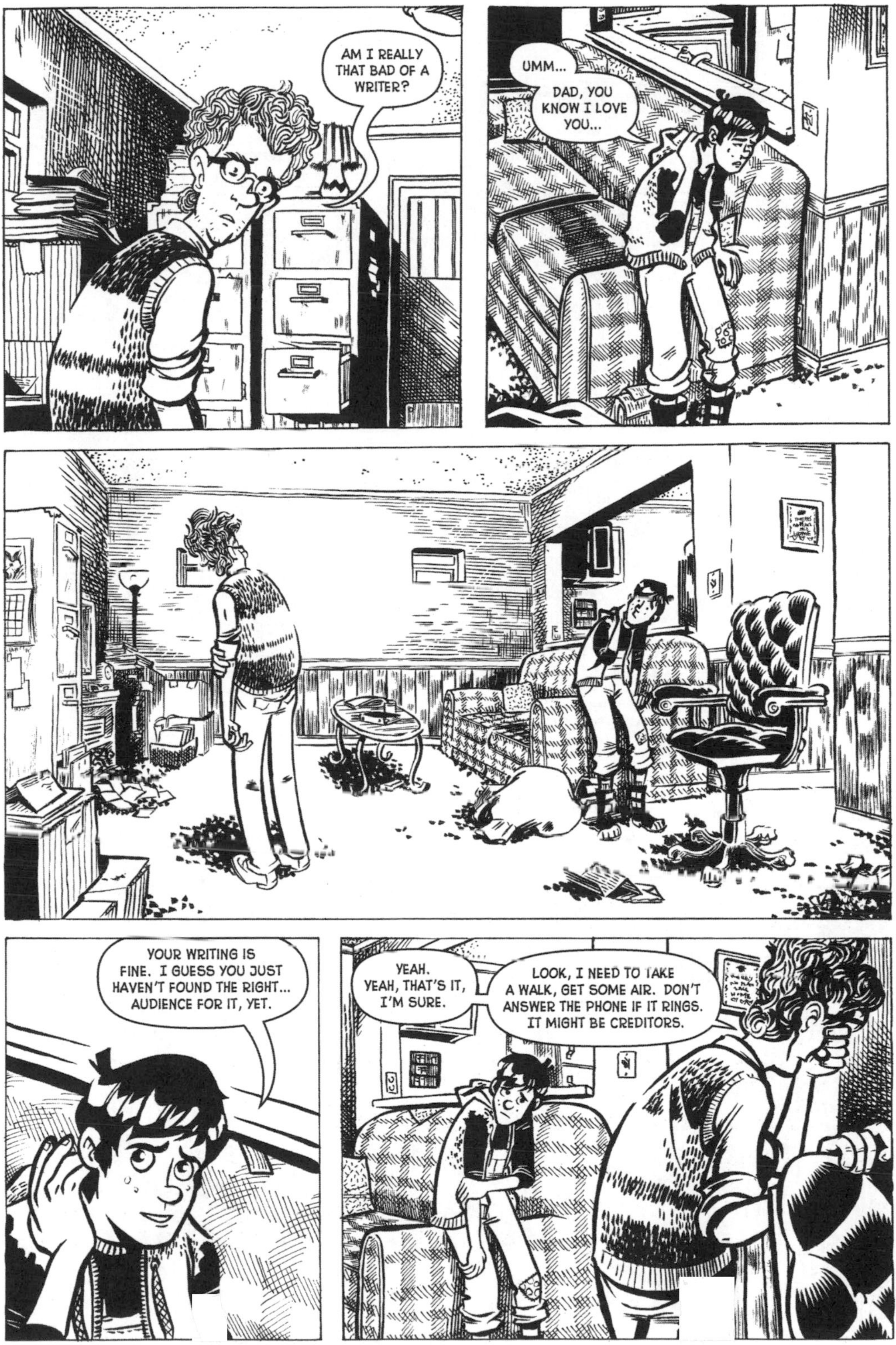
AM I REALLY THAT BAD OF A WRITER?
UMM...
DAD, YOU KNOW I LOVE YOU...
YOUR WRITING IS FINE. I GUESS YOU JUST HAVEN'T FOUND THE RIGHT... AUDIENCE FOR IT, YET.
YEAH. YEAH, THAT'S IT, I'M SURE.
LOOK, I NEED TO TAKE A WALK, GET SOME AIR. DON'T ANSWER THE PHONE IF IT RINGS. IT MIGHT BE CREDITORS.

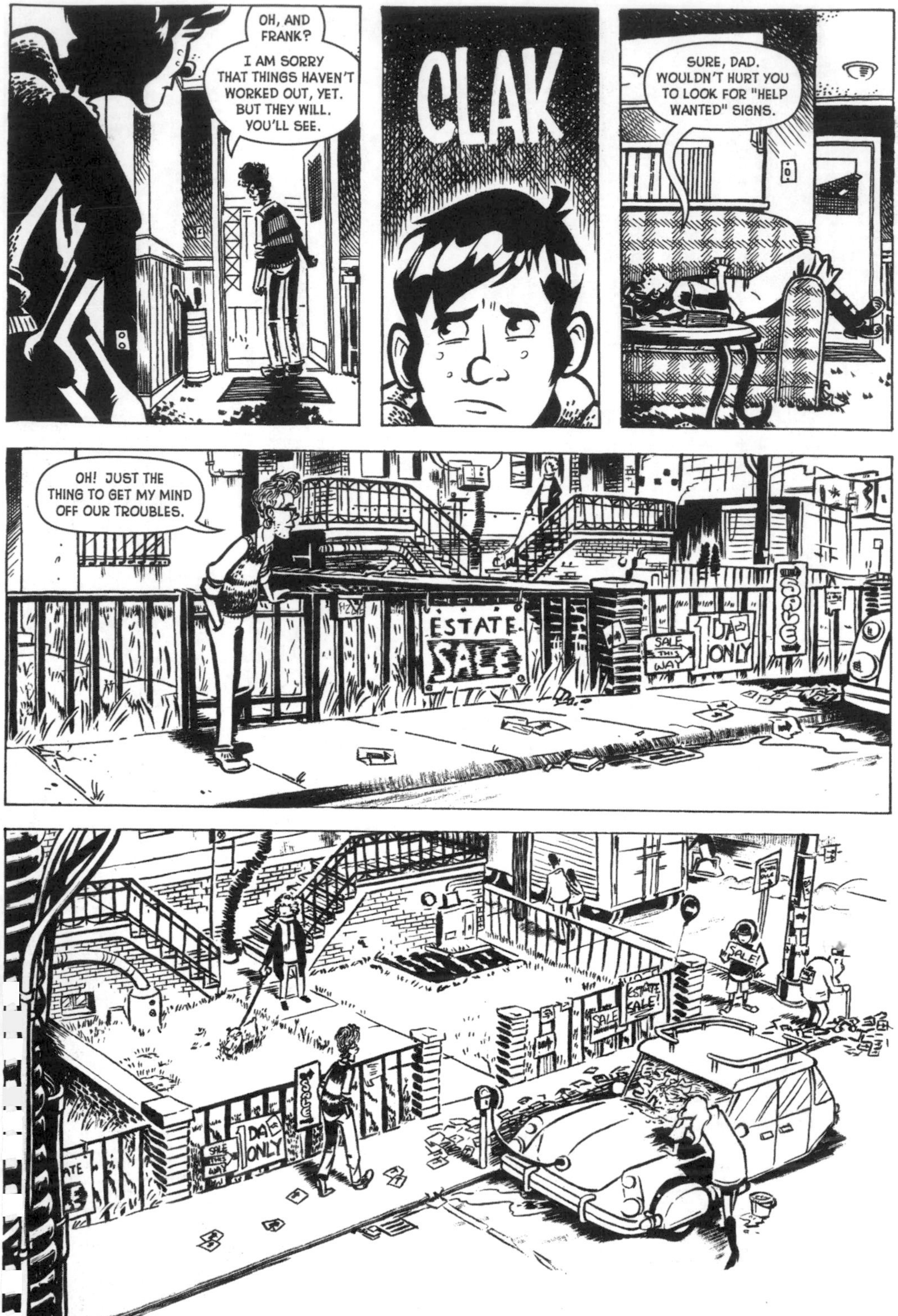
OH, AND FRANK? I AM SORRY THAT THINGS HAVEN'T WORKED OUT, YET. BUT THEY WILL. YOU'LL SEE.
CLAK
SURE, DAD. WOULDN'T HURT YOU TO LOOK FOR "HELP WANTED" SIGNS.
OH! JUST THE THING TO GET MY MIND OFF OUR TROUBLES.
ESTATE SALE
SALE THIS WAY
SALE!

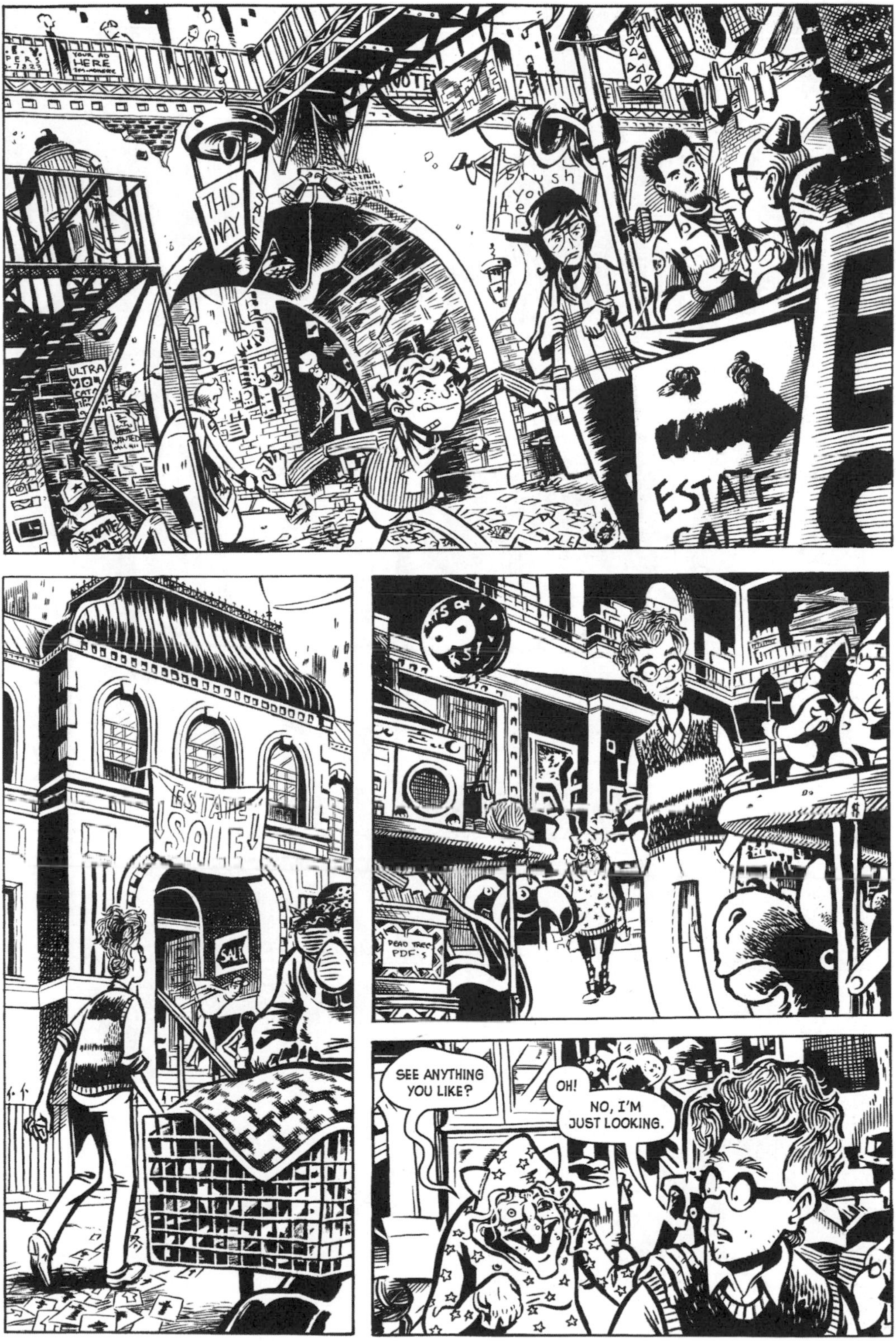
YOUR AD HERE
VOTE
SALE
THIS WAY
ULTRA
WANTED
ESTATE SALE!
ESTATE SALE
SALE
DEAD TREE PDF's
SEE ANYTHING YOU LIKE?
OH!
NO, I'M JUST LOOKING.

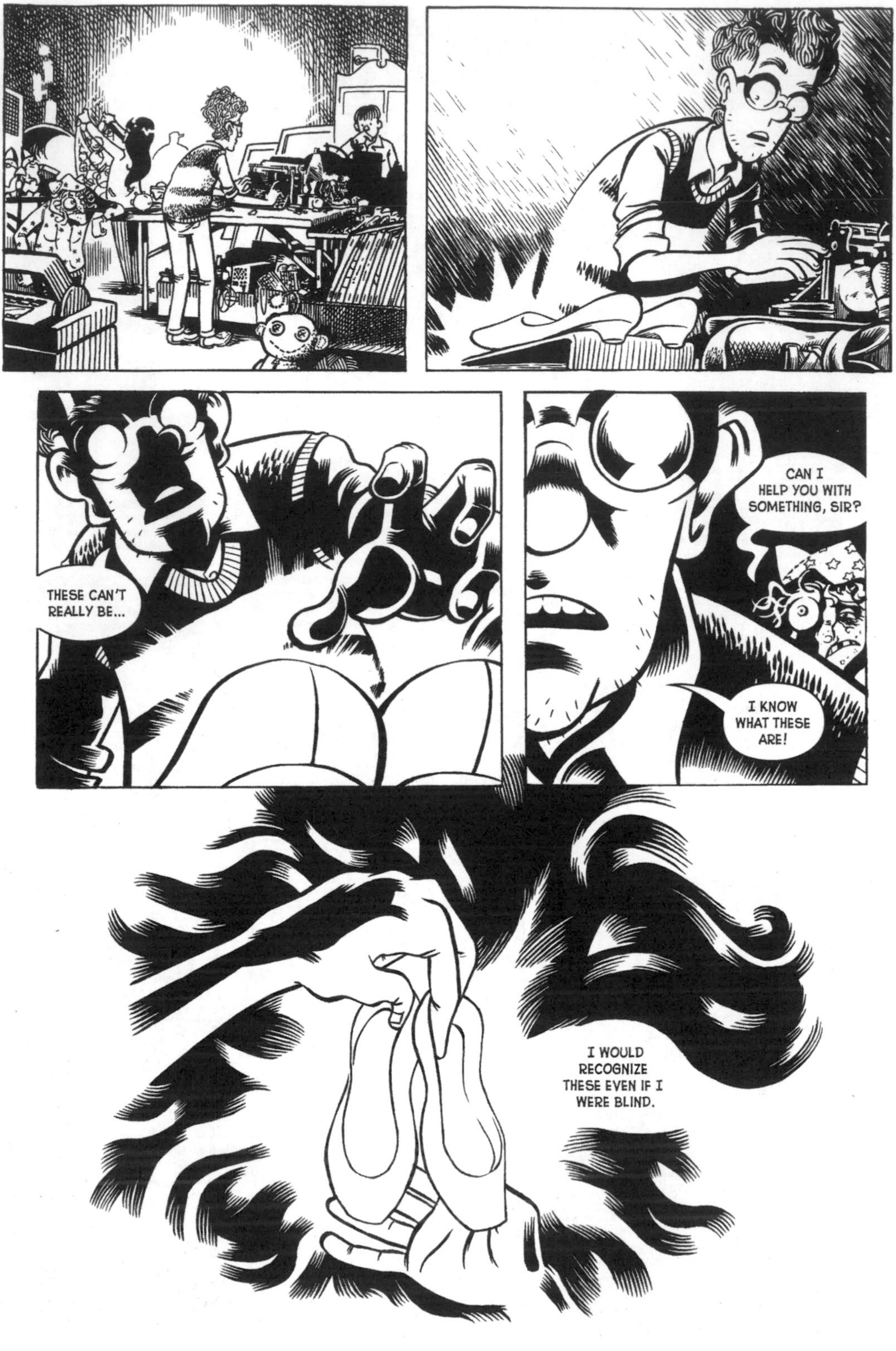
THESE CAN'T REALLY BE...
CAN I HELP YOU WITH SOMETHING, SIR?
I KNOW WHAT THESE ARE!
I WOULD RECOGNIZE THESE EVEN IF I WERE BLIND.

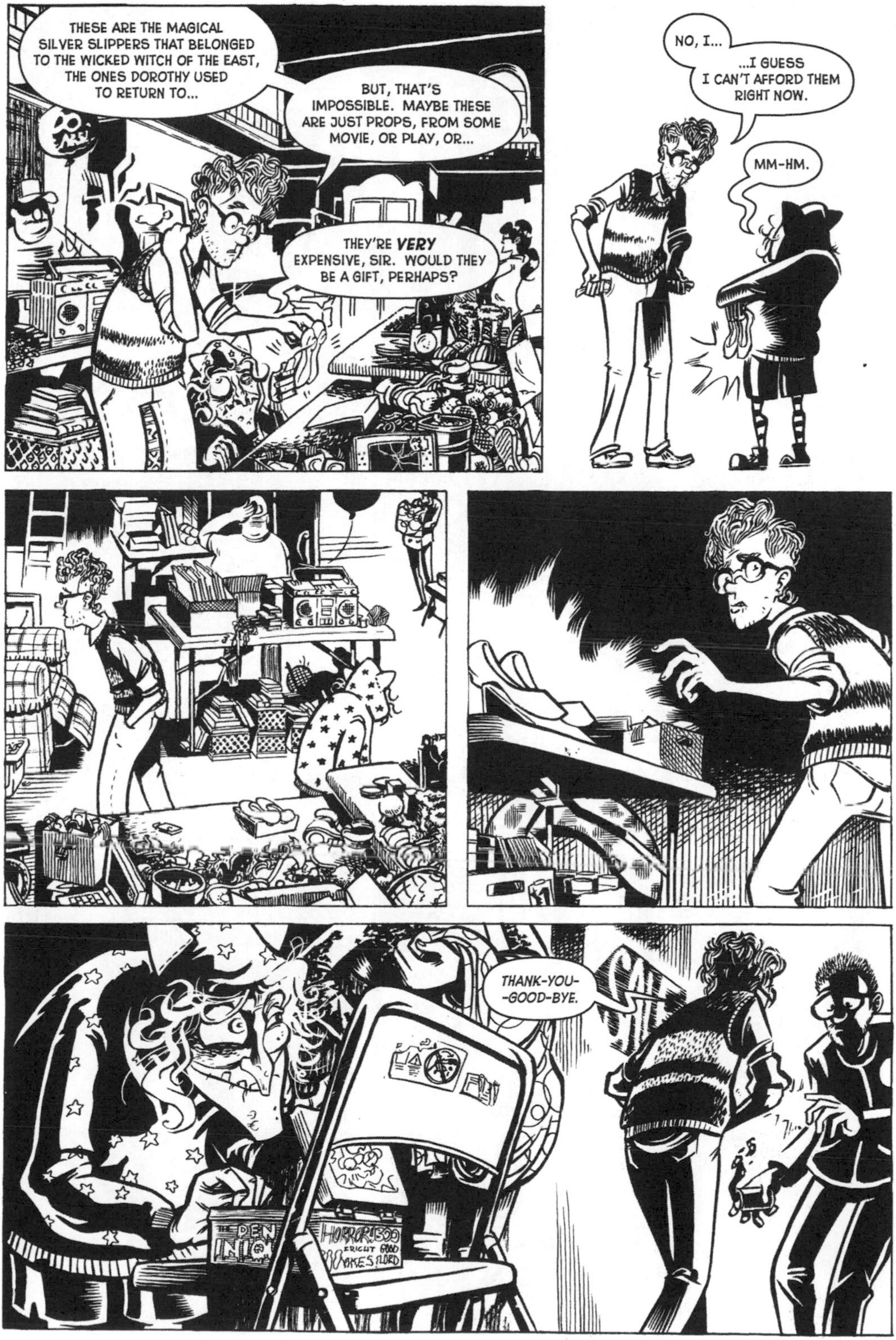
THESE ARE THE MAGICAL SILVER SLIPPERS THAT BELONGED TO THE WICKED WITCH OF THE EAST, THE ONES DOROTHY USED TO RETURN TO...
BUT, THAT'S IMPOSSIBLE. MAYBE THESE ARE JUST PROPS, FROM SOME MOVIE, OR PLAY, OR...
THEY'RE **VERY** EXPENSIVE, SIR. WOULD THEY BE A GIFT, PERHAPS?
NO, I...
...I GUESS I CAN'T AFFORD THEM RIGHT NOW.
MM-HM.
THANK-YOU- -GOOD-BYE.

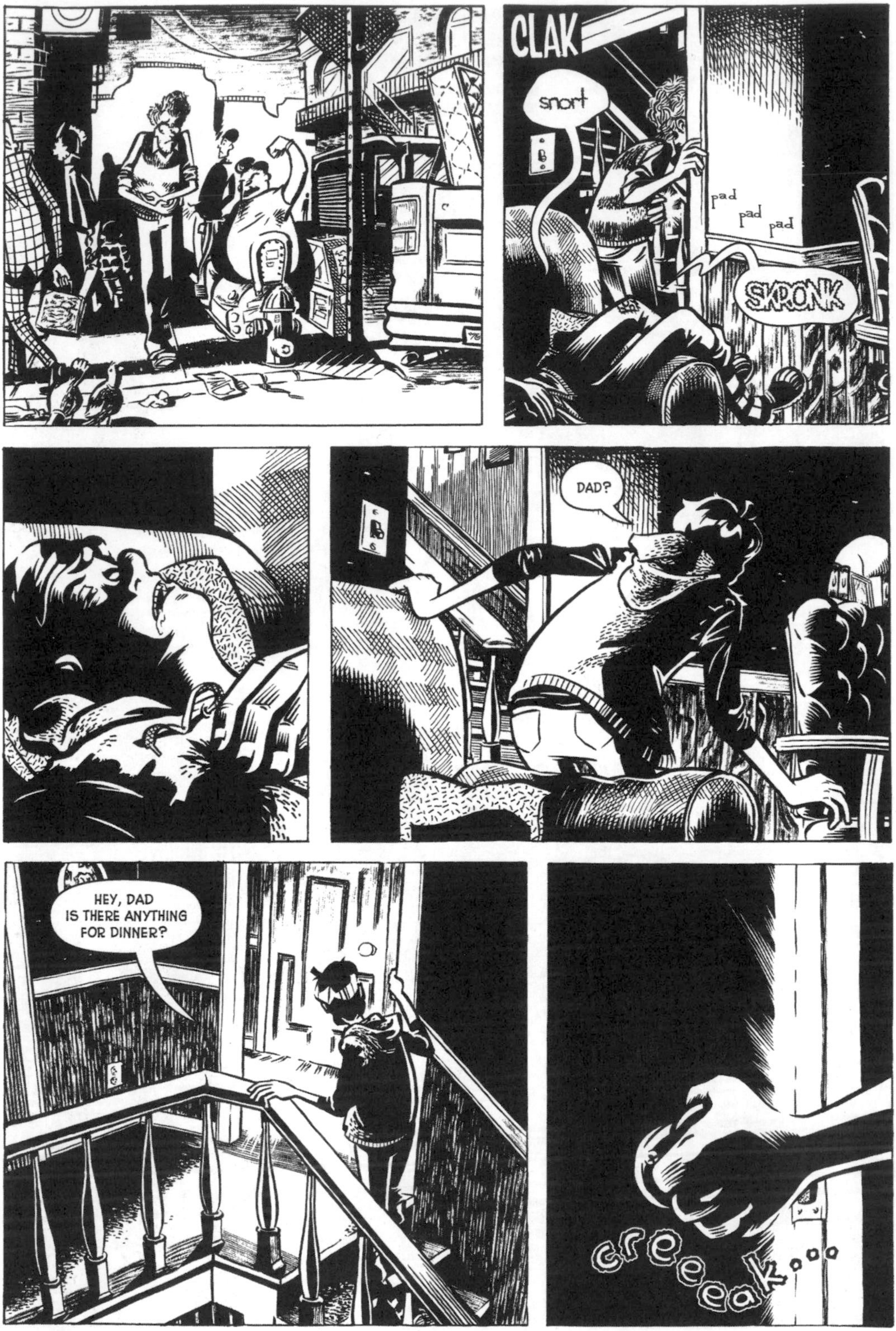
CLAK
snort
pad
pad
pad
SKRONK
DAD?
HEY, DAD IS THERE ANYTHING FOR DINNER?
creeeak...

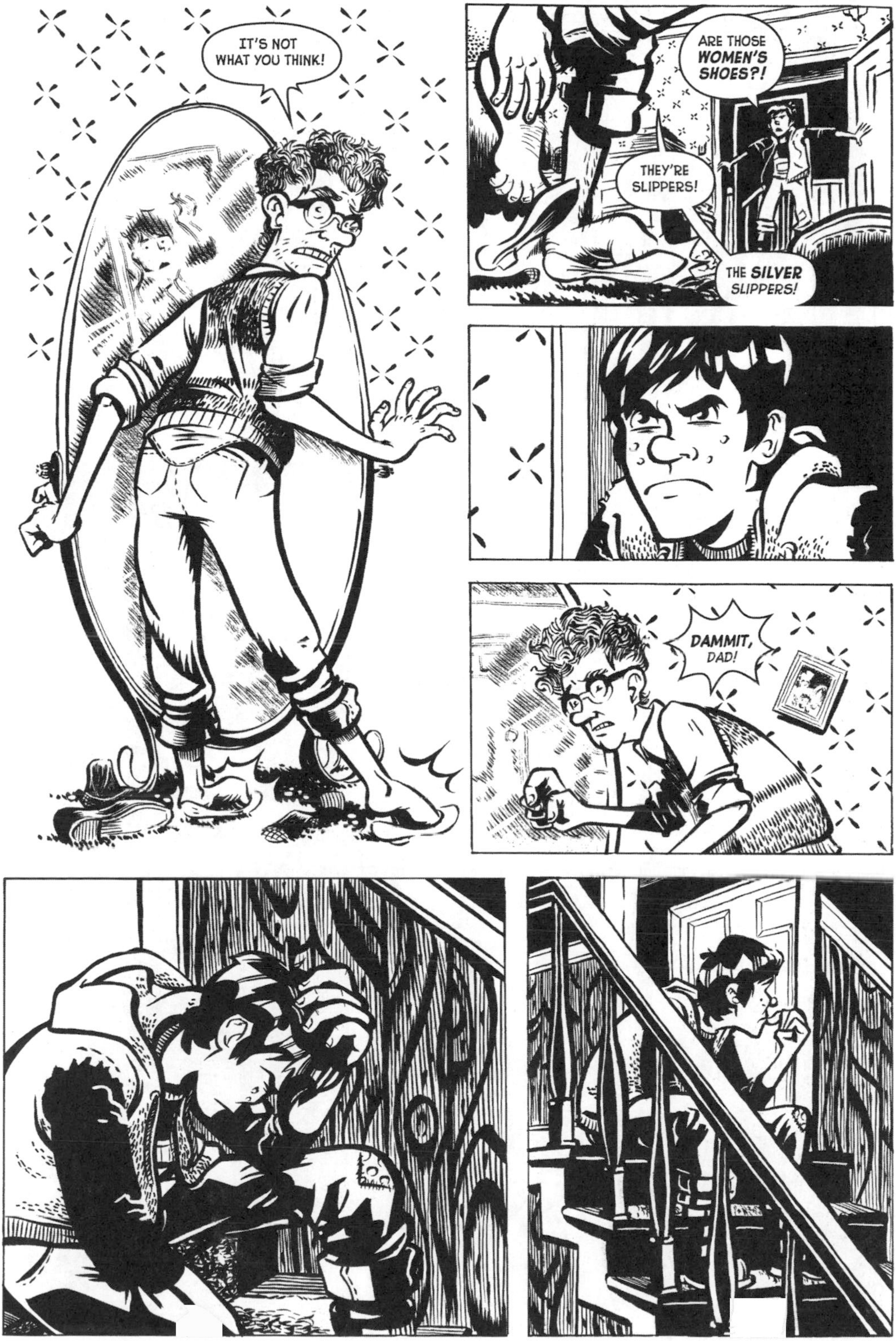
IT'S NOT WHAT YOU THINK!
ARE THOSE WOMEN'S SHOES?!
THEY'RE SLIPPERS!
THE SILVER SLIPPERS!
DAMMIT, DAD!

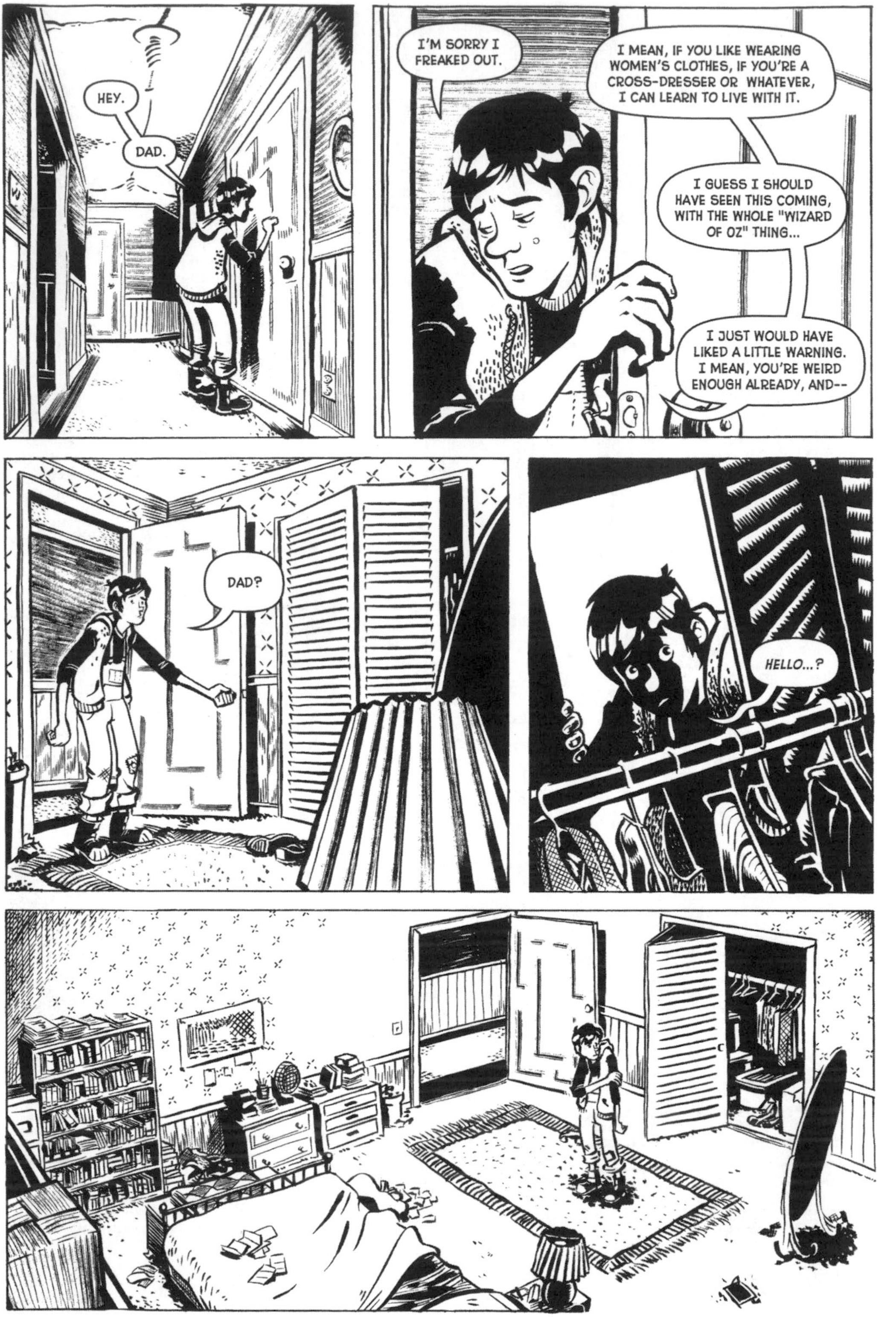
HEY.
DAD.
I'M SORRY I FREAKED OUT.
I MEAN, IF YOU LIKE WEARING WOMEN'S CLOTHES, IF YOU'RE A CROSS-DRESSER OR WHATEVER, I CAN LEARN TO LIVE WITH IT.
I GUESS I SHOULD HAVE SEEN THIS COMING, WITH THE WHOLE "WIZARD OF OZ" THING...
I JUST WOULD HAVE LIKED A LITTLE WARNING. I MEAN, YOU'RE WEIRD ENOUGH ALREADY, AND--
DAD?
HELLO...?

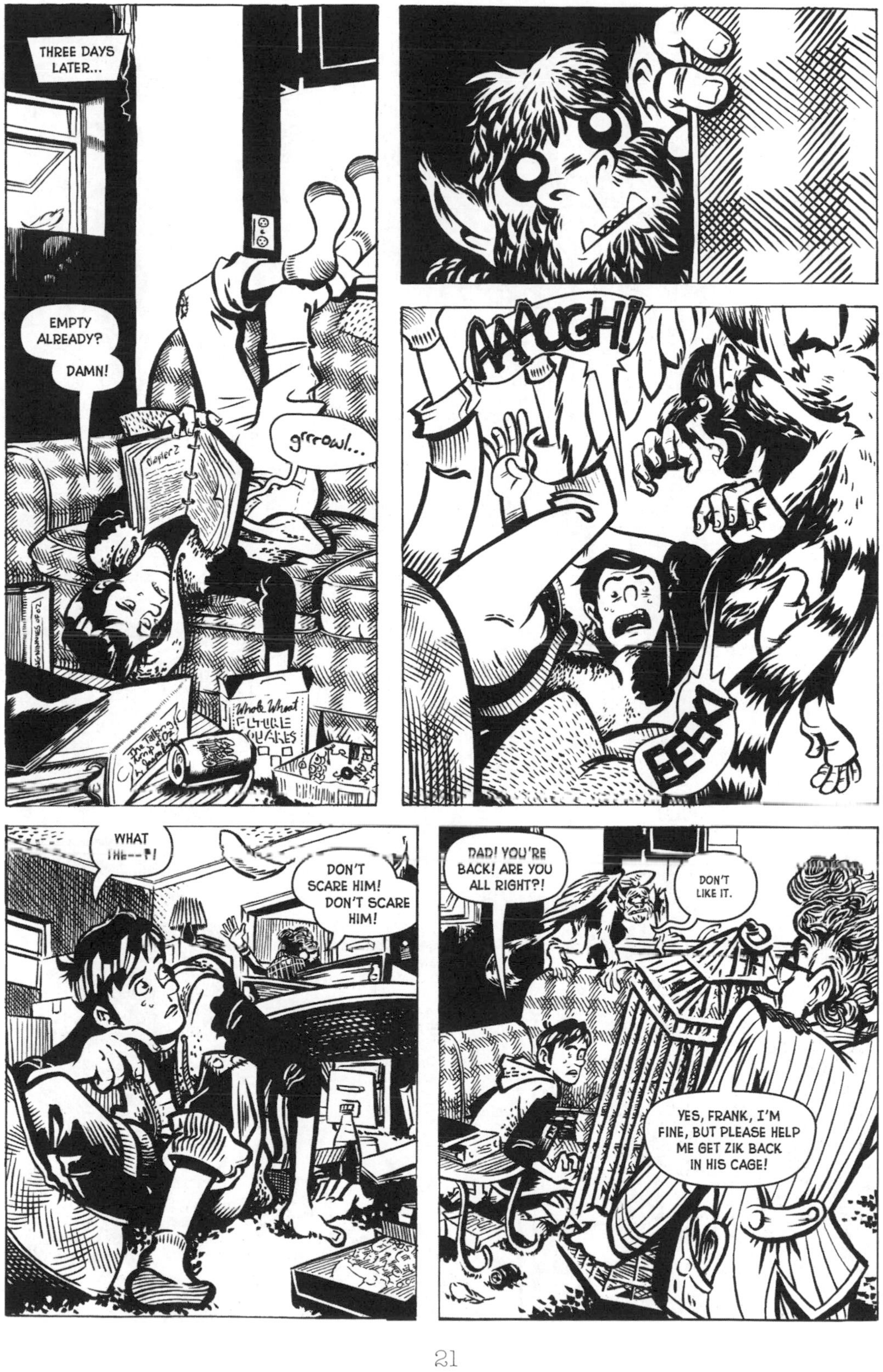

THREE DAYS LATER...
EMPTY ALREADY?
DAMN!
grrrowl...
Whole Wheat FUTURE SQUARES
AAAUGH!
EEEK!
WHAT THE--?!
DON'T SCARE HIM! DON'T SCARE HIM!
DAD! YOU'RE BACK! ARE YOU ALL RIGHT?!
DON'T LIKE IT.
YES, FRANK, I'M FINE, BUT PLEASE HELP ME GET ZIK BACK IN HIS CAGE!

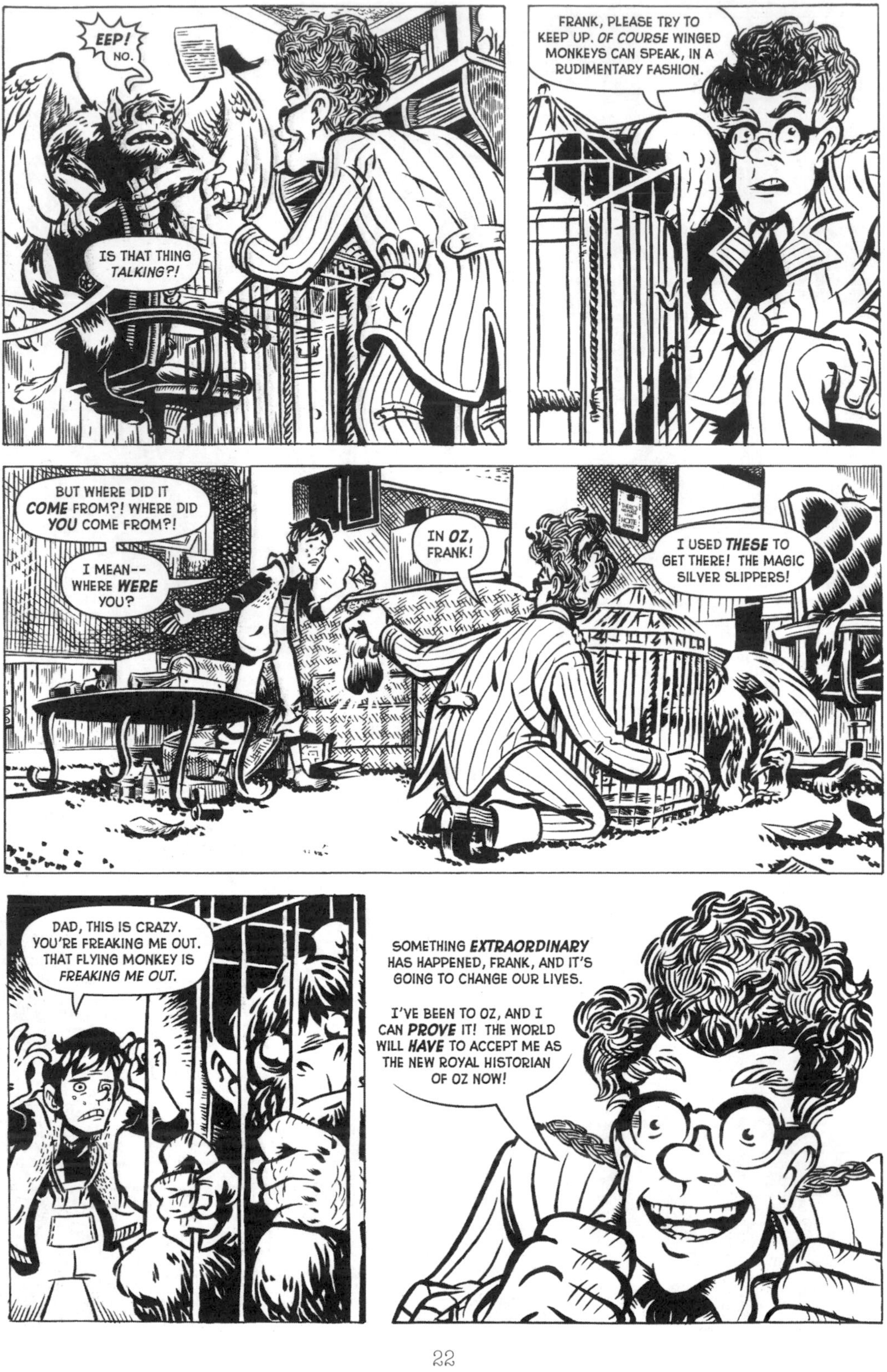
EEP! NO.
IS THAT THING *TALKING?!*
FRANK, PLEASE TRY TO KEEP UP. *OF COURSE* WINGED MONKEYS CAN SPEAK, IN A RUDIMENTARY FASHION.
BUT WHERE DID IT **COME** FROM?! WHERE DID **YOU** COME FROM?!
I MEAN-- WHERE **WERE** YOU?
IN *OZ*, FRANK!
I USED **THESE** TO GET THERE! THE MAGIC SILVER SLIPPERS!
DAD, THIS IS CRAZY. YOU'RE FREAKING ME OUT. THAT FLYING MONKEY IS *FREAKING ME OUT.*
SOMETHING **EXTRAORDINARY** HAS HAPPENED, FRANK, AND IT'S GOING TO CHANGE OUR LIVES.
I'VE BEEN TO OZ, AND I CAN **PROVE** IT! THE WORLD WILL **HAVE** TO ACCEPT ME AS THE NEW ROYAL HISTORIAN OF OZ NOW!

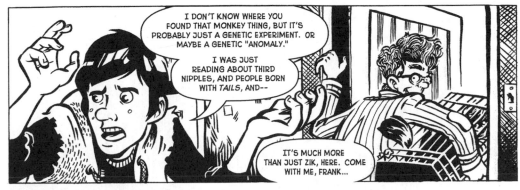

I DON'T KNOW WHERE YOU FOUND THAT MONKEY THING, BUT IT'S PROBABLY JUST A GENETIC EXPERIMENT. OR MAYBE A GENETIC "ANOMALY."

I WAS JUST READING ABOUT THIRD NIPPLES, AND PEOPLE BORN WITH *TAILS*, AND--

IT'S MUCH MORE THAN JUST ZIK, HERE. COME WITH ME, FRANK...

WHAT THE...?!

COME AND SEE WHAT I'VE BROUGHT BACK!

HOW... HOW IS IT SO MUCH LARGER INSIDE THAN OUT?

IT'S AN *ENCHANTMENT!* I BARTERED IT FROM A WINKIE WIZARD.

OH.

OZ *EXISTS*, FRANK! IT'S NOT JUST A DREAM, OR A DUSTY OLD BOOK, IT'S AN *UN-CORRUPTED PARADISE!*

IT'S BEEN SITTING THERE ALL THIS TIME, WAITING FOR SOMEONE LIKE *ME* TO BRING NEW STORIES TO OUR WORLD.

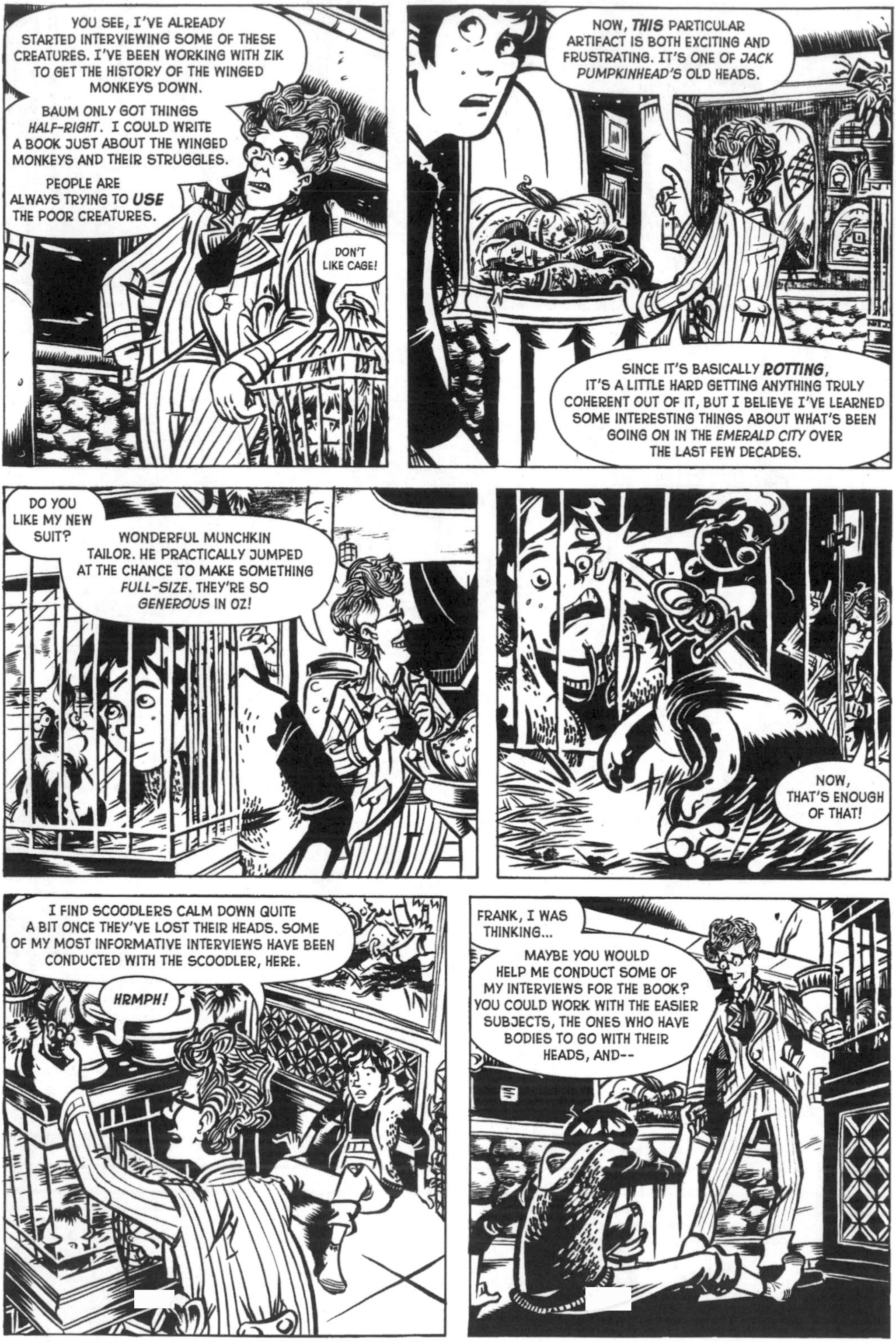
YOU SEE, I'VE ALREADY STARTED INTERVIEWING SOME OF THESE CREATURES. I'VE BEEN WORKING WITH ZIK TO GET THE HISTORY OF THE WINGED MONKEYS DOWN.
BAUM ONLY GOT THINGS *HALF-RIGHT*. I COULD WRITE A BOOK JUST ABOUT THE WINGED MONKEYS AND THEIR STRUGGLES.
PEOPLE ARE ALWAYS TRYING TO ***USE*** THE POOR CREATURES.
DON'T LIKE CAGE!
NOW, ***THIS*** PARTICULAR ARTIFACT IS BOTH EXCITING AND FRUSTRATING. IT'S ONE OF *JACK PUMPKINHEAD'S* OLD HEADS.
SINCE IT'S BASICALLY ***ROTTING***, IT'S A LITTLE HARD GETTING ANYTHING TRULY COHERENT OUT OF IT, BUT I BELIEVE I'VE LEARNED SOME INTERESTING THINGS ABOUT WHAT'S BEEN GOING ON IN THE *EMERALD CITY* OVER THE LAST FEW DECADES.
DO YOU LIKE MY NEW SUIT?
WONDERFUL MUNCHKIN TAILOR. HE PRACTICALLY JUMPED AT THE CHANCE TO MAKE SOMETHING *FULL-SIZE*. THEY'RE SO *GENEROUS* IN OZ!
NOW, THAT'S ENOUGH OF THAT!
I FIND SCOODLERS CALM DOWN QUITE A BIT ONCE THEY'VE LOST THEIR HEADS. SOME OF MY MOST INFORMATIVE INTERVIEWS HAVE BEEN CONDUCTED WITH THE SCOODLER, HERE.
HRMPH!
FRANK, I WAS THINKING...
MAYBE YOU WOULD HELP ME CONDUCT SOME OF MY INTERVIEWS FOR THE BOOK? YOU COULD WORK WITH THE EASIER SUBJECTS, THE ONES WHO HAVE BODIES TO GO WITH THEIR HEADS, AND--

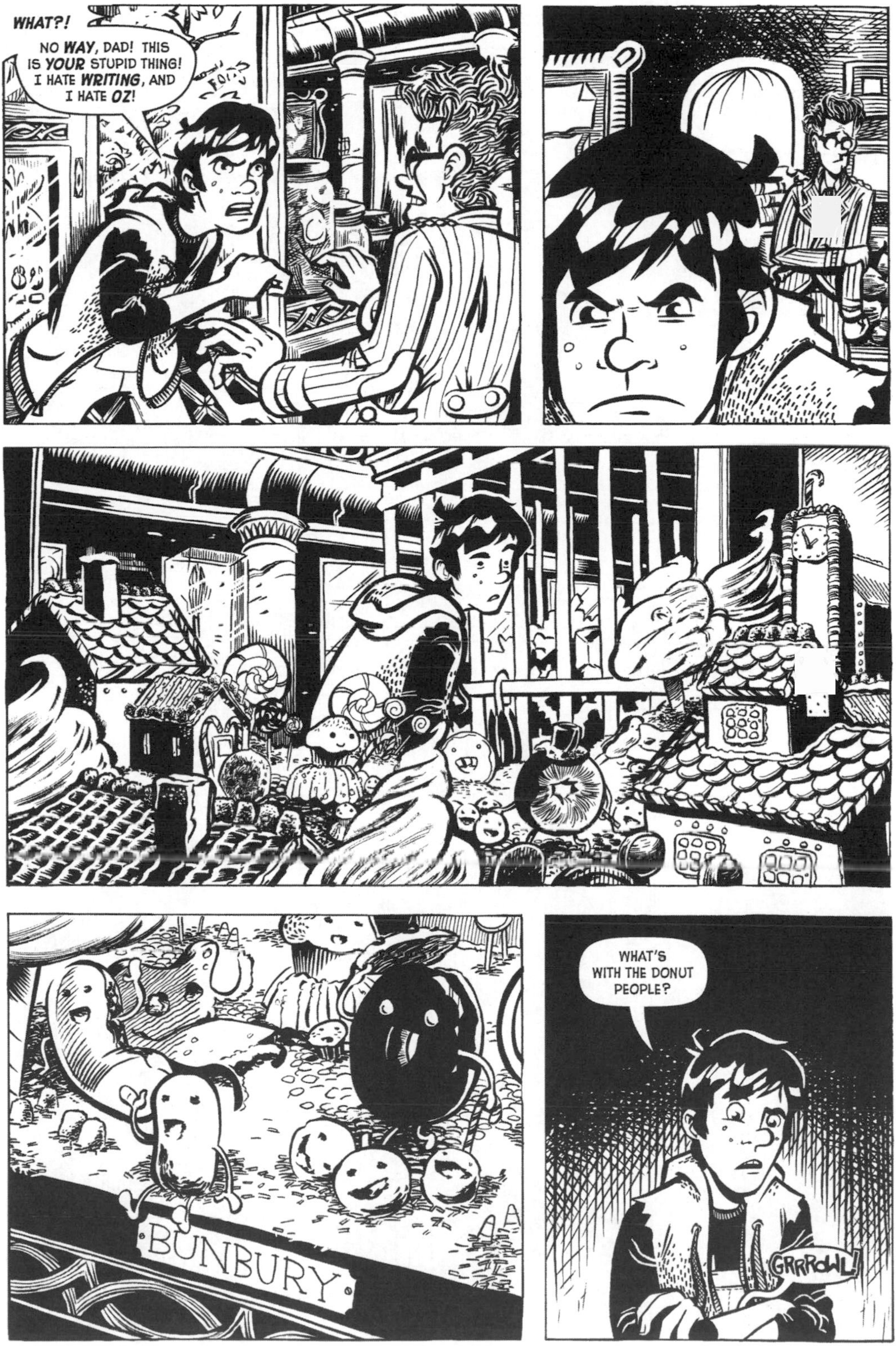
WHAT?!
NO WAY, DAD! THIS IS YOUR STUPID THING! I HATE WRITING, AND I HATE OZ!
BUNBURY
WHAT'S WITH THE DONUT PEOPLE?
GRRROWL!

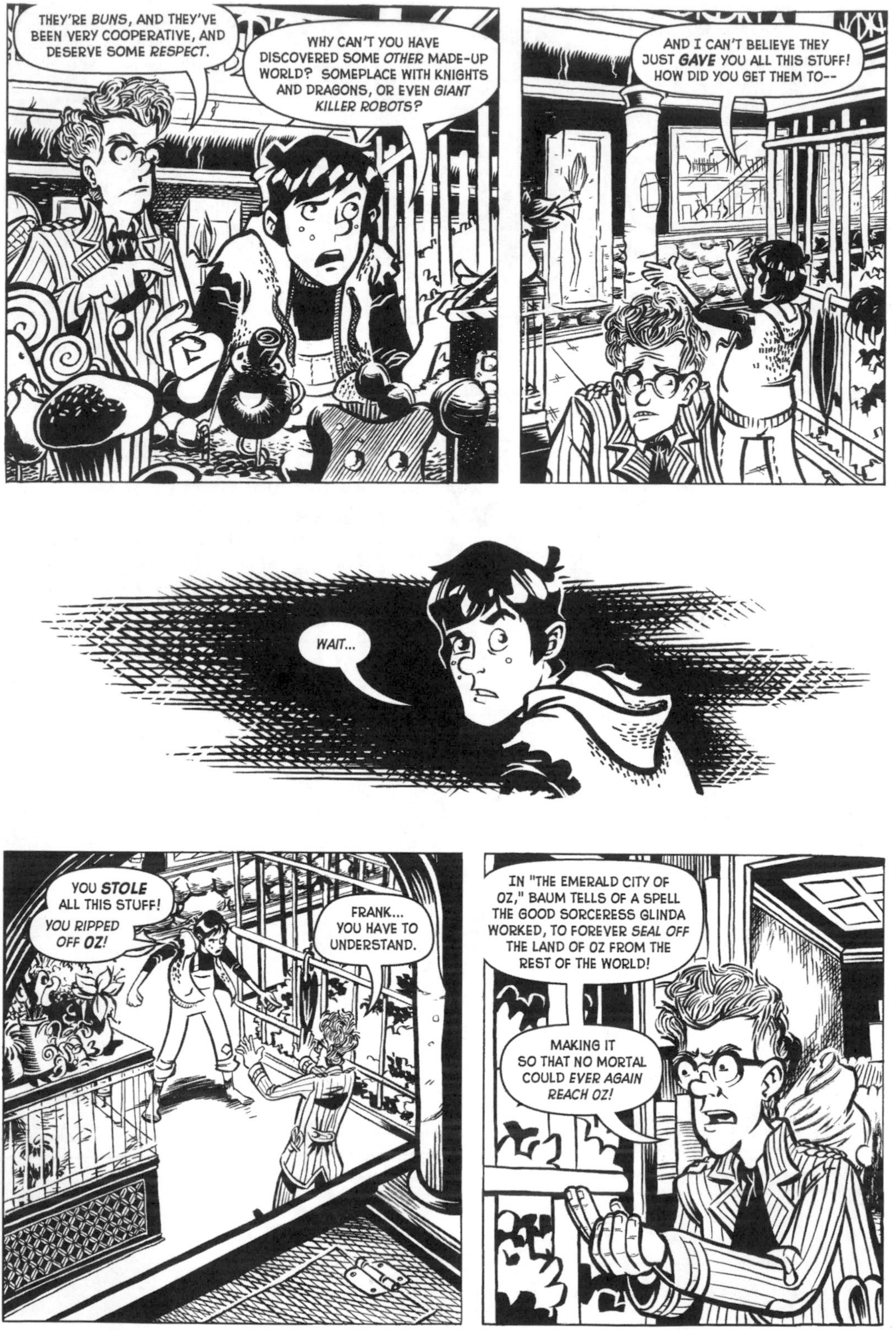
THEY'RE BUNS, AND THEY'VE BEEN VERY COOPERATIVE, AND DESERVE SOME RESPECT.
WHY CAN'T YOU HAVE DISCOVERED SOME OTHER MADE-UP WORLD? SOMEPLACE WITH KNIGHTS AND DRAGONS, OR EVEN GIANT KILLER ROBOTS?
AND I CAN'T BELIEVE THEY JUST GAVE YOU ALL THIS STUFF! HOW DID YOU GET THEM TO--
WAIT...
YOU STOLE ALL THIS STUFF!
YOU RIPPED OFF OZ!
FRANK... YOU HAVE TO UNDERSTAND.
IN "THE EMERALD CITY OF OZ," BAUM TELLS OF A SPELL THE GOOD SORCERESS GLINDA WORKED, TO FOREVER SEAL OFF THE LAND OF OZ FROM THE REST OF THE WORLD!
MAKING IT SO THAT NO MORTAL COULD EVER AGAIN REACH OZ!

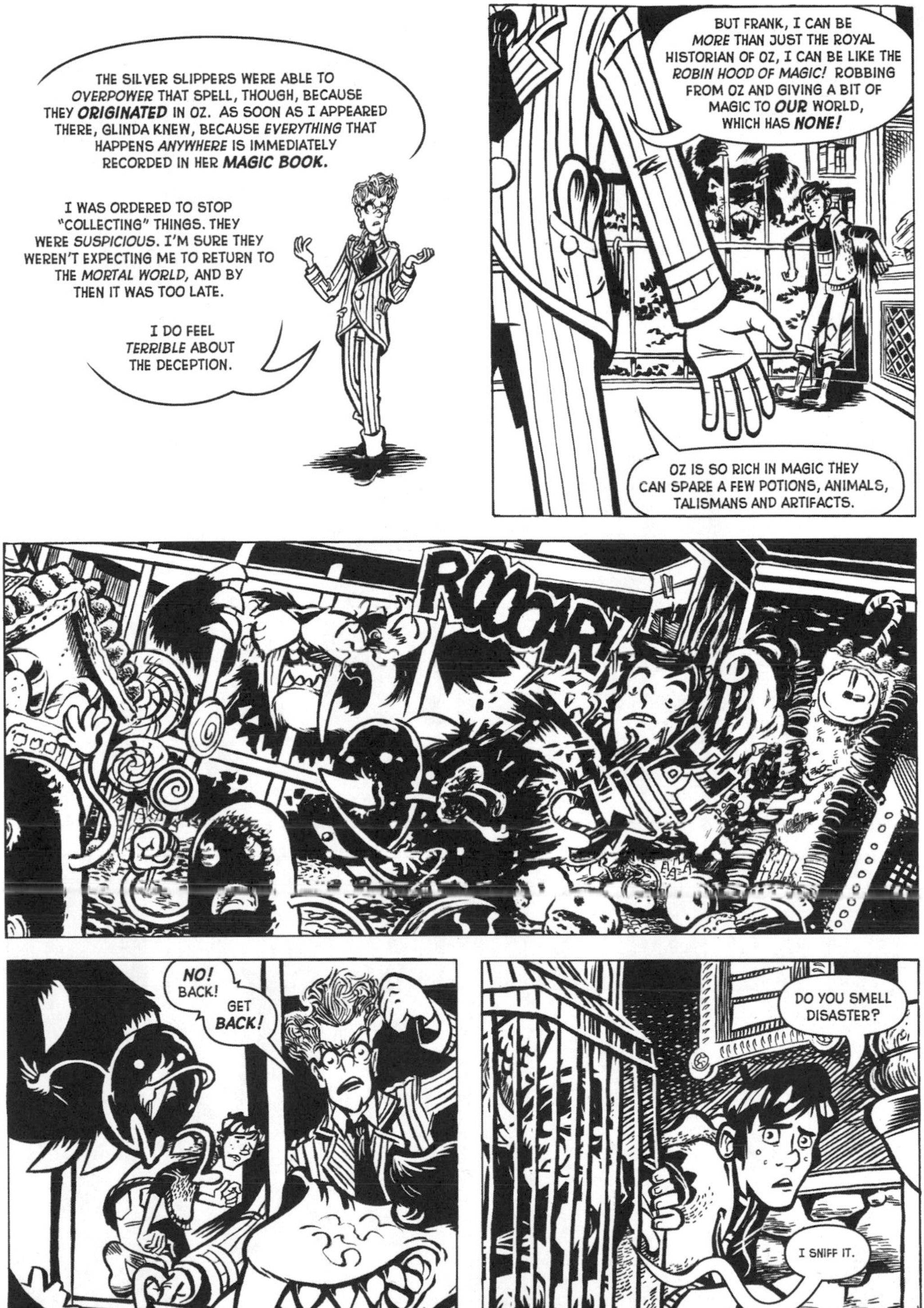
THE SILVER SLIPPERS WERE ABLE TO *OVERPOWER* THAT SPELL, THOUGH, BECAUSE THEY ***ORIGINATED*** IN OZ. AS SOON AS I APPEARED THERE, GLINDA KNEW, BECAUSE *EVERYTHING* THAT HAPPENS *ANYWHERE* IS IMMEDIATELY RECORDED IN HER ***MAGIC BOOK.***
I WAS ORDERED TO STOP "COLLECTING" THINGS. THEY WERE *SUSPICIOUS*. I'M SURE THEY WEREN'T EXPECTING ME TO RETURN TO THE *MORTAL WORLD,* AND BY THEN IT WAS TOO LATE.
I DO FEEL *TERRIBLE* ABOUT THE DECEPTION.
BUT FRANK, I CAN BE *MORE* THAN JUST THE ROYAL HISTORIAN OF OZ, I CAN BE LIKE THE *ROBIN HOOD OF MAGIC!* ROBBING FROM OZ AND GIVING A BIT OF MAGIC TO ***OUR*** WORLD, WHICH HAS ***NONE!***
OZ IS SO RICH IN MAGIC THEY CAN SPARE A FEW POTIONS, ANIMALS, TALISMANS AND ARTIFACTS.
ROOOAR!
NO! BACK! GET ***BACK!***
DO YOU SMELL DISASTER?
I SNIFF IT.

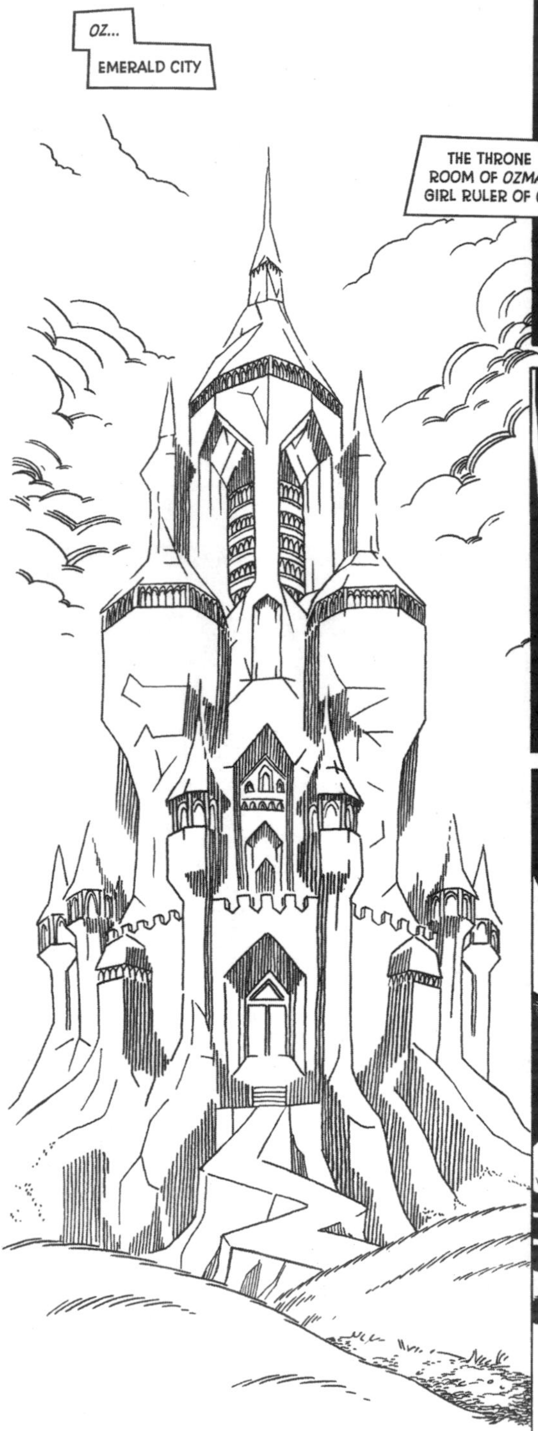
OZ...
EMERALD CITY

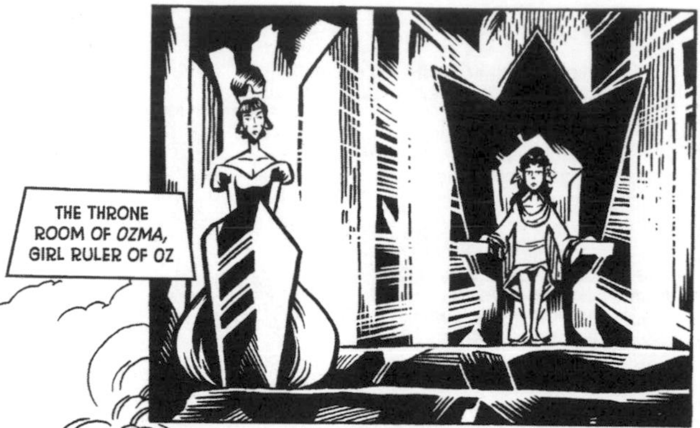
THE THRONE ROOM OF *OZMA*, GIRL RULER OF OZ

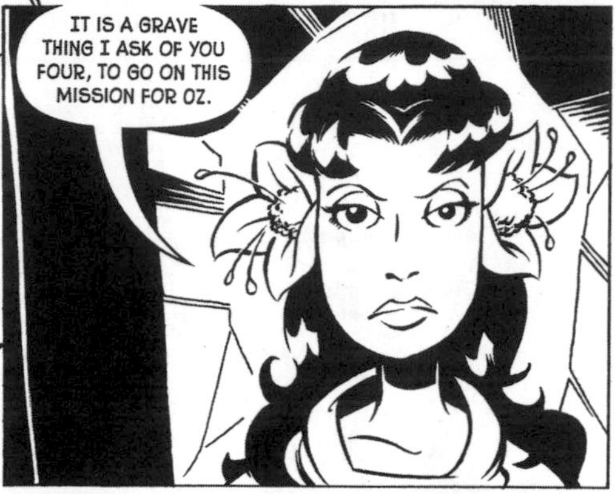
IT IS A GRAVE THING I ASK OF YOU FOUR, TO GO ON THIS MISSION FOR OZ.

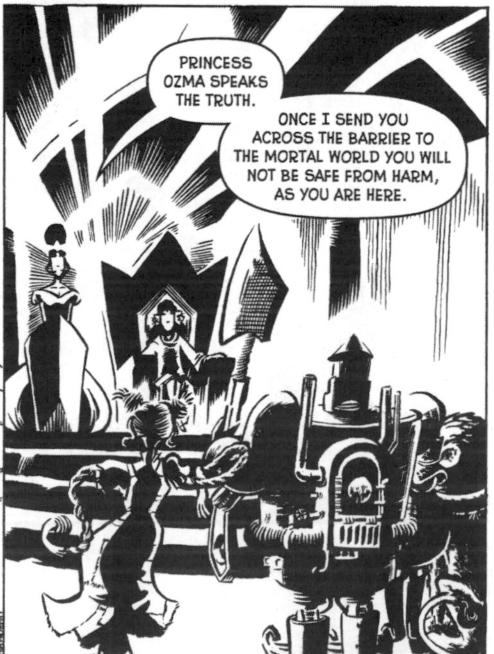
PRINCESS OZMA SPEAKS THE TRUTH.
ONCE I SEND YOU ACROSS THE BARRIER TO THE MORTAL WORLD YOU WILL NOT BE SAFE FROM HARM, AS YOU ARE HERE.

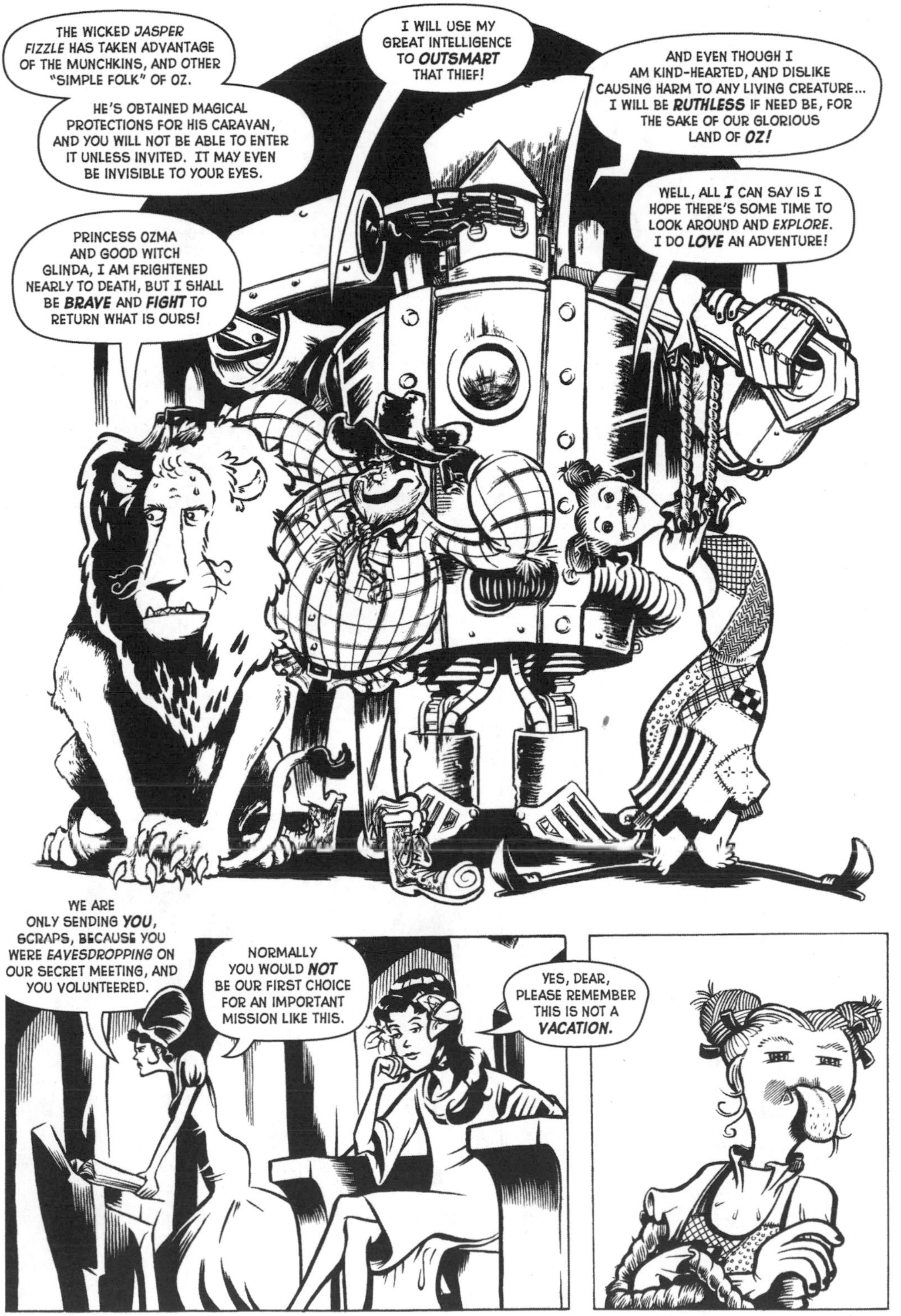
THE WICKED *JASPER FIZZLE* HAS TAKEN ADVANTAGE OF THE MUNCHKINS, AND OTHER "SIMPLE FOLK" OF OZ.
HE'S OBTAINED MAGICAL PROTECTIONS FOR HIS CARAVAN, AND YOU WILL NOT BE ABLE TO ENTER IT UNLESS INVITED. IT MAY EVEN BE INVISIBLE TO YOUR EYES.
I WILL USE MY GREAT INTELLIGENCE TO ***OUTSMART*** THAT THIEF!
AND EVEN THOUGH I AM KIND-HEARTED, AND DISLIKE CAUSING HARM TO ANY LIVING CREATURE... I WILL BE ***RUTHLESS*** IF NEED BE, FOR THE SAKE OF OUR GLORIOUS LAND OF ***OZ!***
PRINCESS OZMA AND GOOD WITCH GLINDA, I AM FRIGHTENED NEARLY TO DEATH, BUT I SHALL BE ***BRAVE*** AND ***FIGHT*** TO RETURN WHAT IS OURS!
WELL, ALL ***I*** CAN SAY IS I HOPE THERE'S SOME TIME TO LOOK AROUND AND *EXPLORE*. I DO ***LOVE*** AN ADVENTURE!
WE ARE ONLY SENDING ***YOU***, SCRAPS, BECAUSE YOU WERE *EAVESDROPPING* ON OUR SECRET MEETING, AND YOU VOLUNTEERED.
NORMALLY YOU WOULD ***NOT*** BE OUR FIRST CHOICE FOR AN IMPORTANT MISSION LIKE THIS.
YES, DEAR, PLEASE REMEMBER THIS IS NOT A ***VACATION.***

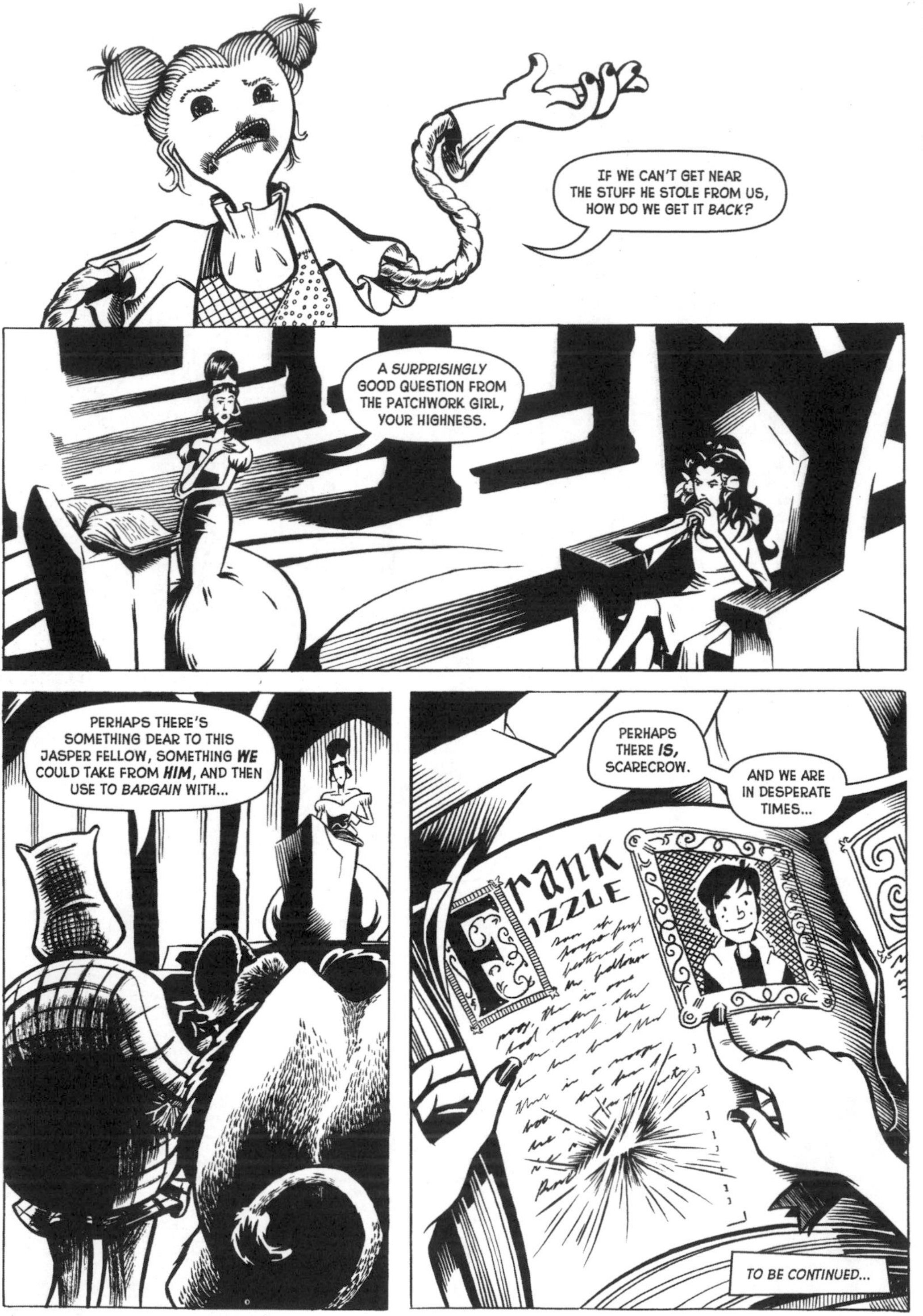
IF WE CAN'T GET NEAR THE STUFF HE STOLE FROM US, HOW DO WE GET IT *BACK?*
A *SURPRISINGLY* GOOD QUESTION FROM THE PATCHWORK GIRL, YOUR HIGHNESS.
PERHAPS THERE'S SOMETHING DEAR TO THIS JASPER FELLOW, SOMETHING ***WE*** COULD TAKE FROM ***HIM***, AND THEN USE TO *BARGAIN* WITH...
PERHAPS THERE ***IS***, SCARECROW.
AND WE ARE IN DESPERATE TIMES...
Frank Fizzle
TO BE CONTINUED...

"Sinister Visitors"

2

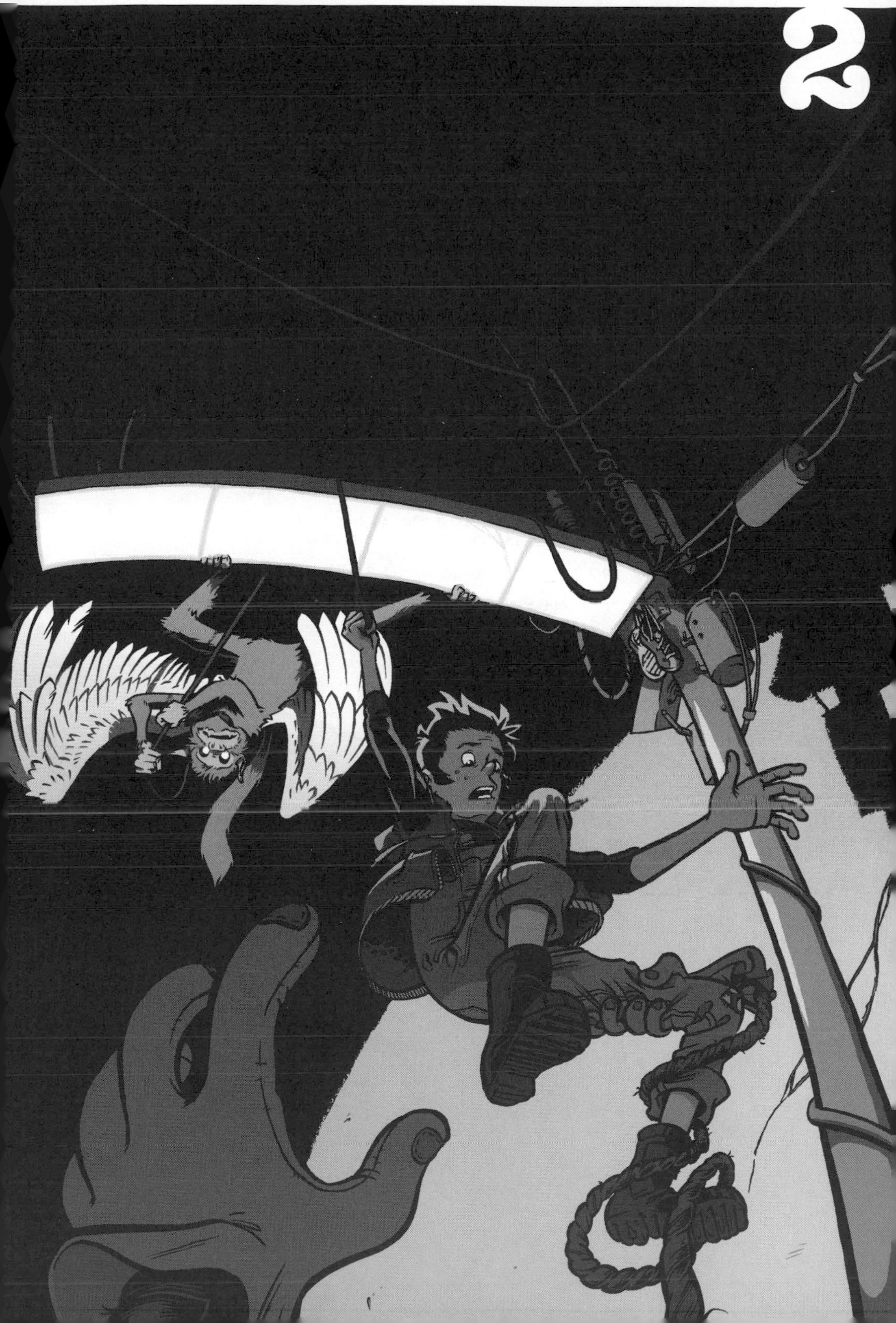

YOU MIGHT THINK THE DISCOVERY OF *ACTUAL MAGIC* -- A WHOLE
COUNTRY *FULL* OF IT -- WOULD MAKE THE REST OF MY BORING, STUPID LIFE SEEM
UNIMPORTANT. BUT WHEN DAD SAID WE HAD TO DROP EVERYTHING AND LEAVE, ALL I
COULD THINK ABOUT WERE MY FRIENDS AND THE PARTY I'D MISS ON SATURDAY NIGHT.

BUT DAD KEEPS INSISTING THAT HE ISN'T READY TO *"GO PUBLIC"* WITH THIS OZ STUFF, YET.
HE DOESN'T REALLY HAVE CONTROL OF THE COLLECTION, DOESN'T UNDERSTAND ALL THE MAGIC,
AND HASN'T FIGURED OUT HOW TO MAKE SURE NOBODY WILL TAKE THIS AWAY FROM HIM.

IN OTHER WORDS: SURPRISE! DAD DOESN'T HAVE A CLUE. *AS USUAL.*

IN THE MEANTIME, THE OZ SOCIETY WILL THROW US IN JAIL FOR DEFYING THEIR *CEASE & DESIST
ORDER* IF THEY SEE DAD'S NEW OZ BOOK, AND SOME PISSED-OFF *MUNCHKINS* MIGHT BE COMING AFTER
US TO GET THEIR FAIRY SPARKLE POTION BACK. SO WE HAVE TO STAY ON THE MOVE AND OFF THE GRID.

AND SOMETHING ELSE IS BOTHERING ME. IT'S HARD TO EXPLAIN, BUT OZ IS DAD'S THING.
IT MAY BE FULL OF AMAZING WONDERS, BUT THEY'RE *DAD'S* WONDERS, NOT MINE.

I DIDN'T HAVE MUCH BEFORE WE LEFT HOME, BUT I HAD A FEW FRIENDS THAT WERE JUST MINE, AND WE
HAD OUR PRIVATE JOKES AND OUR SECRET NICKNAMES, AND THIS REALLY COOL ABANDONED SUBWAY
TUNNEL THAT DAD DOESN'T EVEN KNOW ABOUT BECAUSE HE'D THINK IT WAS TOO DANGEROUS.

NOW I'M LIVING IN DAD'S WORLD 24/7.

BUT I'M A SUPER-AWESOME SON WHO WOULD *NEVER* ABANDON HIS DAD,
AND IT MEANS EVERYTHING TO ME TO SEE HIM SO HAPPY FINALLY.

ACTUALLY, THAT'S TOTAL B.S. I THINK ABOUT DITCHING HIM
AND RUNNING BACK HOME EVERY SINGLE DAY.

AND EVERY TIME I THINK ABOUT IT, I FEEL HORRIBLE.

AT LEAST I HAVE A NEW FRIEND. PET?

WELL, WHATEVER ZIK IS.

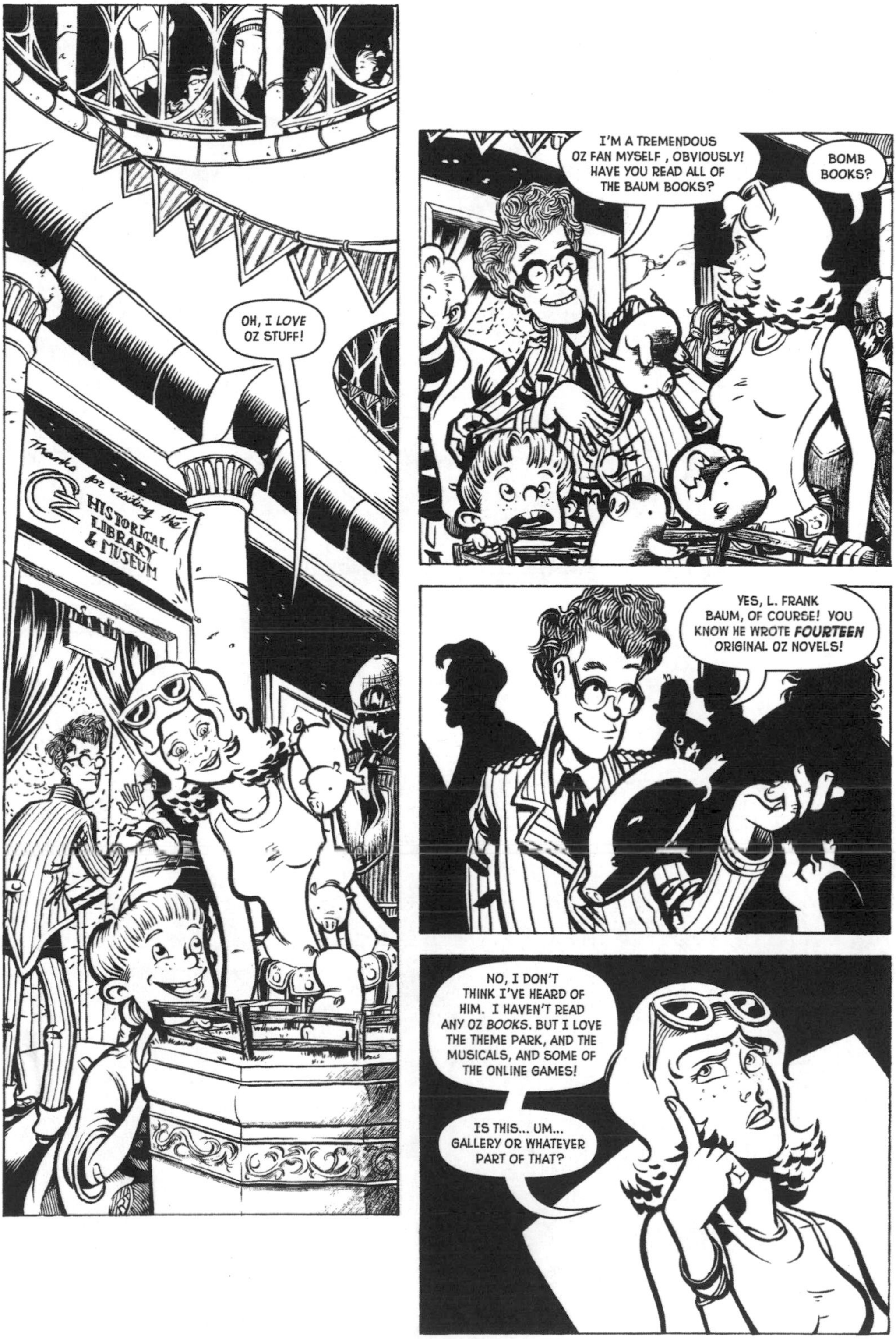
Thanks for visiting the
OZ HISTORICAL LIBRARY & MUSEUM
OH, I *LOVE* OZ STUFF!
I'M A TREMENDOUS OZ FAN MYSELF , OBVIOUSLY! HAVE YOU READ ALL OF THE BAUM BOOKS?
BOMB BOOKS?
YES, L. FRANK BAUM, OF COURSE! YOU KNOW HE WROTE **FOURTEEN** ORIGINAL OZ NOVELS!
NO, I DON'T THINK I'VE HEARD OF HIM. I HAVEN'T READ ANY OZ *BOOKS*. BUT I LOVE THE THEME PARK, AND THE MUSICALS, AND SOME OF THE ONLINE GAMES!
IS THIS... UM... GALLERY OR WHATEVER PART OF THAT?

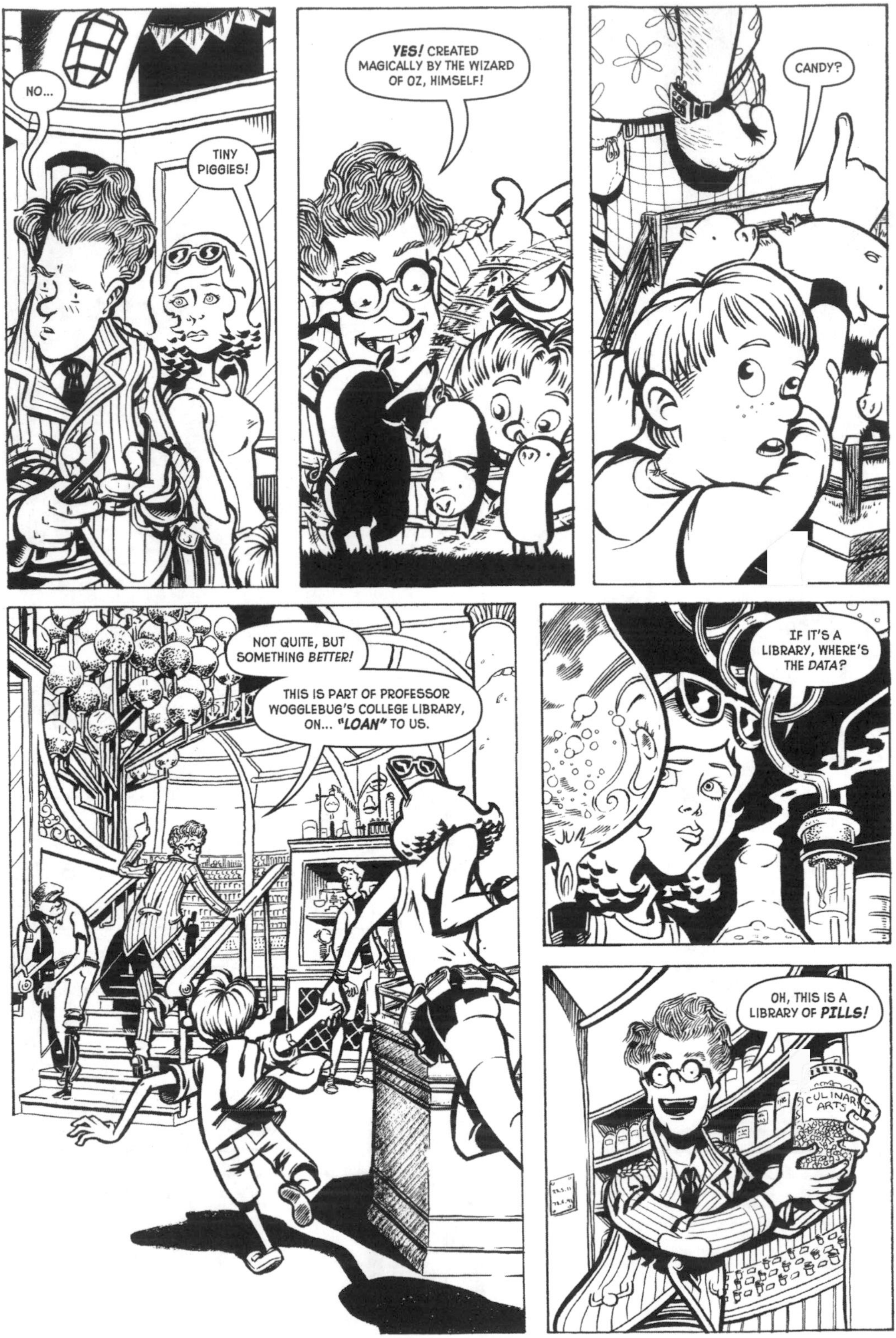
NO...
TINY PIGGIES!
YES! CREATED MAGICALLY BY THE WIZARD OF OZ, HIMSELF!
CANDY?
NOT QUITE, BUT SOMETHING BETTER!
THIS IS PART OF PROFESSOR WOGGLEBUG'S COLLEGE LIBRARY, ON... "LOAN" TO US.
IF IT'S A LIBRARY, WHERE'S THE DATA?
OH, THIS IS A LIBRARY OF PILLS!
CULINARY ARTS

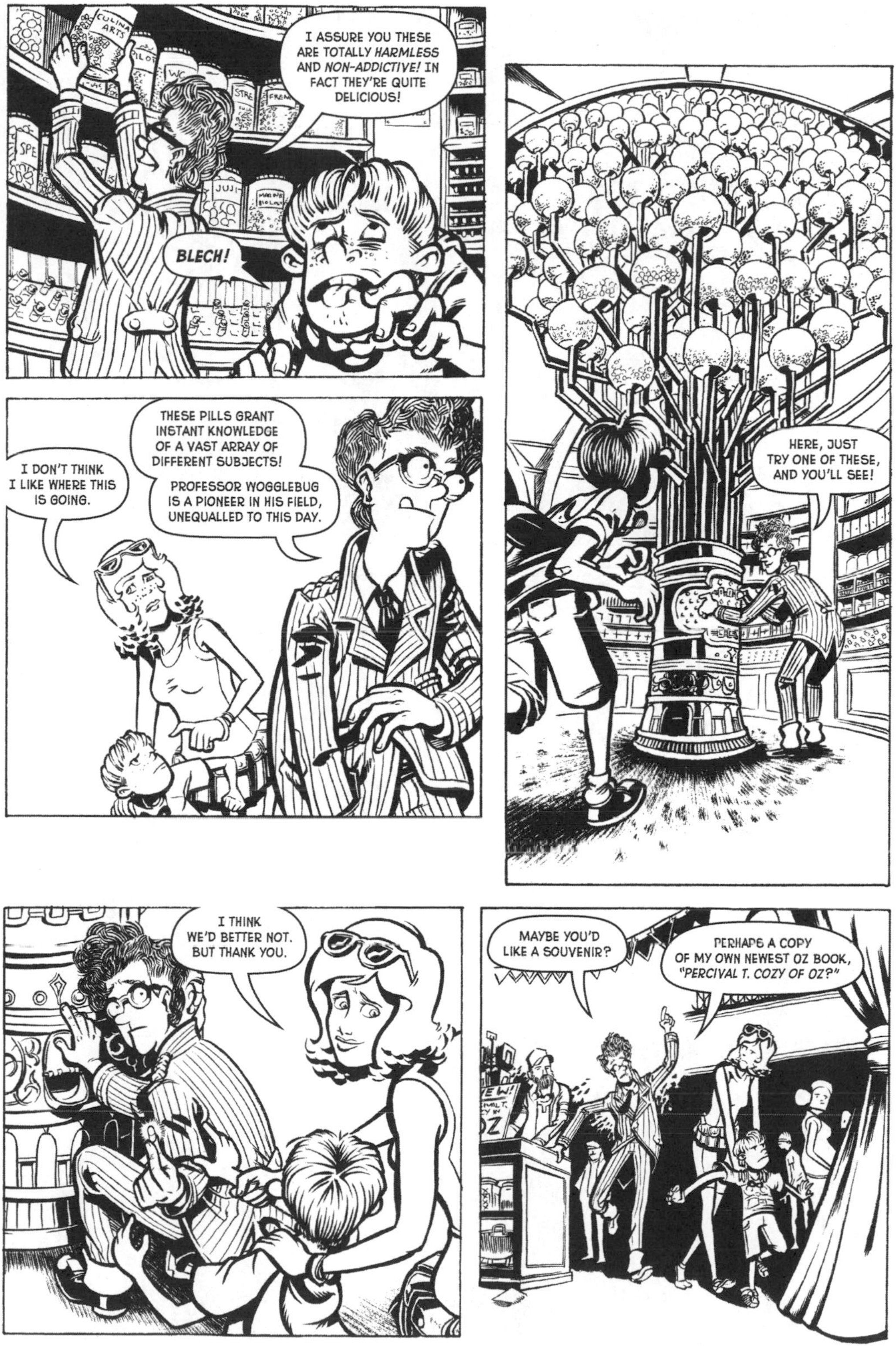
I ASSURE YOU THESE ARE TOTALLY *HARMLESS* AND *NON-ADDICTIVE!* IN FACT THEY'RE QUITE DELICIOUS!
BLECH!
THESE PILLS GRANT INSTANT KNOWLEDGE OF A VAST ARRAY OF DIFFERENT SUBJECTS!
PROFESSOR WOGGLEBUG IS A PIONEER IN HIS FIELD, UNEQUALLED TO THIS DAY.
I DON'T THINK I LIKE WHERE THIS IS GOING.
HERE, JUST TRY ONE OF THESE, AND YOU'LL SEE!
I THINK WE'D BETTER NOT. BUT THANK YOU.
MAYBE YOU'D LIKE A SOUVENIR?
PERHAPS A COPY OF MY OWN NEWEST OZ BOOK, *"PERCIVAL T. COZY OF OZ?"*

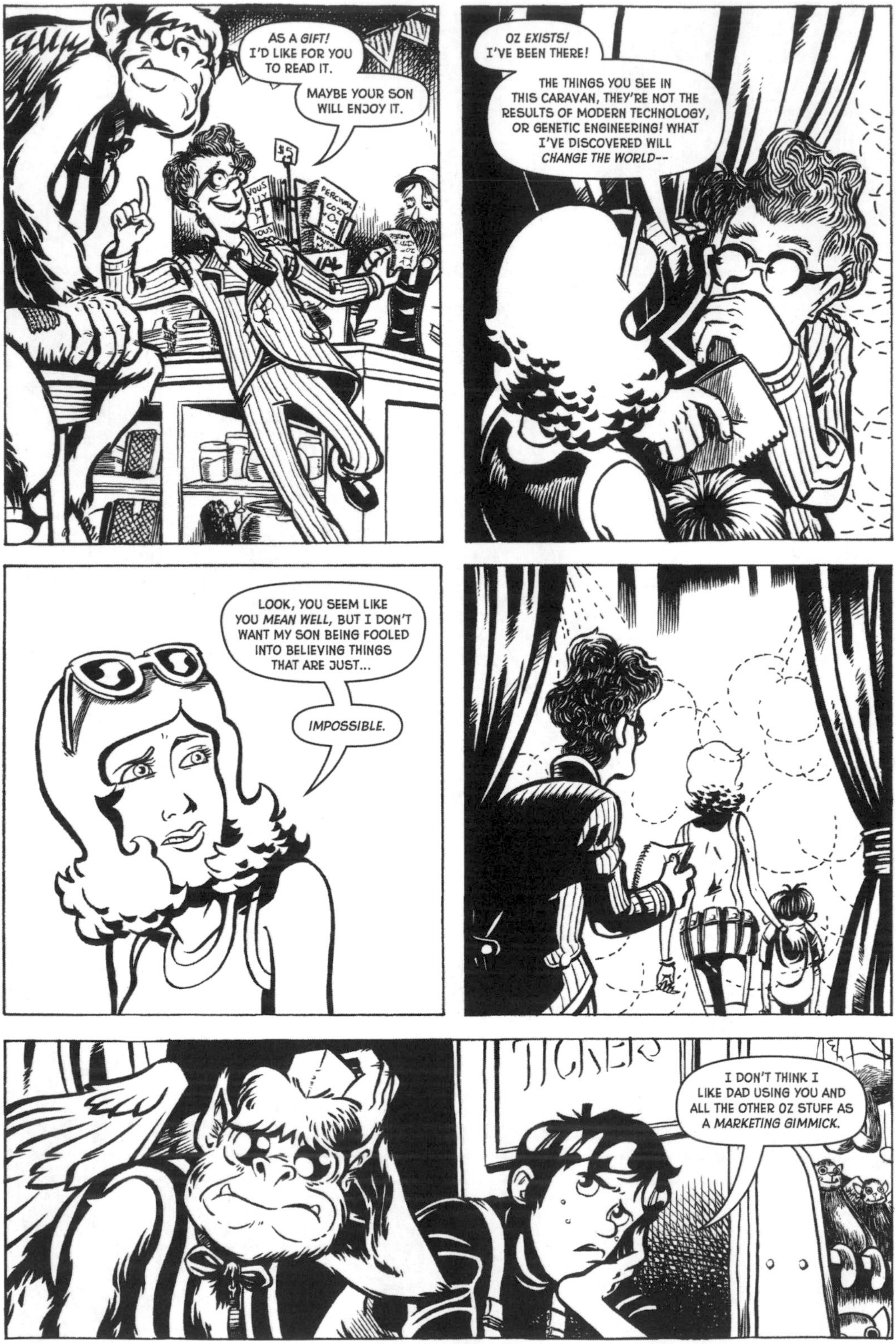
AS A *GIFT!* I'D LIKE FOR YOU TO READ IT.
MAYBE YOUR SON WILL ENJOY IT.
OZ *EXISTS!* I'VE BEEN THERE!
THE THINGS YOU SEE IN THIS CARAVAN, THEY'RE NOT THE RESULTS OF MODERN TECHNOLOGY, OR GENETIC ENGINEERING! WHAT I'VE DISCOVERED WILL *CHANGE THE WORLD--*
LOOK, YOU SEEM LIKE YOU *MEAN WELL,* BUT I DON'T WANT MY SON BEING FOOLED INTO BELIEVING THINGS THAT ARE JUST...
IMPOSSIBLE.
I DON'T THINK I LIKE DAD USING YOU AND ALL THE OTHER OZ STUFF AS A *MARKETING GIMMICK.*

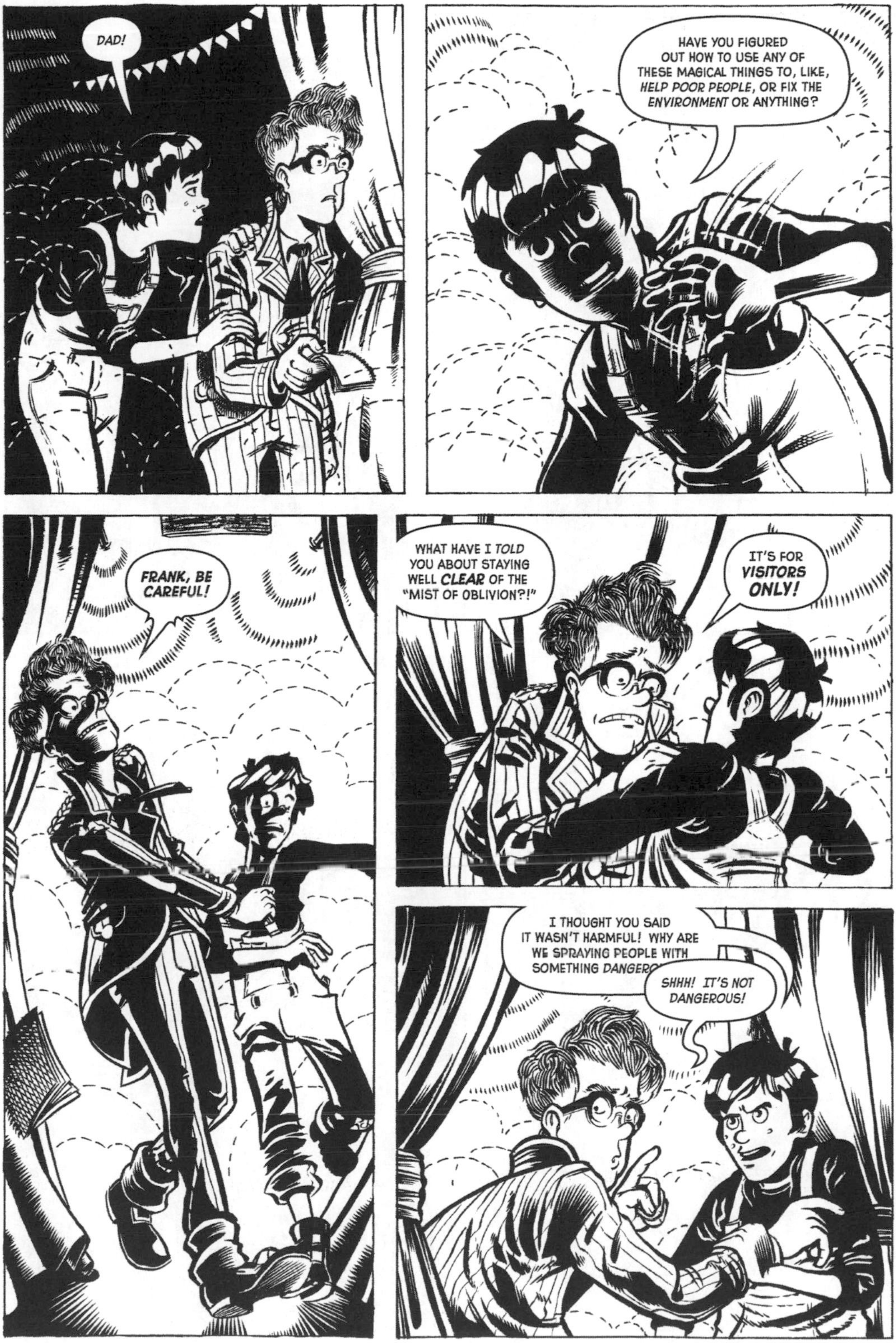
DAD!
HAVE YOU FIGURED OUT HOW TO USE ANY OF THESE MAGICAL THINGS TO, LIKE, HELP POOR PEOPLE, OR FIX THE ENVIRONMENT OR ANYTHING?
FRANK, BE CAREFUL!
WHAT HAVE I TOLD YOU ABOUT STAYING WELL CLEAR OF THE "MIST OF OBLIVION?!"
IT'S FOR VISITORS ONLY!
I THOUGHT YOU SAID IT WASN'T HARMFUL! WHY ARE WE SPRAYING PEOPLE WITH SOMETHING DANGERO
SHHH! IT'S NOT DANGEROUS!

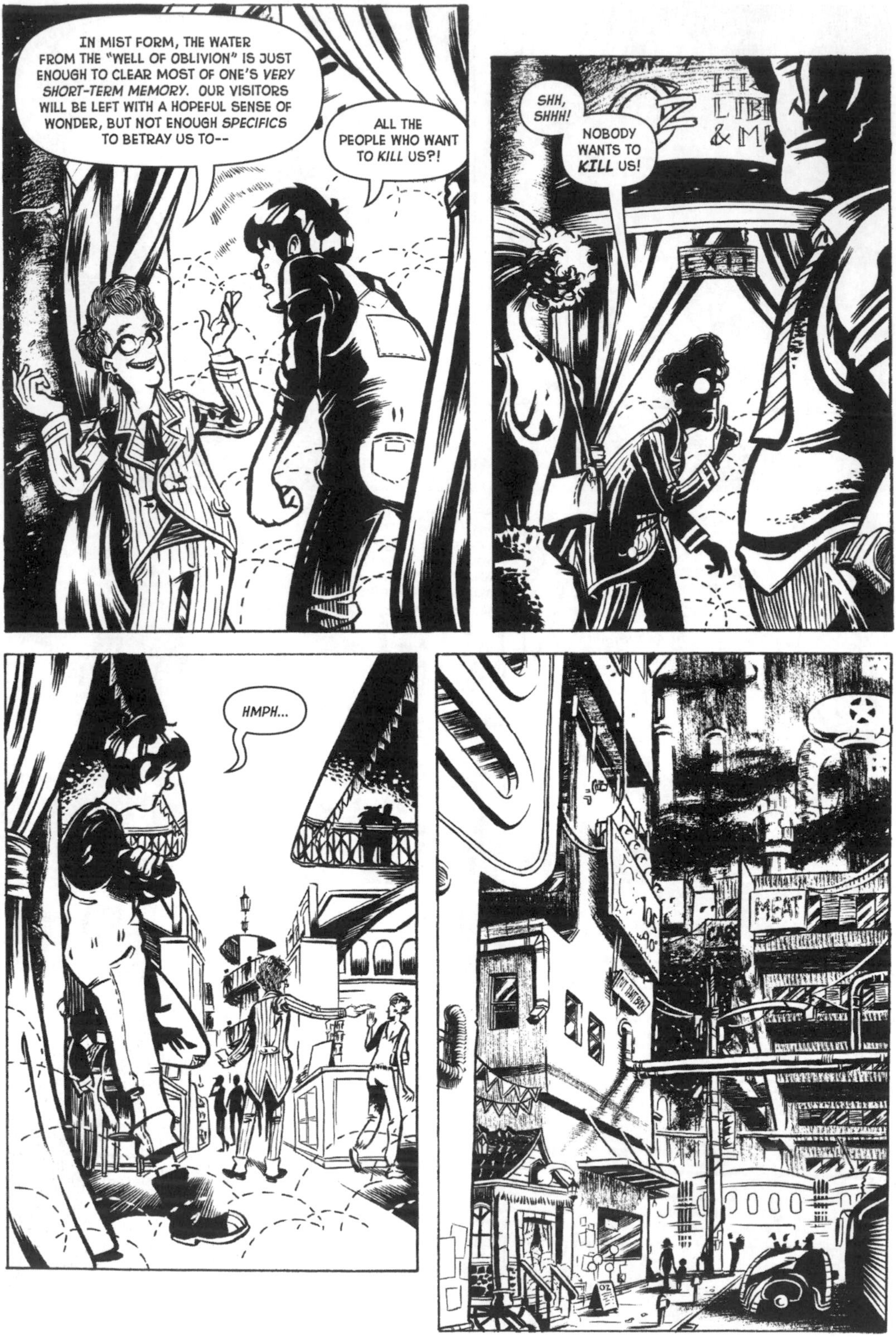
IN MIST FORM, THE WATER FROM THE "WELL OF OBLIVION" IS JUST ENOUGH TO CLEAR MOST OF ONE'S *VERY SHORT-TERM MEMORY*. OUR VISITORS WILL BE LEFT WITH A HOPEFUL SENSE OF WONDER, BUT NOT ENOUGH *SPECIFICS* TO BETRAY US TO--
ALL THE PEOPLE WHO WANT TO *KILL* US?!
SHH, SHHH!
NOBODY WANTS TO ***KILL*** US!
EXIT
HMPH...
MEAT
OZ

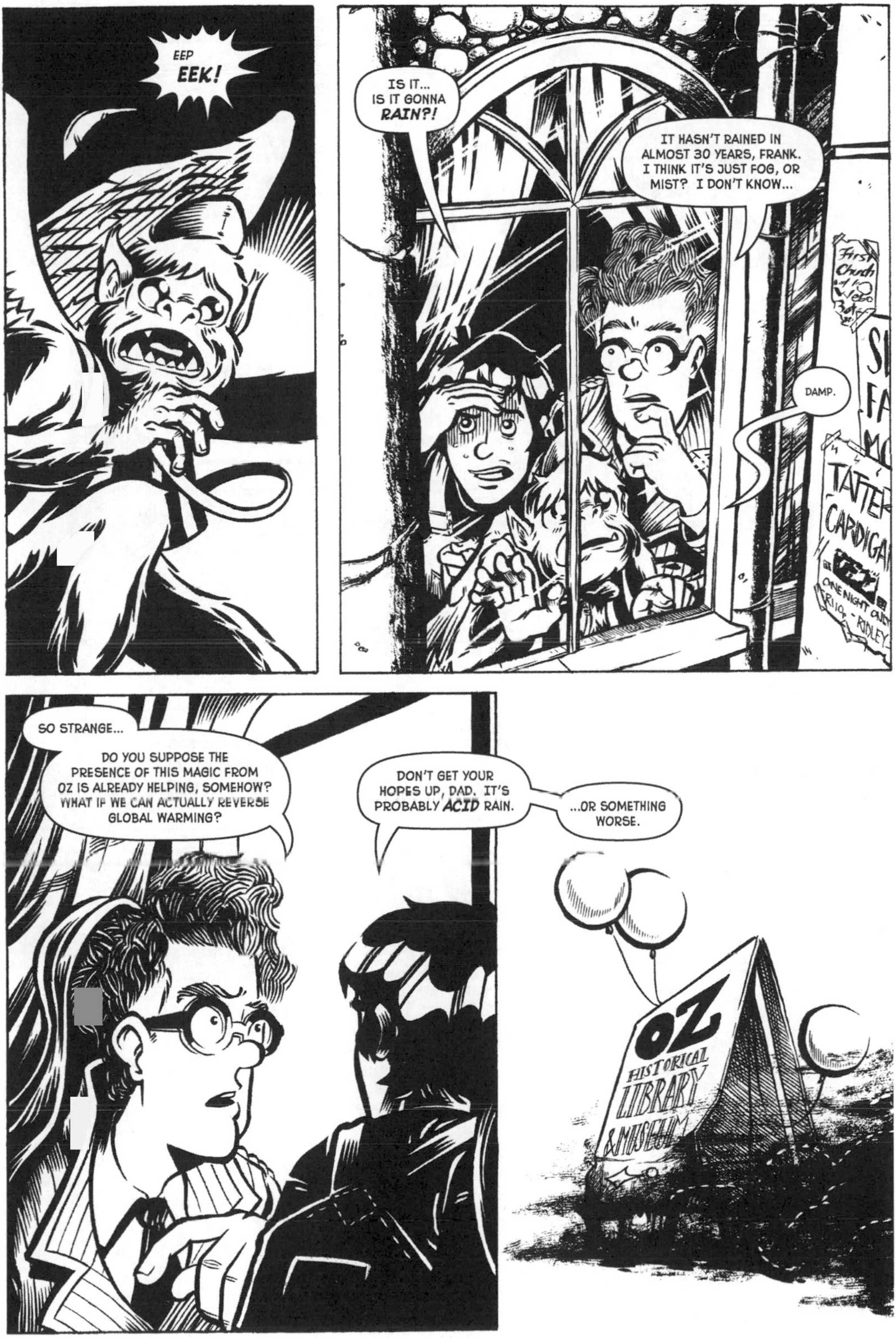
EEP
EEK!
IS IT... IS IT GONNA RAIN?!
IT HASN'T RAINED IN ALMOST 30 YEARS, FRANK. I THINK IT'S JUST FOG, OR MIST? I DON'T KNOW...
DAMP.
SO STRANGE...
DO YOU SUPPOSE THE PRESENCE OF THIS MAGIC FROM OZ IS ALREADY HELPING, SOMEHOW? WHAT IF WE CAN ACTUALLY REVERSE GLOBAL WARMING?
DON'T GET YOUR HOPES UP, DAD. IT'S PROBABLY ACID RAIN.
...OR SOMETHING WORSE.
OZ HISTORICAL LIBRARY & MUSEUM

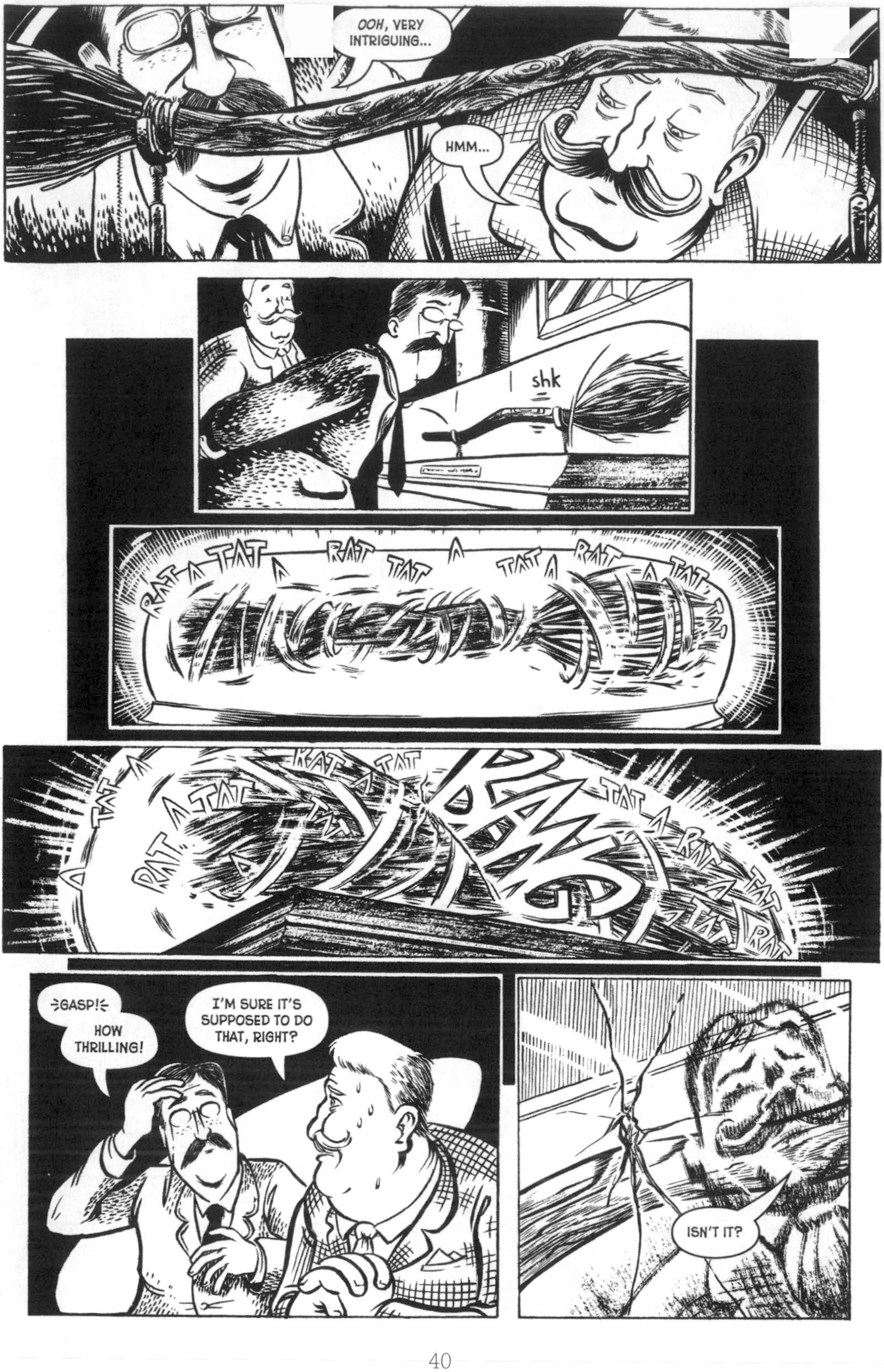
OOH, VERY INTRIGUING...
HMM...
shk
RAT A TAT A RAT TAT A TAT A RAT A TAT TAT
A TAT A RAT A TAT RAT A TAT BANG TAT A RAT A TAT RAT TAT
⋞GASP!⋟ HOW THRILLING!
I'M SURE IT'S SUPPOSED TO DO THAT, RIGHT?
ISN'T IT?

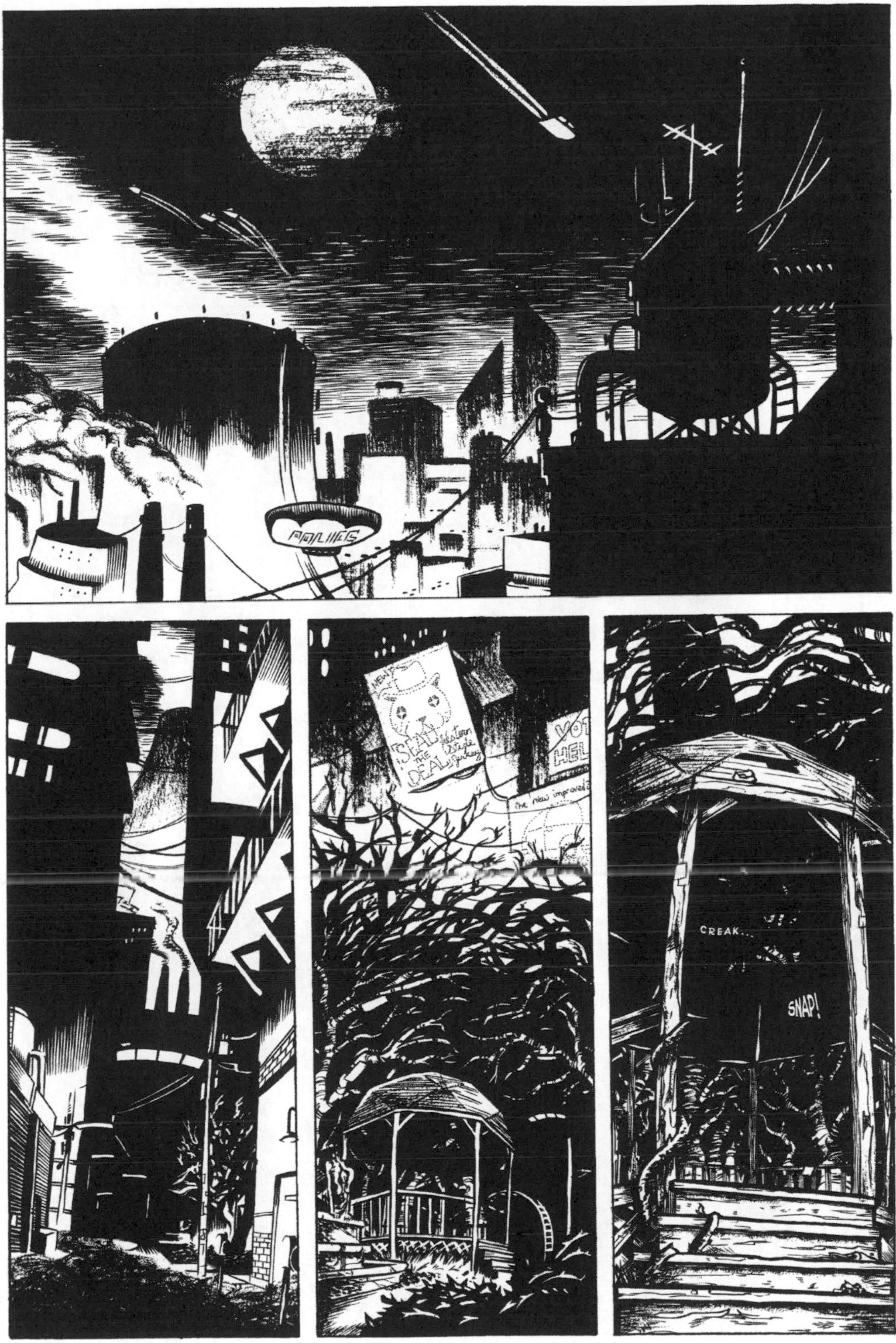

NEWS
SEAL THE DEAL
Western Lifestyle Jockey
the new improved
CREAK...
SNAP!

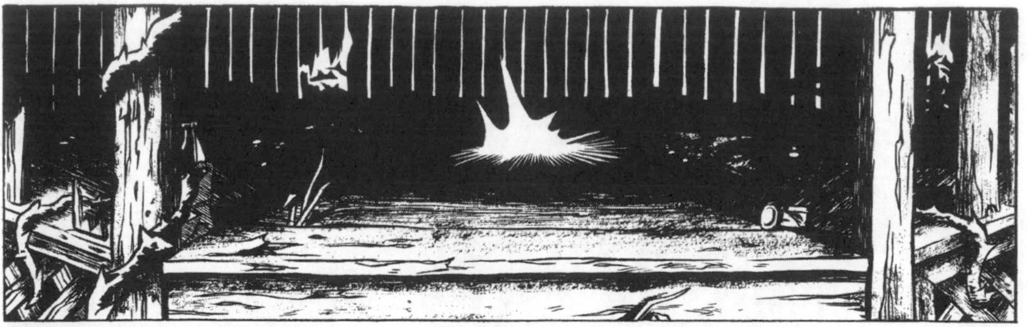

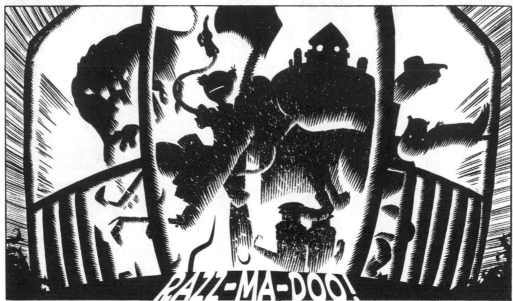

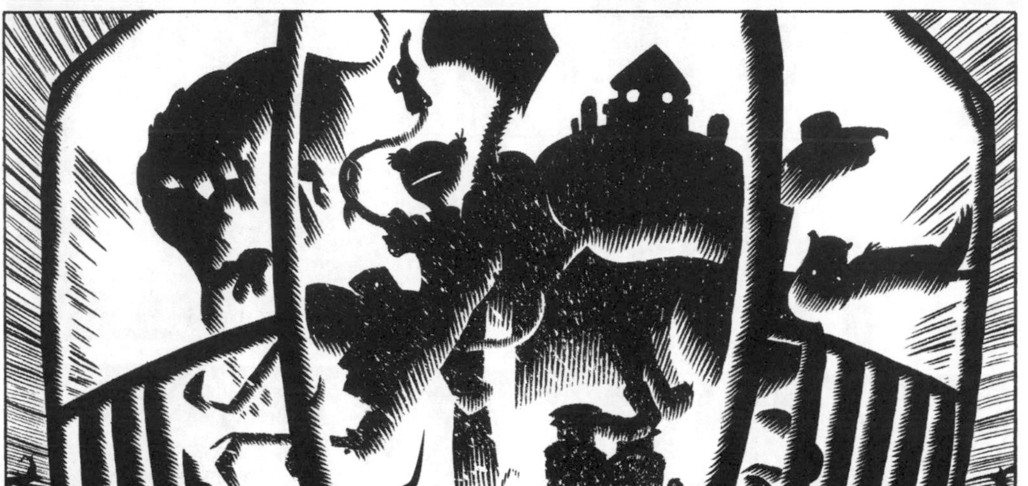
RAZZ-MA-DOO!

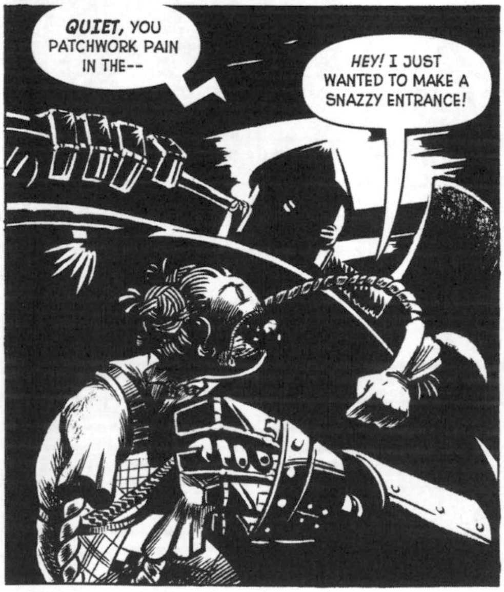
QUIET, YOU PATCHWORK PAIN IN THE--
HEY! I JUST WANTED TO MAKE A SNAZZY ENTRANCE!

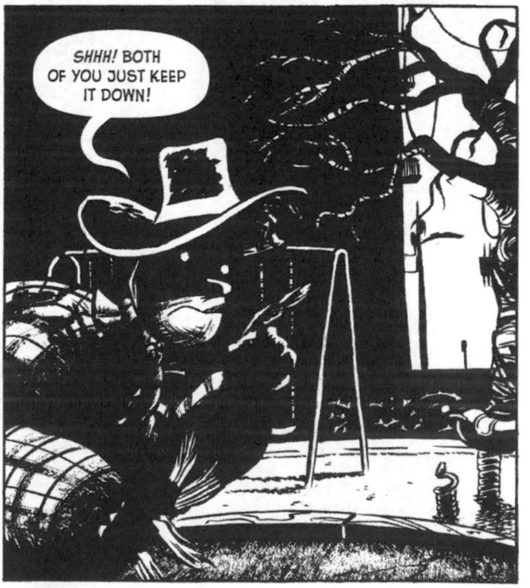
SHHH! BOTH OF YOU JUST KEEP IT DOWN!

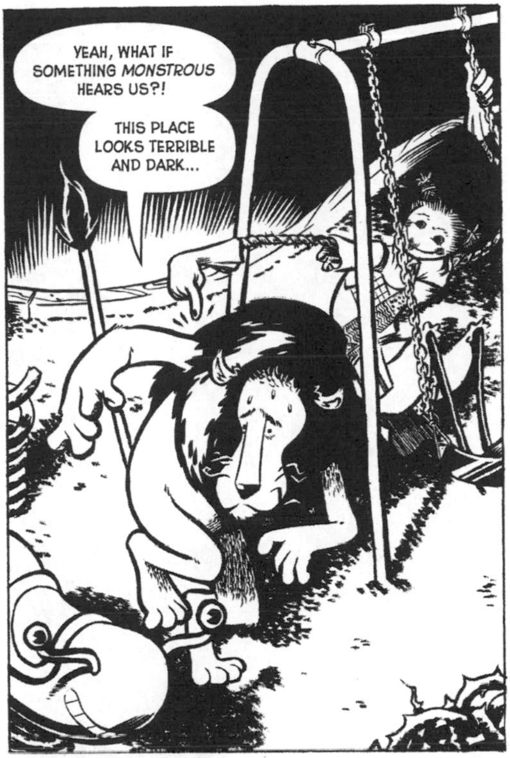
YEAH, WHAT IF SOMETHING *MONSTROUS* HEARS US?!
THIS PLACE LOOKS TERRIBLE AND DARK...

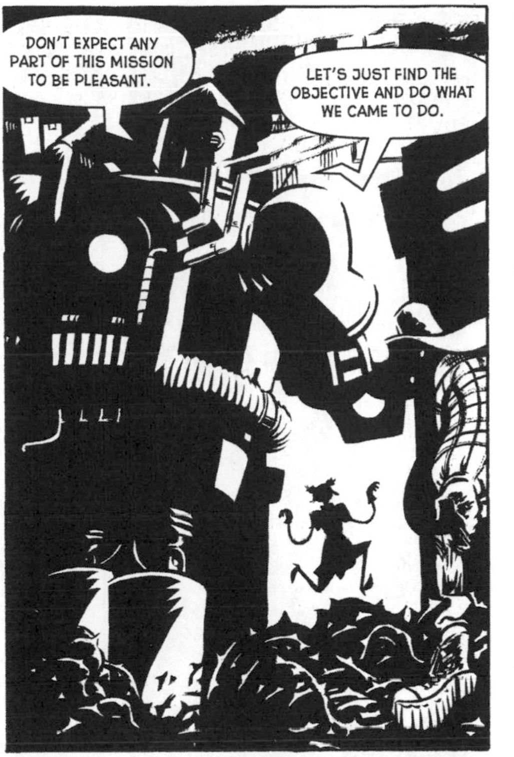
DON'T EXPECT ANY PART OF THIS MISSION TO BE PLEASANT.
LET'S JUST FIND THE OBJECTIVE AND DO WHAT WE CAME TO DO.

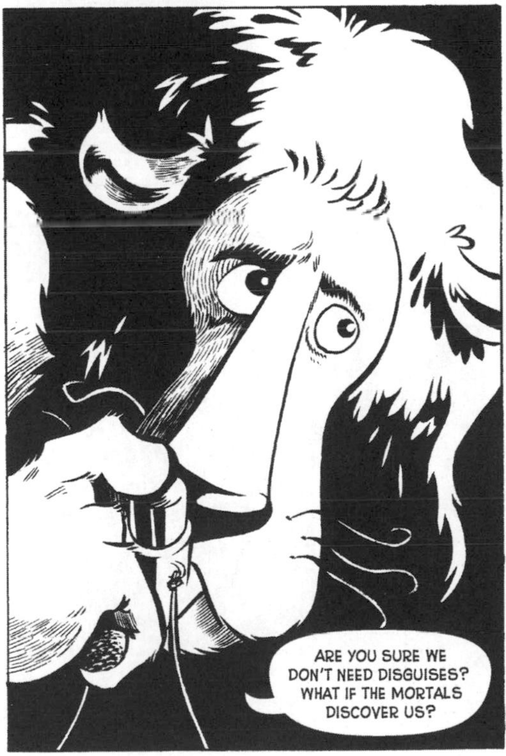
ARE YOU SURE WE DON'T NEED DISGUISES? WHAT IF THE MORTALS DISCOVER US?

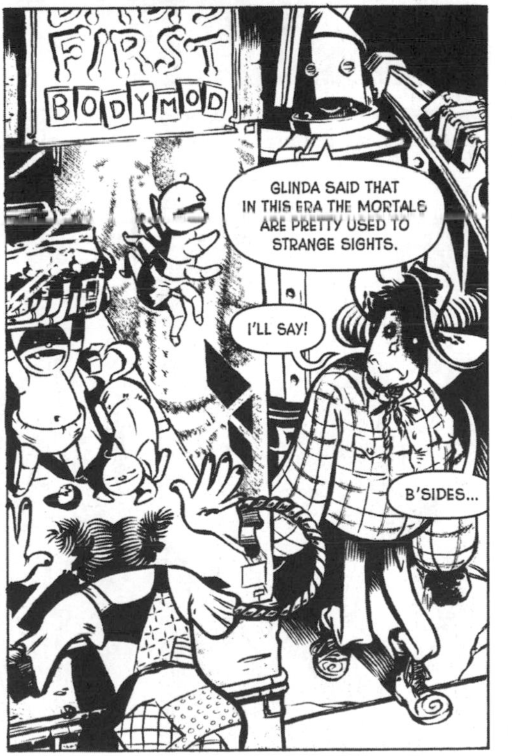
FIRST
BODYMOD
GLINDA SAID THAT IN THIS ERA THE MORTALS ARE PRETTY USED TO STRANGE SIGHTS.
I'LL SAY!
B'SIDES...

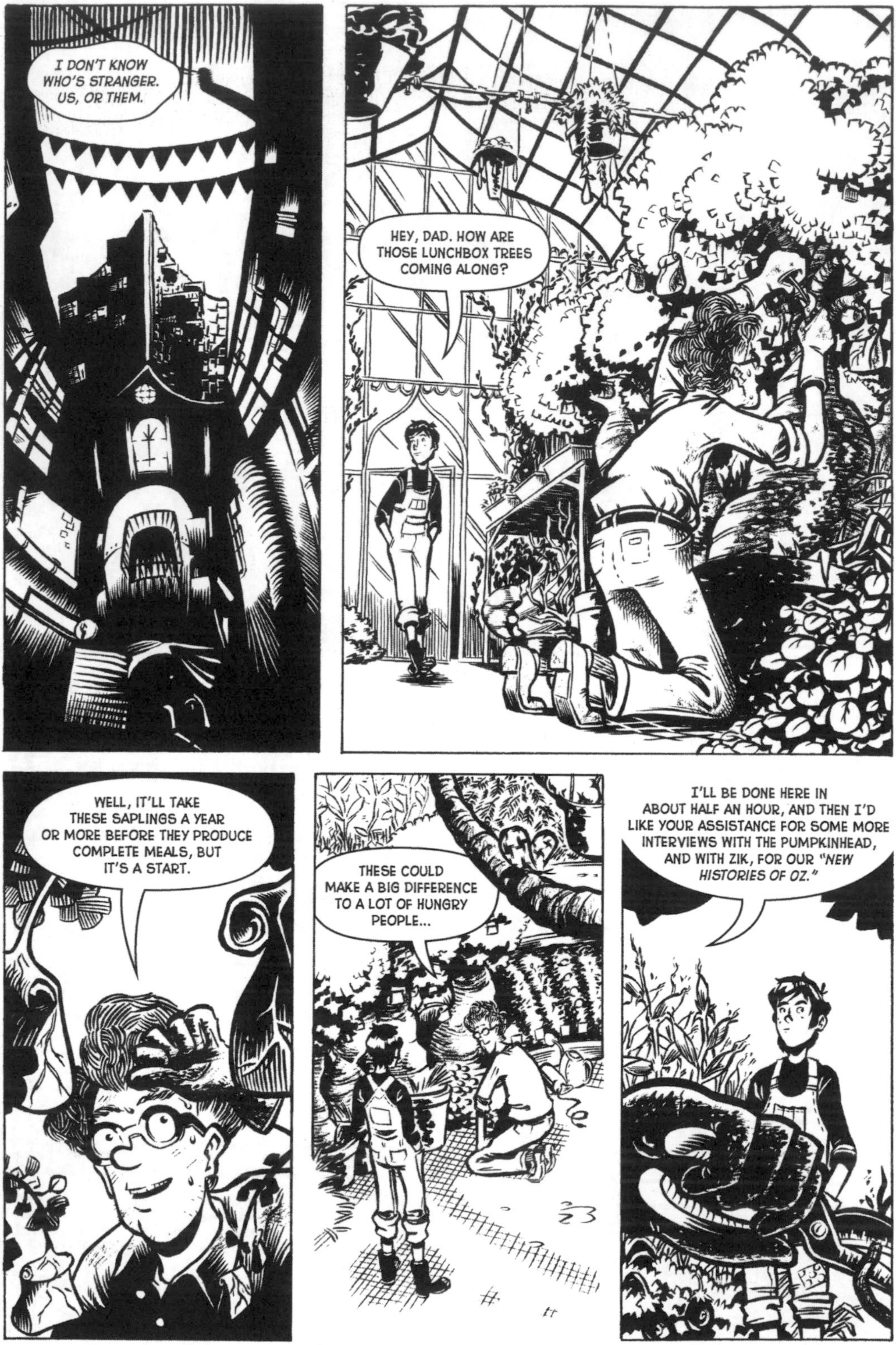
I DON'T KNOW WHO'S STRANGER. US, OR THEM.
HEY, DAD. HOW ARE THOSE LUNCHBOX TREES COMING ALONG?
WELL, IT'LL TAKE THESE SAPLINGS A YEAR OR MORE BEFORE THEY PRODUCE COMPLETE MEALS, BUT IT'S A START.
THESE COULD MAKE A BIG DIFFERENCE TO A LOT OF HUNGRY PEOPLE...
I'LL BE DONE HERE IN ABOUT HALF AN HOUR, AND THEN I'D LIKE YOUR ASSISTANCE FOR SOME MORE INTERVIEWS WITH THE PUMPKINHEAD, AND WITH ZIK, FOR OUR "NEW HISTORIES OF OZ."

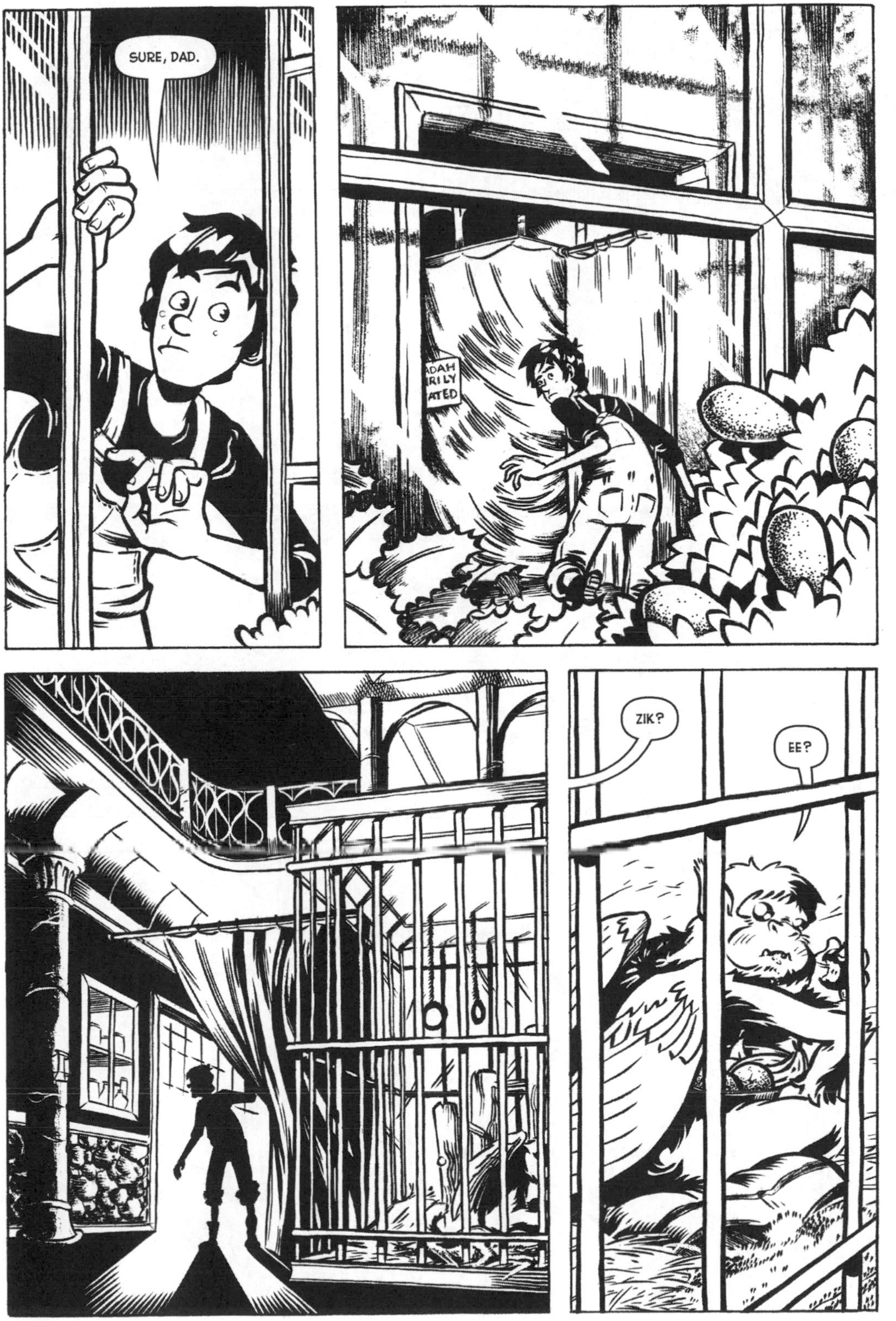
SURE, DAD.
ZIK?
EE?

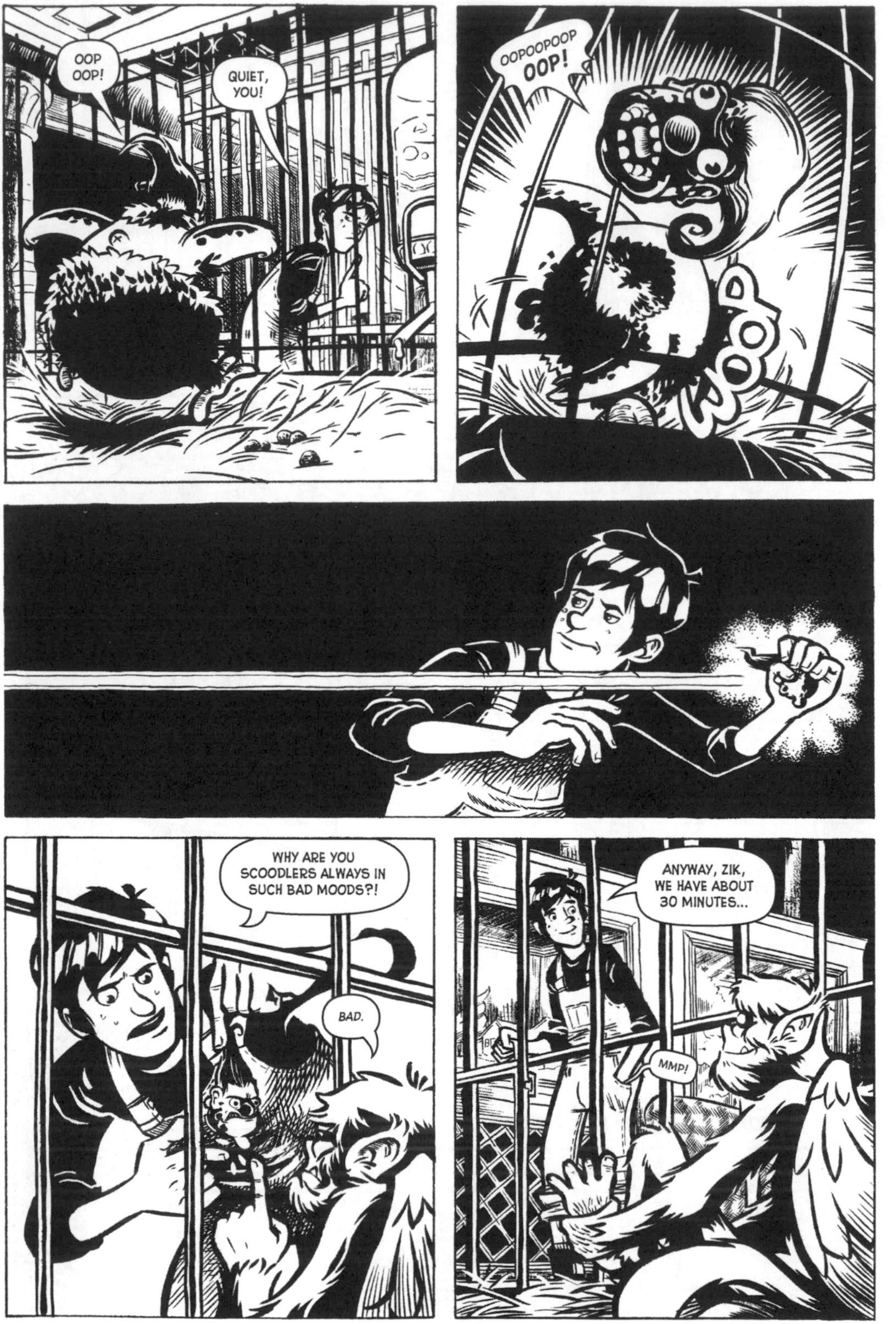
OOP OOP!
QUIET, YOU!
OOPOOPOOP OOP!
WOOP
WHY ARE YOU SCOODLERS ALWAYS IN SUCH BAD MOODS?!
BAD.
ANYWAY, ZIK, WE HAVE ABOUT 30 MINUTES...
MMP!

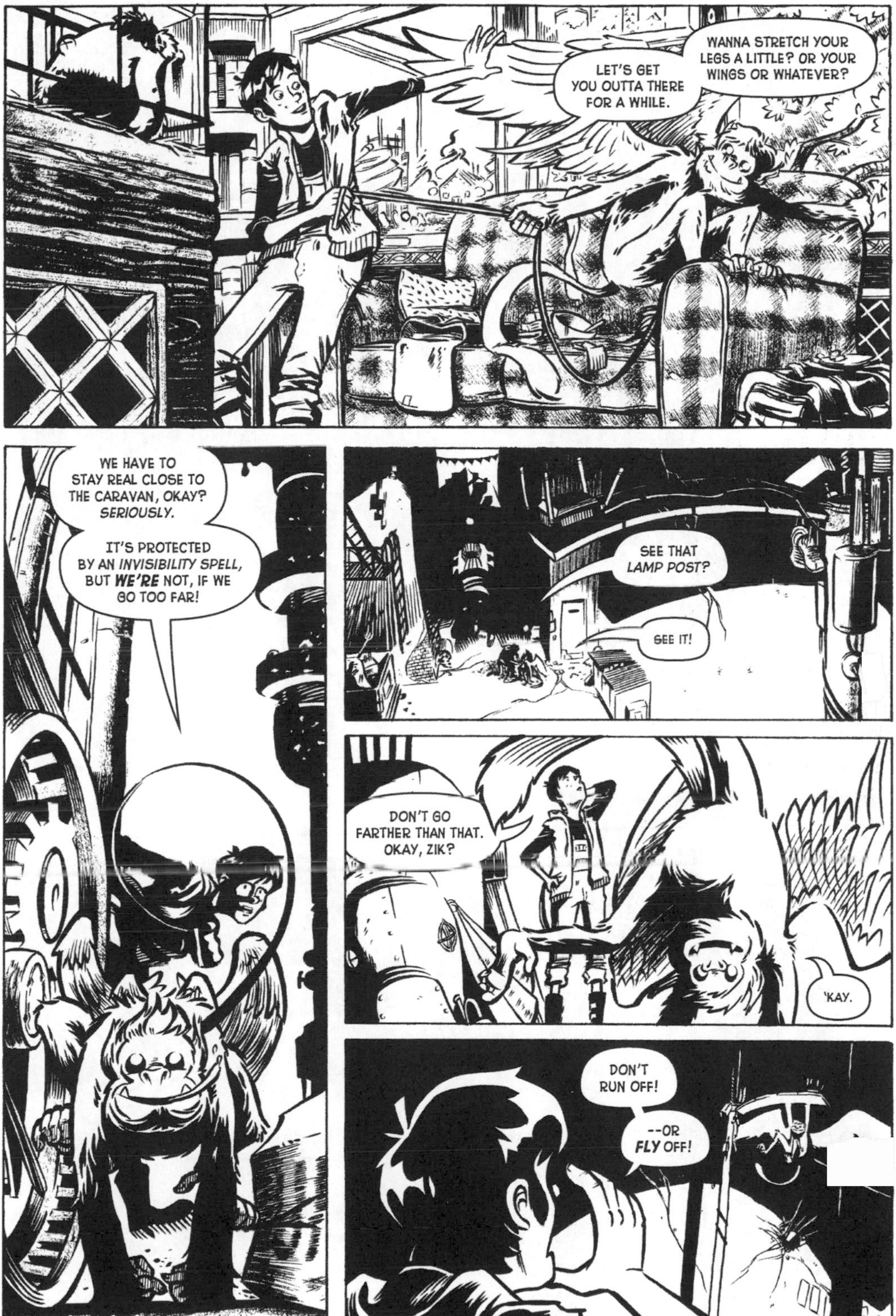
LET'S GET YOU OUTTA THERE FOR A WHILE.
WANNA STRETCH YOUR LEGS A LITTLE? OR YOUR WINGS OR WHATEVER?
WE HAVE TO STAY REAL CLOSE TO THE CARAVAN, OKAY? *SERIOUSLY.*
IT'S PROTECTED BY AN *INVISIBILITY SPELL,* BUT ***WE'RE*** NOT, IF WE GO TOO FAR!
SEE THAT *LAMP POST?*
SEE IT!
DON'T GO FARTHER THAN THAT. OKAY, ZIK?
'KAY.
DON'T RUN OFF!
--OR ***FLY*** OFF!

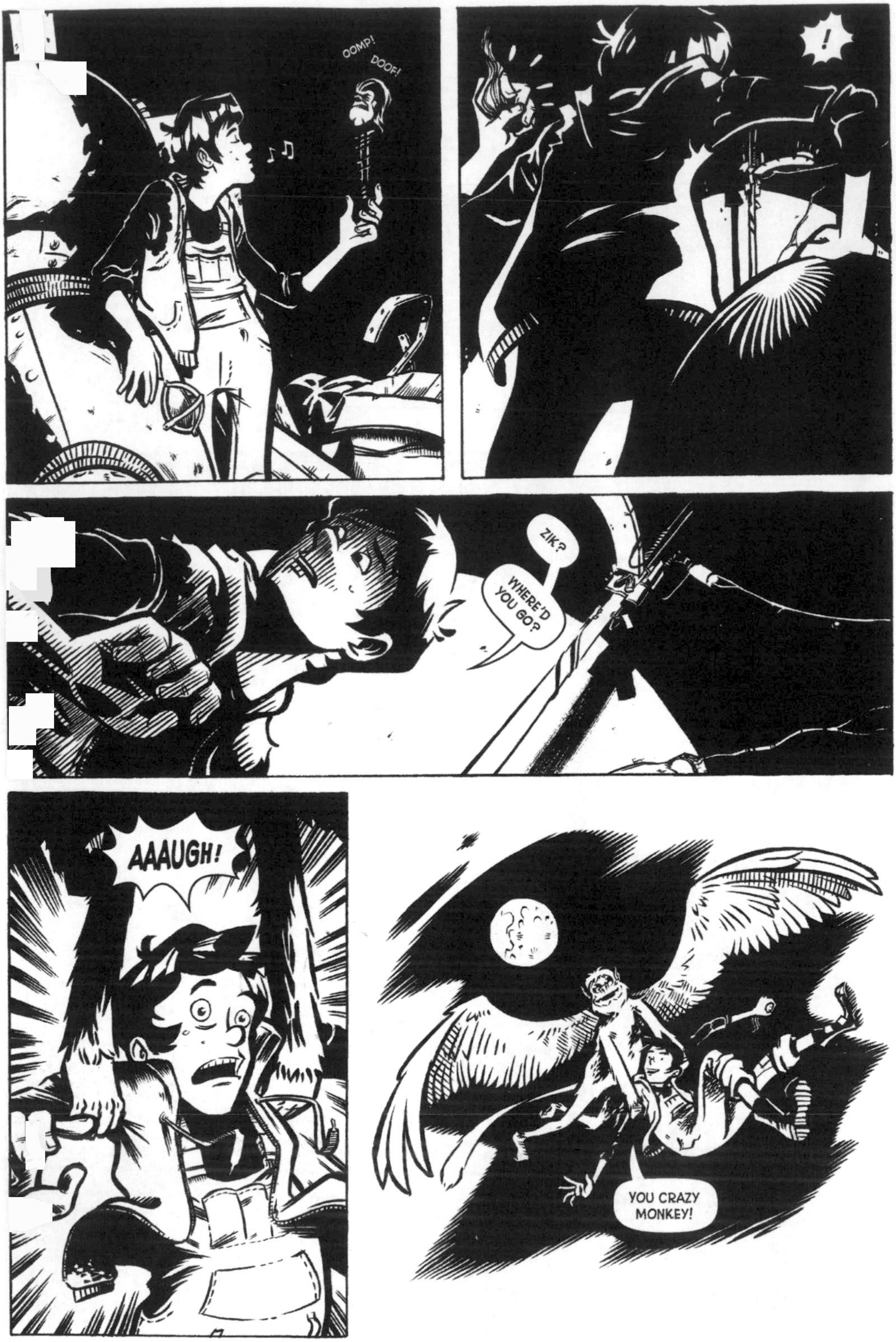
OOMP!
DOOF!
!
ZIK?
WHERE'D YOU GO?
AAAUGH!
YOU CRAZY MONKEY!

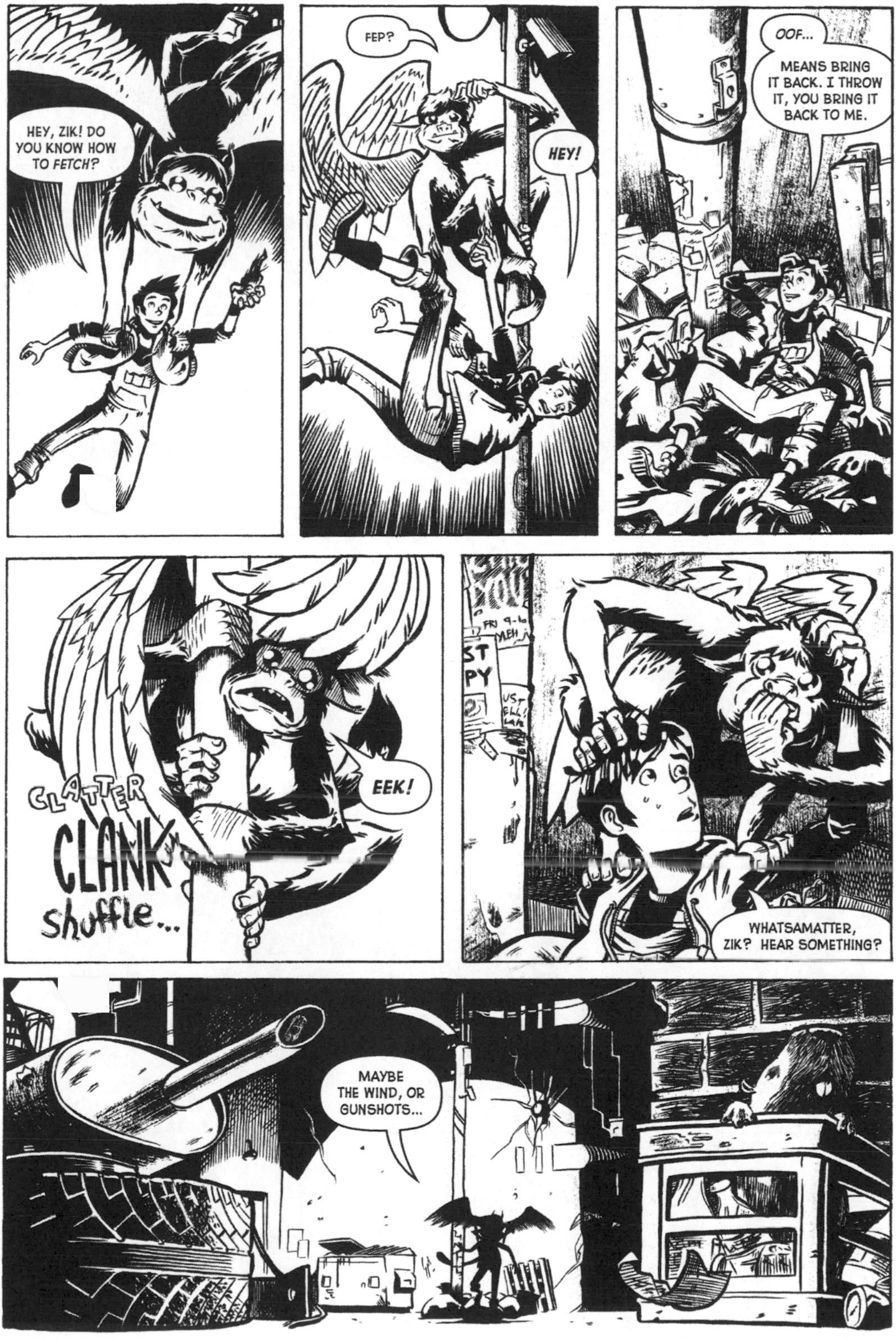
HEY, ZIK! DO YOU KNOW HOW TO *FETCH*?
FEP?
HEY!
OOF...
MEANS BRING IT BACK. I THROW IT, YOU BRING IT BACK TO ME.
CLATTER
CLANK
shuffle...
EEK!
FRI 9-10
WHATSAMATTER, ZIK? HEAR SOMETHING?
MAYBE THE WIND, OR GUNSHOTS...

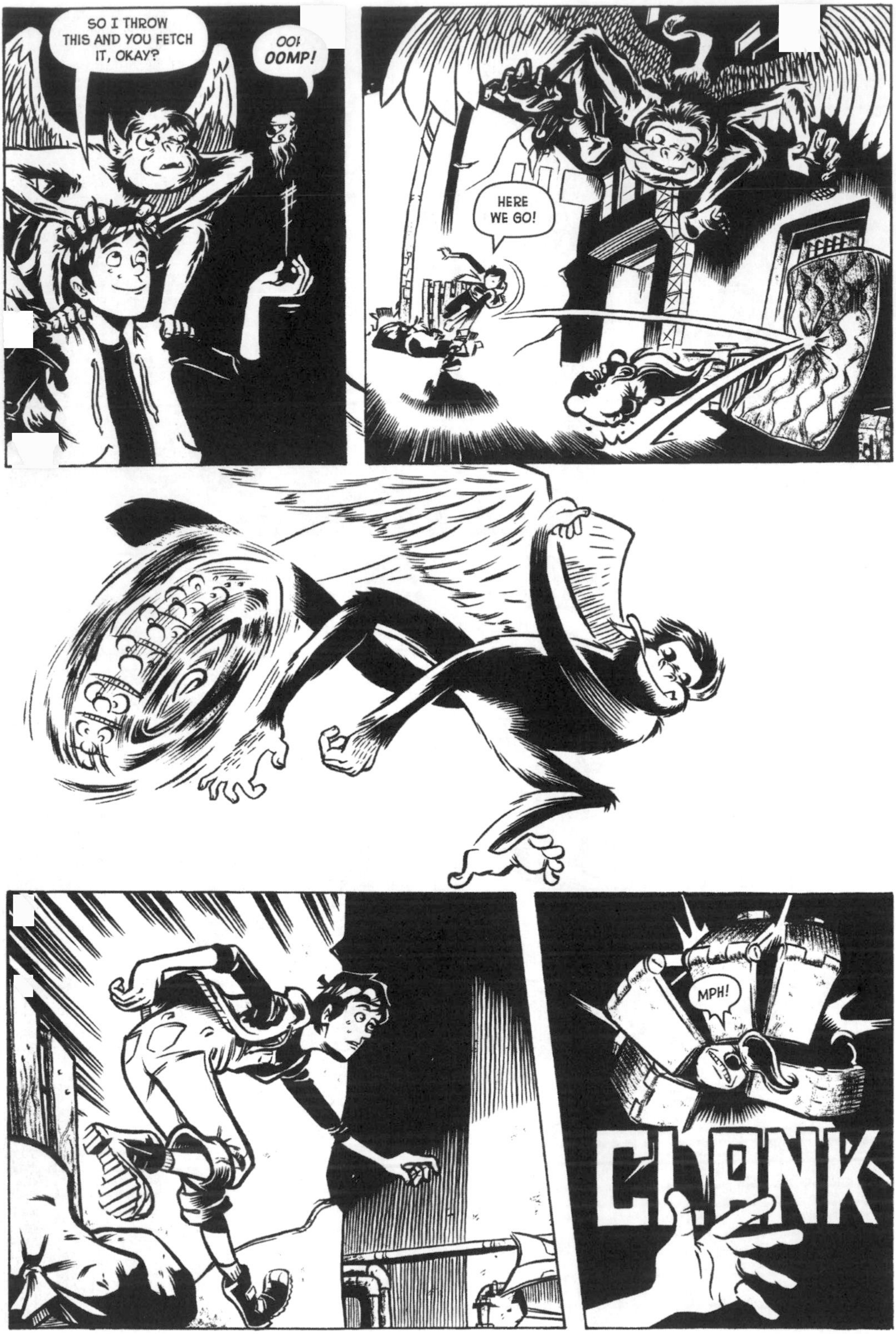
SO I THROW THIS AND YOU FETCH IT, OKAY?
OO! OOMP!
HERE WE GO!
MPH!
CLANK

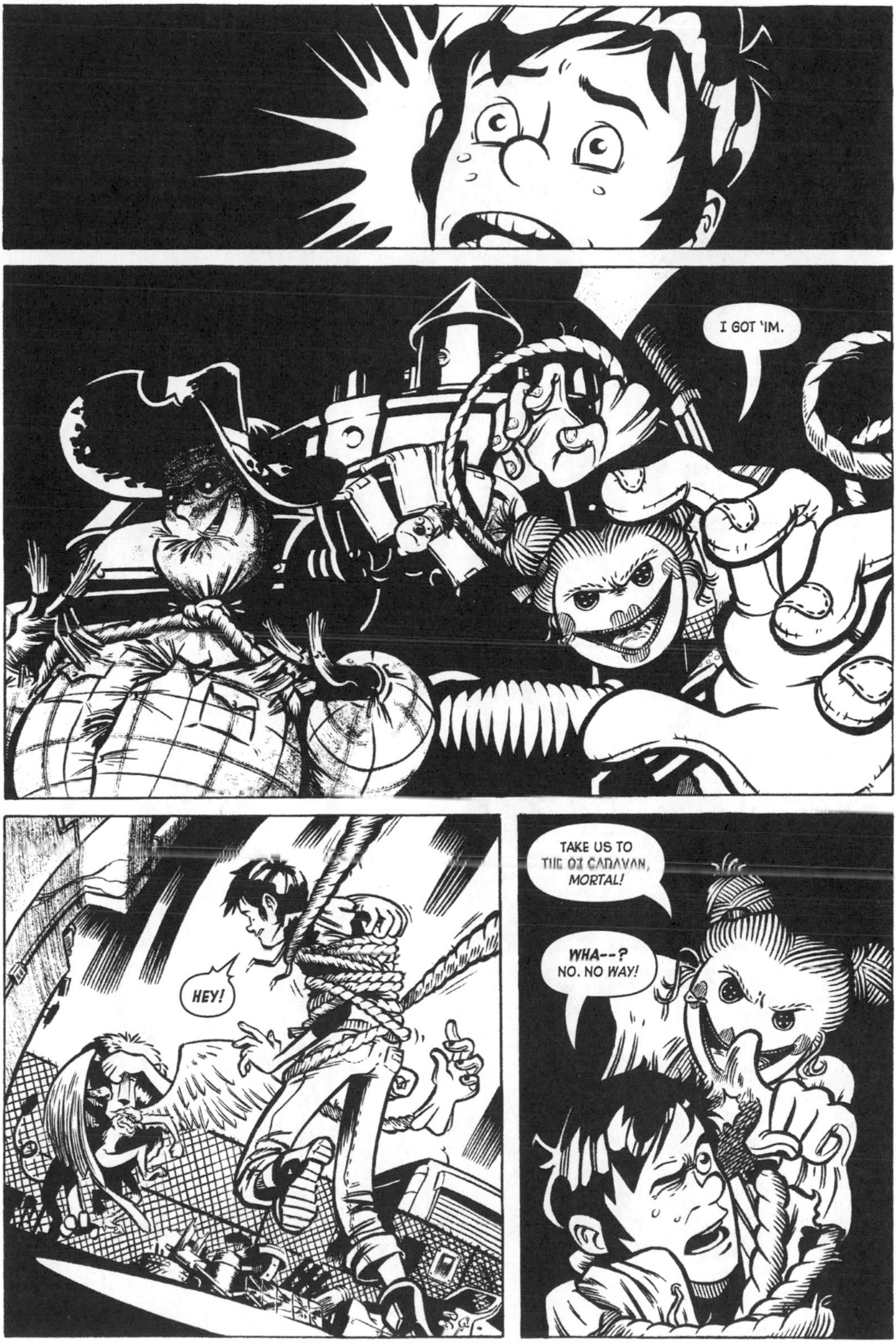
I GOT 'IM.
HEY!
TAKE US TO THE OZ CARAVAN, *MORTAL!*
WHA--? NO. NO WAY!

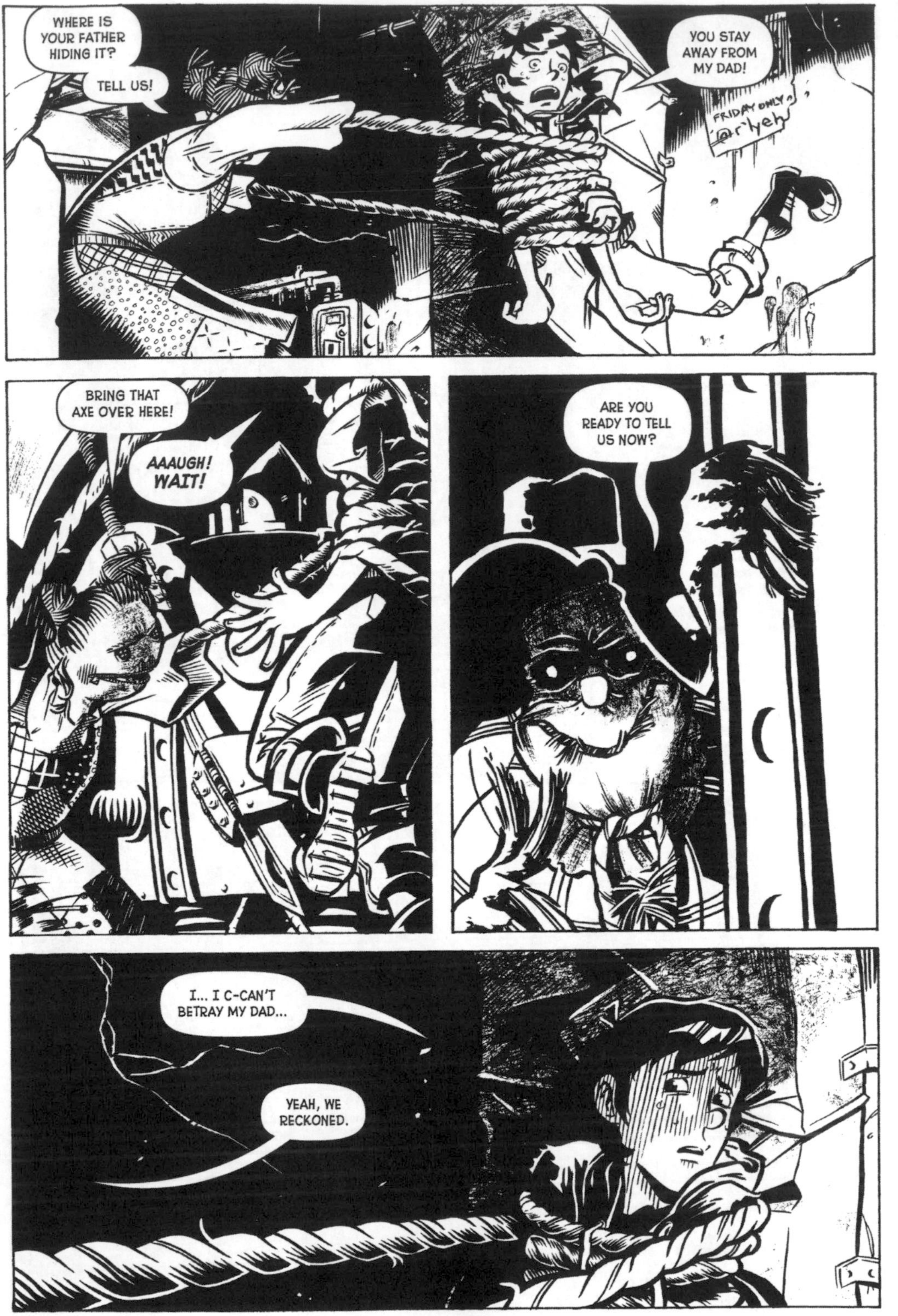
WHERE IS YOUR FATHER HIDING IT?
TELL US!
YOU STAY AWAY FROM MY DAD!
FRIDAY ONLY
BRING THAT AXE OVER HERE!
AAAUGH! WAIT!
ARE YOU READY TO TELL US NOW?
I... I C-CAN'T BETRAY MY DAD...
YEAH, WE RECKONED.

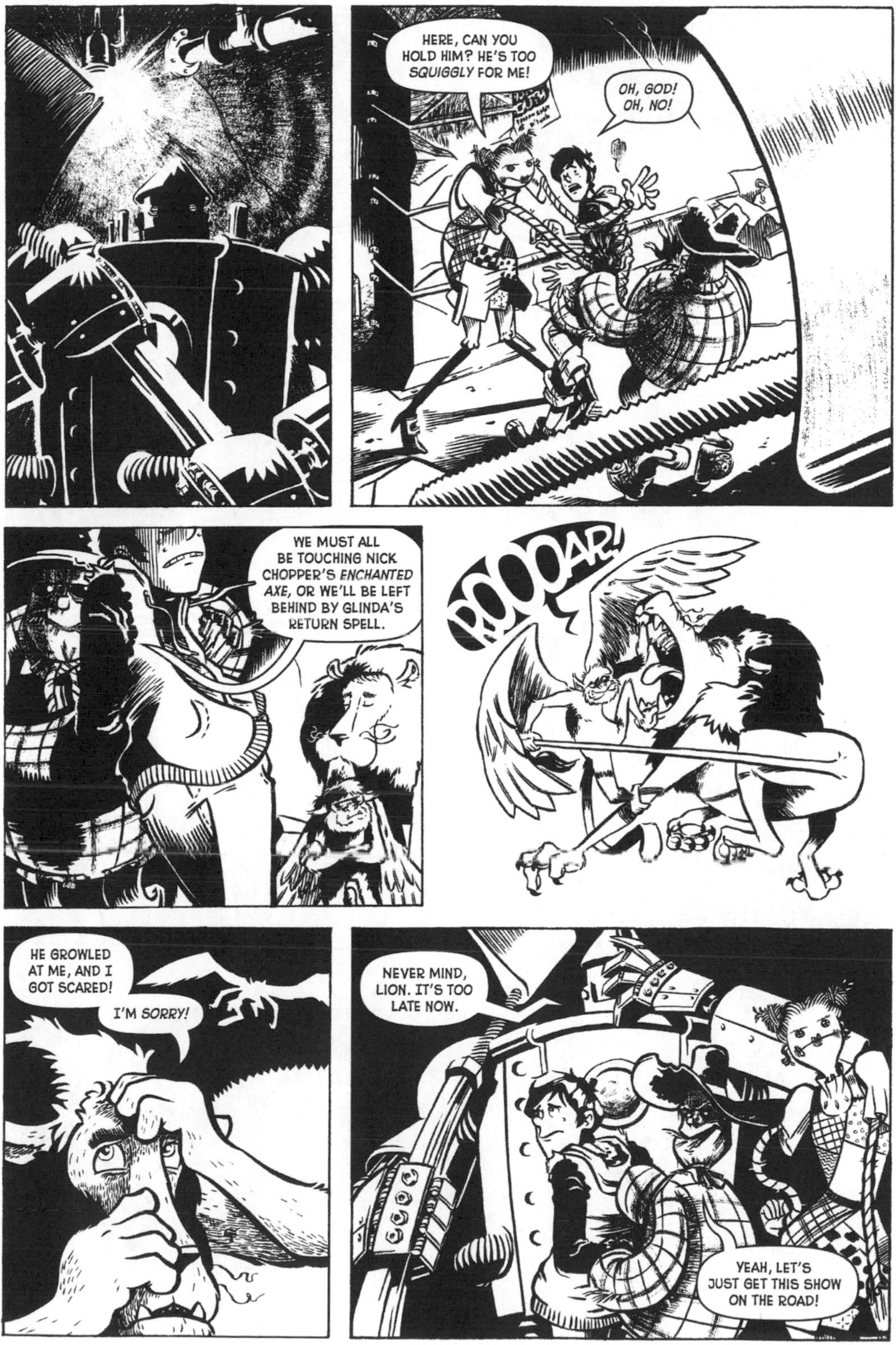
HERE, CAN YOU HOLD HIM? HE'S TOO *SQUIGGLY* FOR ME!
OH, GOD! OH, NO!
WE MUST ALL BE TOUCHING NICK CHOPPER'S *ENCHANTED AXE*, OR WE'LL BE LEFT BEHIND BY GLINDA'S RETURN SPELL.
ROOOAR!
HE GROWLED AT ME, AND I GOT SCARED!
I'M *SORRY!*
NEVER MIND, LION. IT'S TOO LATE NOW.
YEAH, LET'S JUST GET THIS SHOW ON THE ROAD!

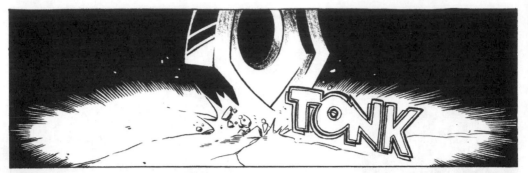

PRINCESS OZMA, WE KNOW YOU ARE WATCHING US RIGHT NOW IN YOUR MAGIC PICTURE THAT SHOWS ANYTHING YOU COMMAND IT TO. PLEASE ASK GLINDA TO BRING US BACK--

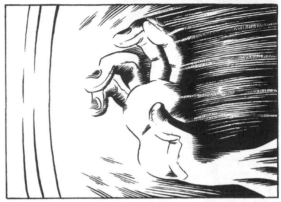

--TO OZ!

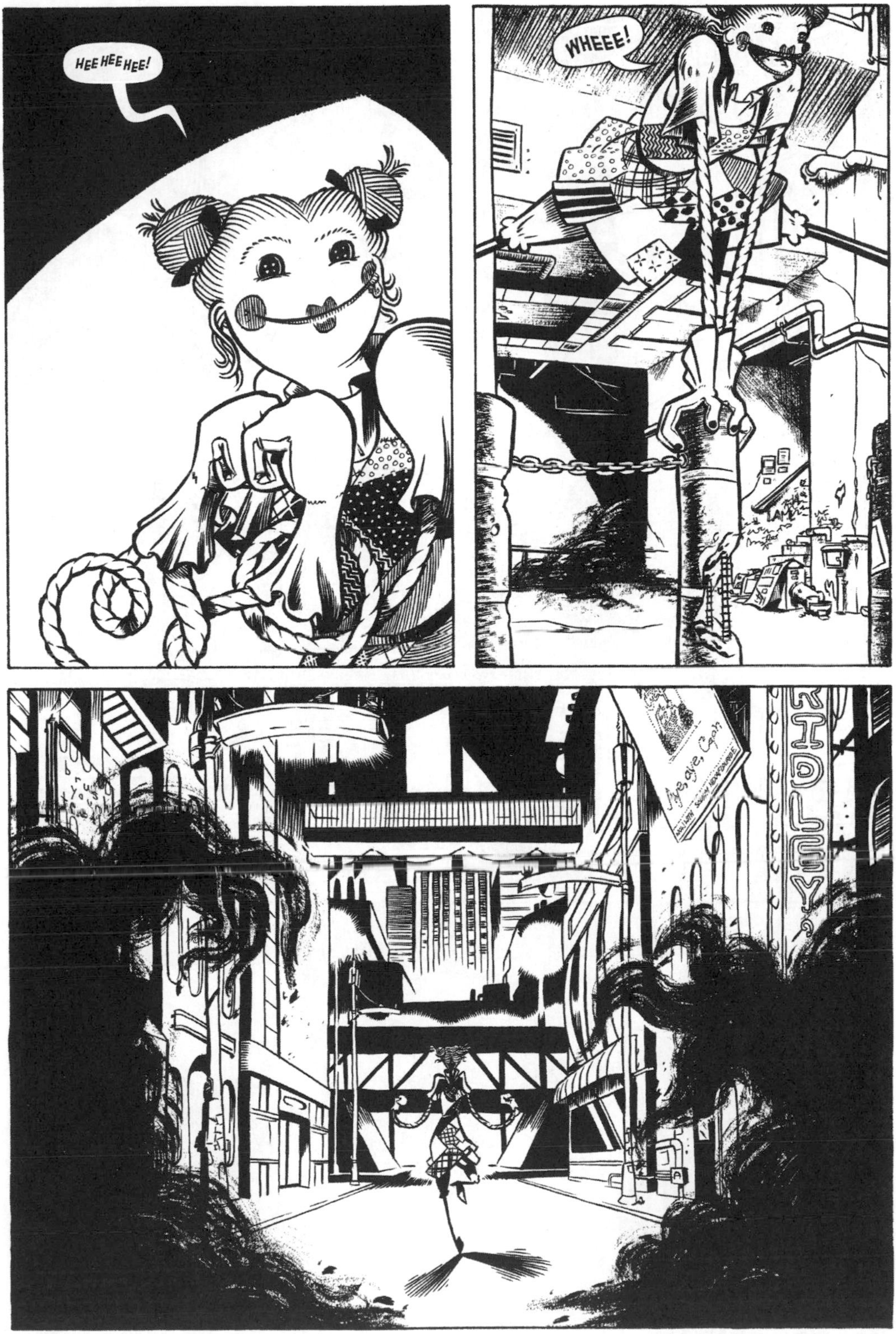
HEE HEE HEE!
WHEEE!
RIDLEY

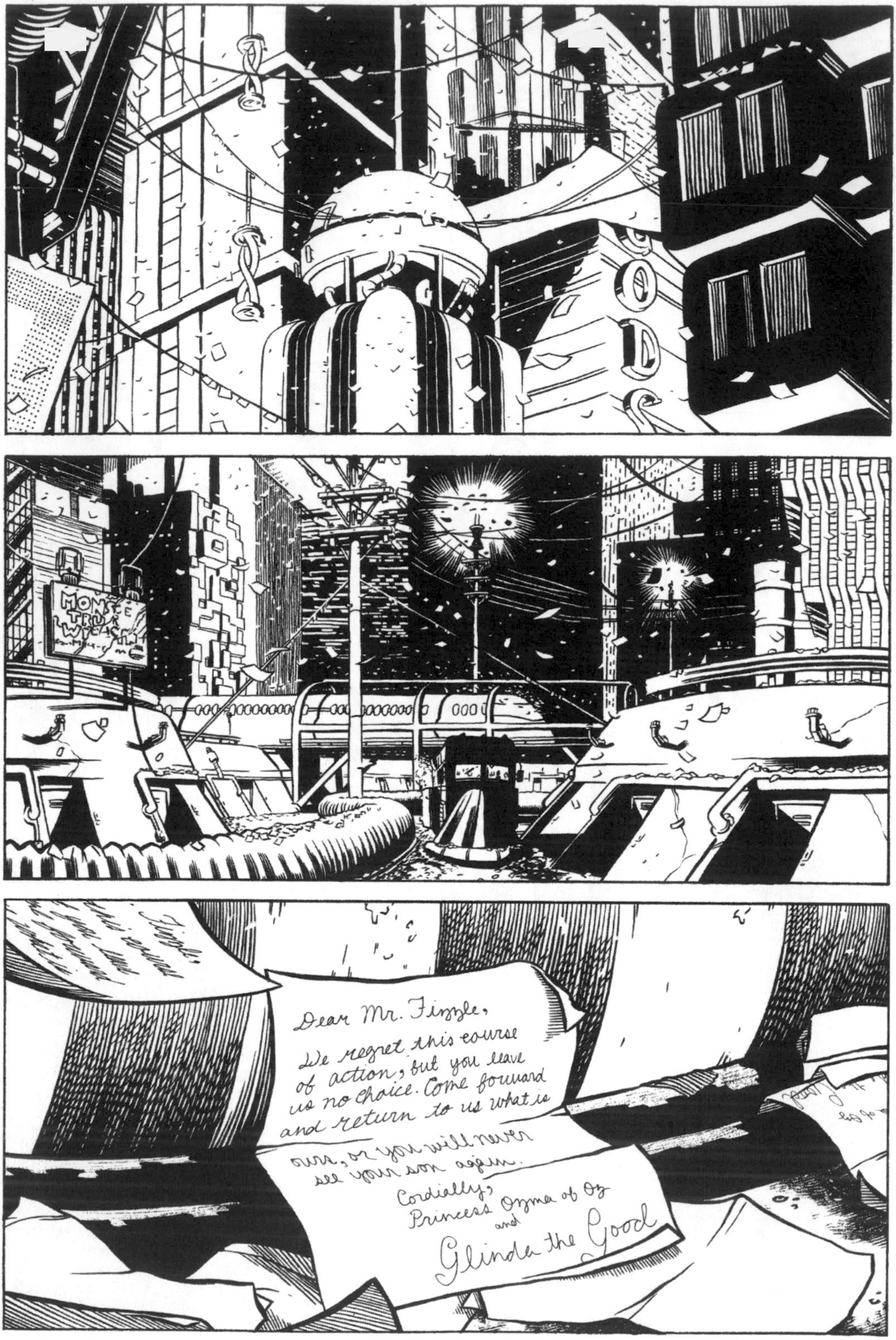
Dear Mr. Fizzle,
We regret this course of action, but you leave us no choice. Come forward and return to us what is ours, or you will never see your son again.
Cordially,
Princess Ozma of Oz
and
Glinda the Good

"Captivity in Oz"

3

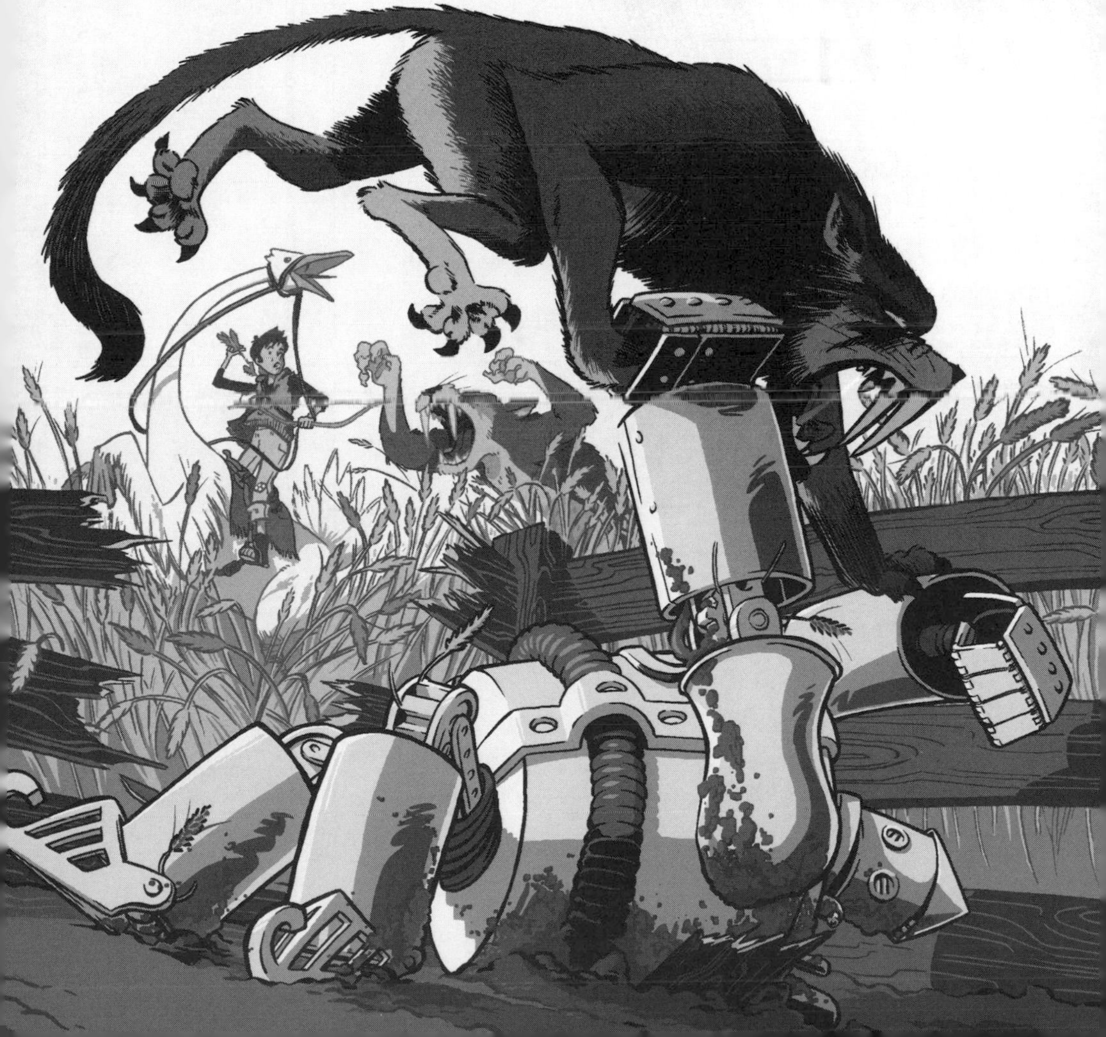

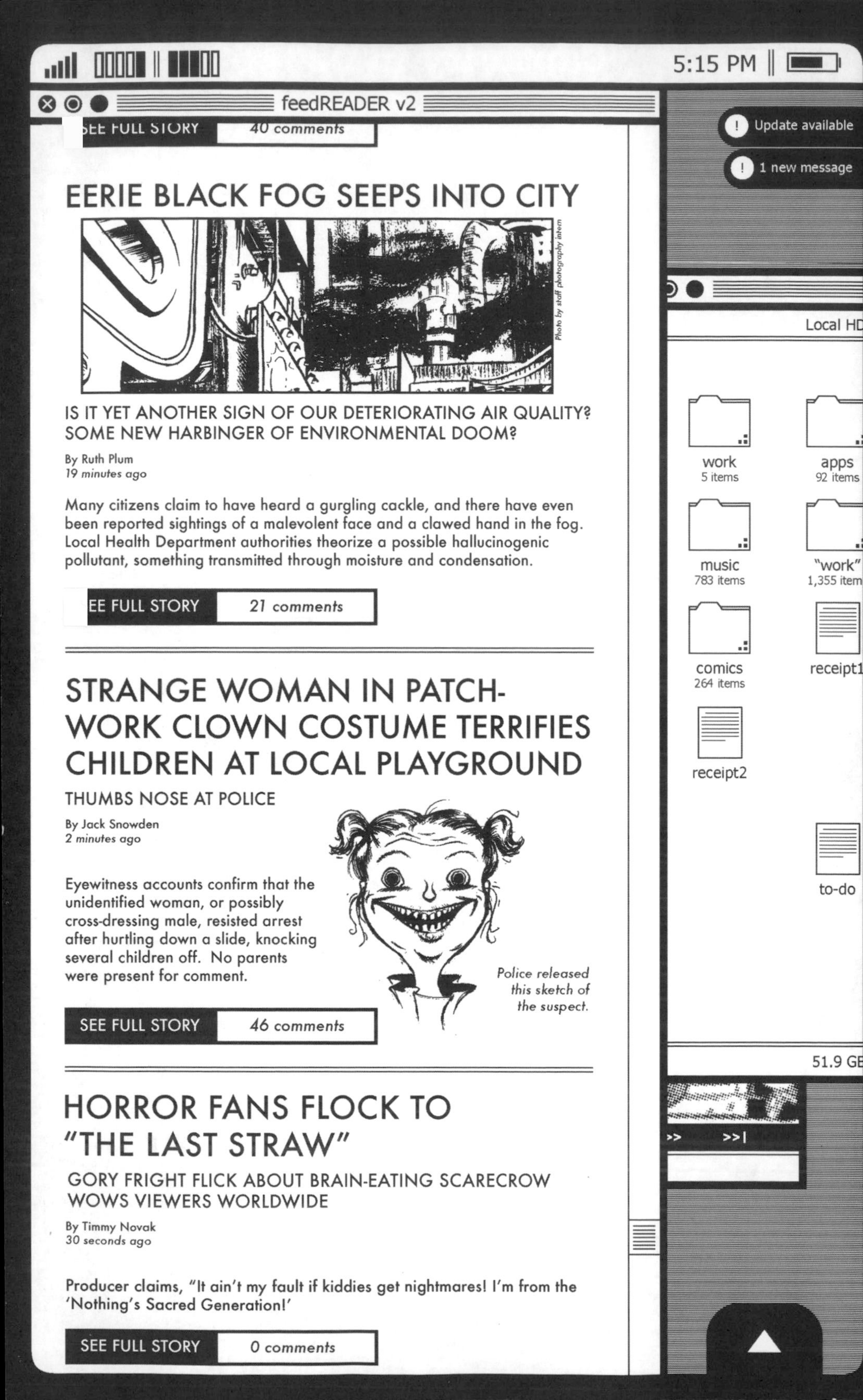
5:15 PM
feedREADER v2
SEE FULL STORY
40 comments
Update available
1 new message
EERIE BLACK FOG SEEPS INTO CITY
Photo by staff photography intern
IS IT YET ANOTHER SIGN OF OUR DETERIORATING AIR QUALITY? SOME NEW HARBINGER OF ENVIRONMENTAL DOOM?
By Ruth Plum
19 minutes ago
Many citizens claim to have heard a gurgling cackle, and there have even been reported sightings of a malevolent face and a clawed hand in the fog. Local Health Department authorities theorize a possible hallucinogenic pollutant, something transmitted through moisture and condensation.
SEE FULL STORY
21 comments
Local HD
work
5 items
apps
92 items
music
783 items
"work"
1,355 items
comics
264 items
receipt1
receipt2
STRANGE WOMAN IN PATCH-WORK CLOWN COSTUME TERRIFIES CHILDREN AT LOCAL PLAYGROUND
THUMBS NOSE AT POLICE
By Jack Snowden
2 minutes ago
Eyewitness accounts confirm that the unidentified woman, or possibly cross-dressing male, resisted arrest after hurtling down a slide, knocking several children off. No parents were present for comment.
Police released this sketch of the suspect.
to-do
SEE FULL STORY
46 comments
51.9 GB
HORROR FANS FLOCK TO "THE LAST STRAW"
GORY FRIGHT FLICK ABOUT BRAIN-EATING SCARECROW WOWS VIEWERS WORLDWIDE
By Timmy Novak
30 seconds ago
Producer claims, "It ain't my fault if kiddies get nightmares! I'm from the 'Nothing's Sacred Generation!'
SEE FULL STORY
0 comments

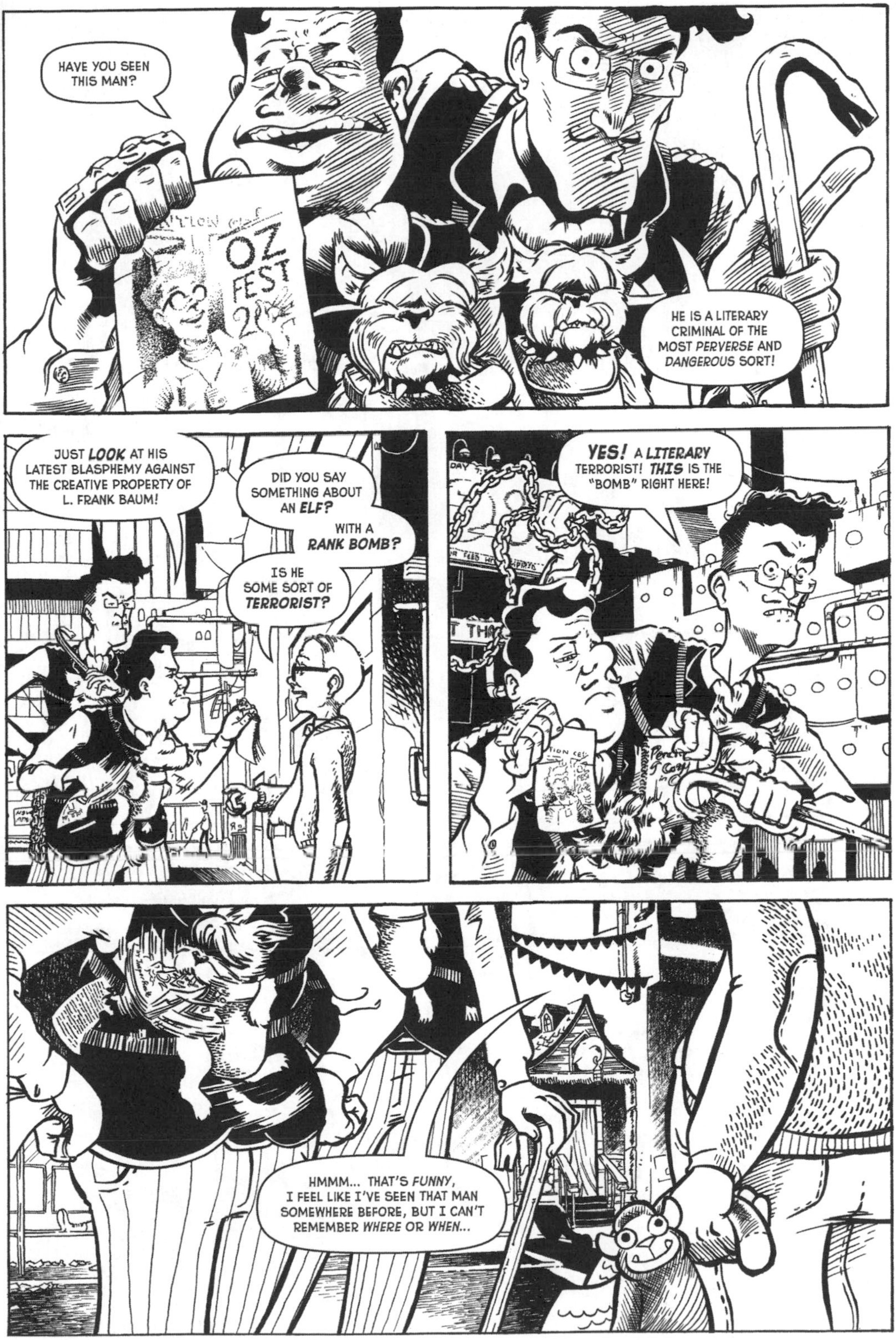
HAVE YOU SEEN THIS MAN?
OZ FEST
HE IS A LITERARY CRIMINAL OF THE MOST *PERVERSE* AND *DANGEROUS* SORT!
JUST **LOOK** AT HIS LATEST BLASPHEMY AGAINST THE CREATIVE PROPERTY OF L. FRANK BAUM!
DID YOU SAY SOMETHING ABOUT AN ***ELF?***
WITH A ***RANK BOMB?***
IS HE SOME SORT OF ***TERRORIST?***
YES! A ***LITERARY*** TERRORIST! ***THIS*** IS THE "BOMB" RIGHT HERE!
HMMM... THAT'S *FUNNY*, I FEEL LIKE I'VE SEEN THAT MAN SOMEWHERE BEFORE, BUT I CAN'T REMEMBER *WHERE* OR *WHEN*...

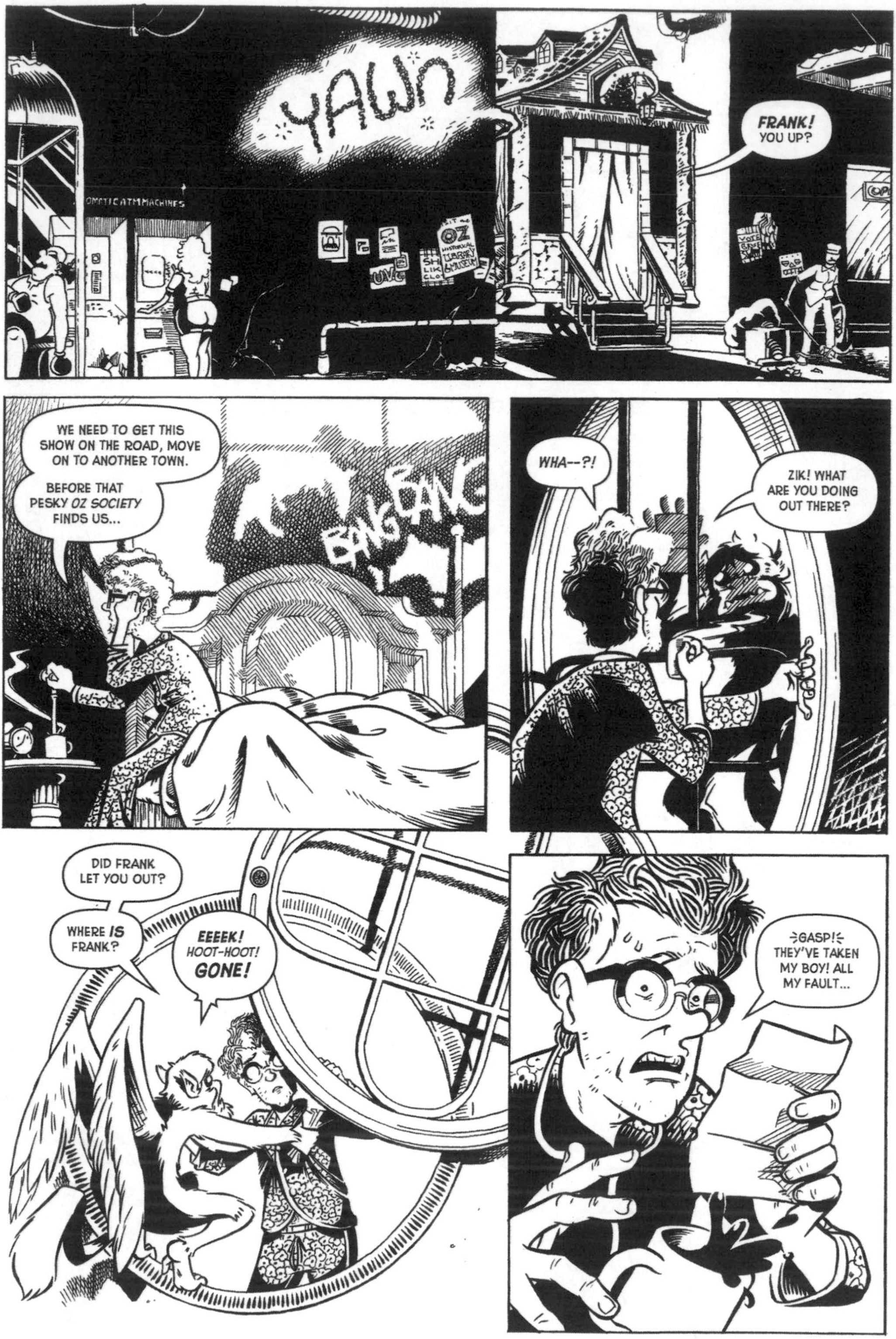

YAWN
OMATIC ATM MACHINES
OZ HISTORICAL LIBRARY & MUSEUM
FRANK! YOU UP?
WE NEED TO GET THIS SHOW ON THE ROAD, MOVE ON TO ANOTHER TOWN.
BEFORE THAT PESKY *OZ SOCIETY* FINDS US...
BANG BANG
WHA--?!
ZIK! WHAT ARE YOU DOING OUT THERE?
DID FRANK LET YOU OUT?
WHERE *IS* FRANK?
EEEEK! HOOT-HOOT! GONE!
GASP! THEY'VE TAKEN MY BOY! ALL MY FAULT...

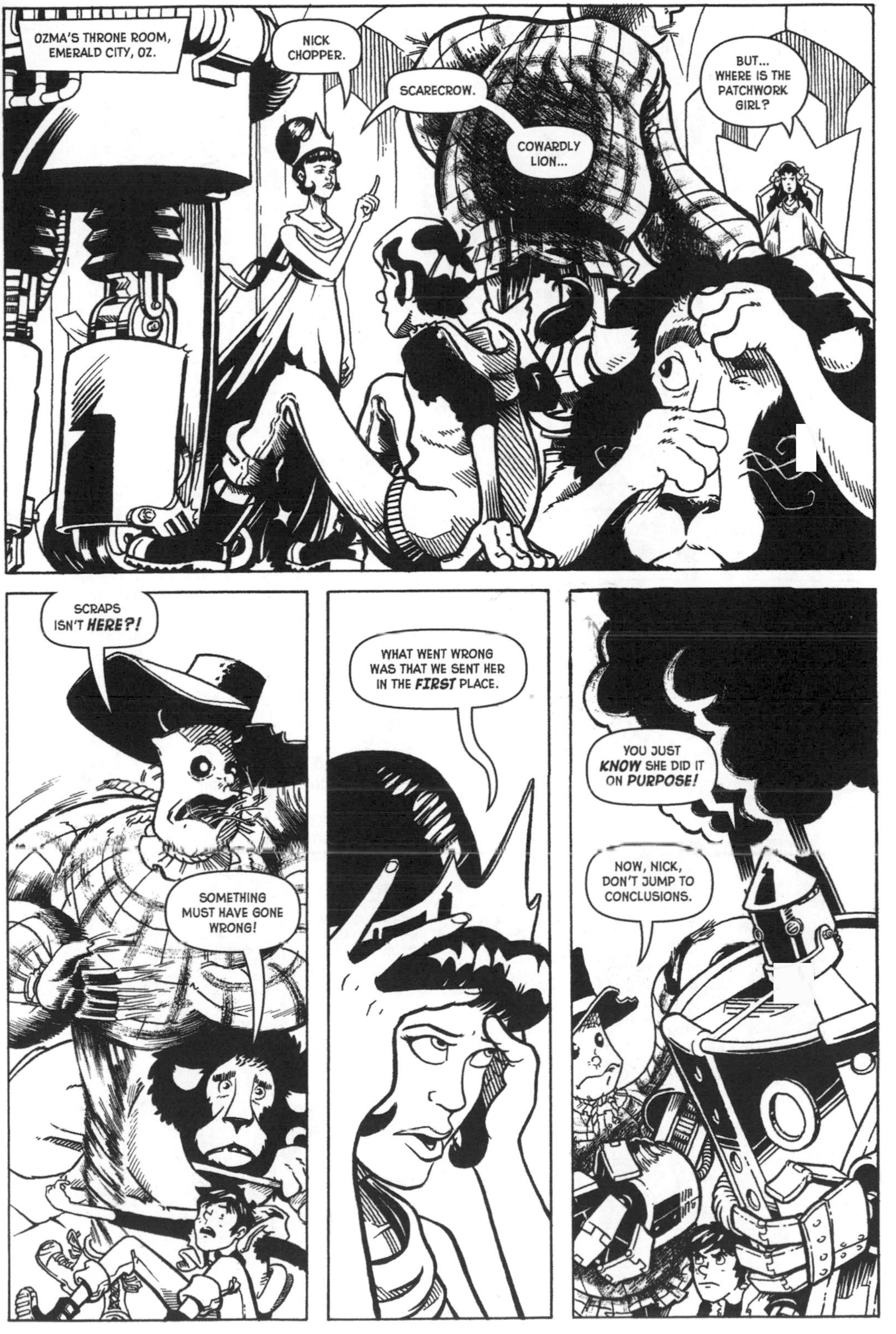
OZMA'S THRONE ROOM, EMERALD CITY, OZ.
NICK CHOPPER.
SCARECROW.
COWARDLY LION...
BUT... WHERE IS THE PATCHWORK GIRL?
SCRAPS ISN'T HERE?!
SOMETHING MUST HAVE GONE WRONG!
WHAT WENT WRONG WAS THAT WE SENT HER IN THE FIRST PLACE.
YOU JUST KNOW SHE DID IT ON PURPOSE!
NOW, NICK, DON'T JUMP TO CONCLUSIONS.

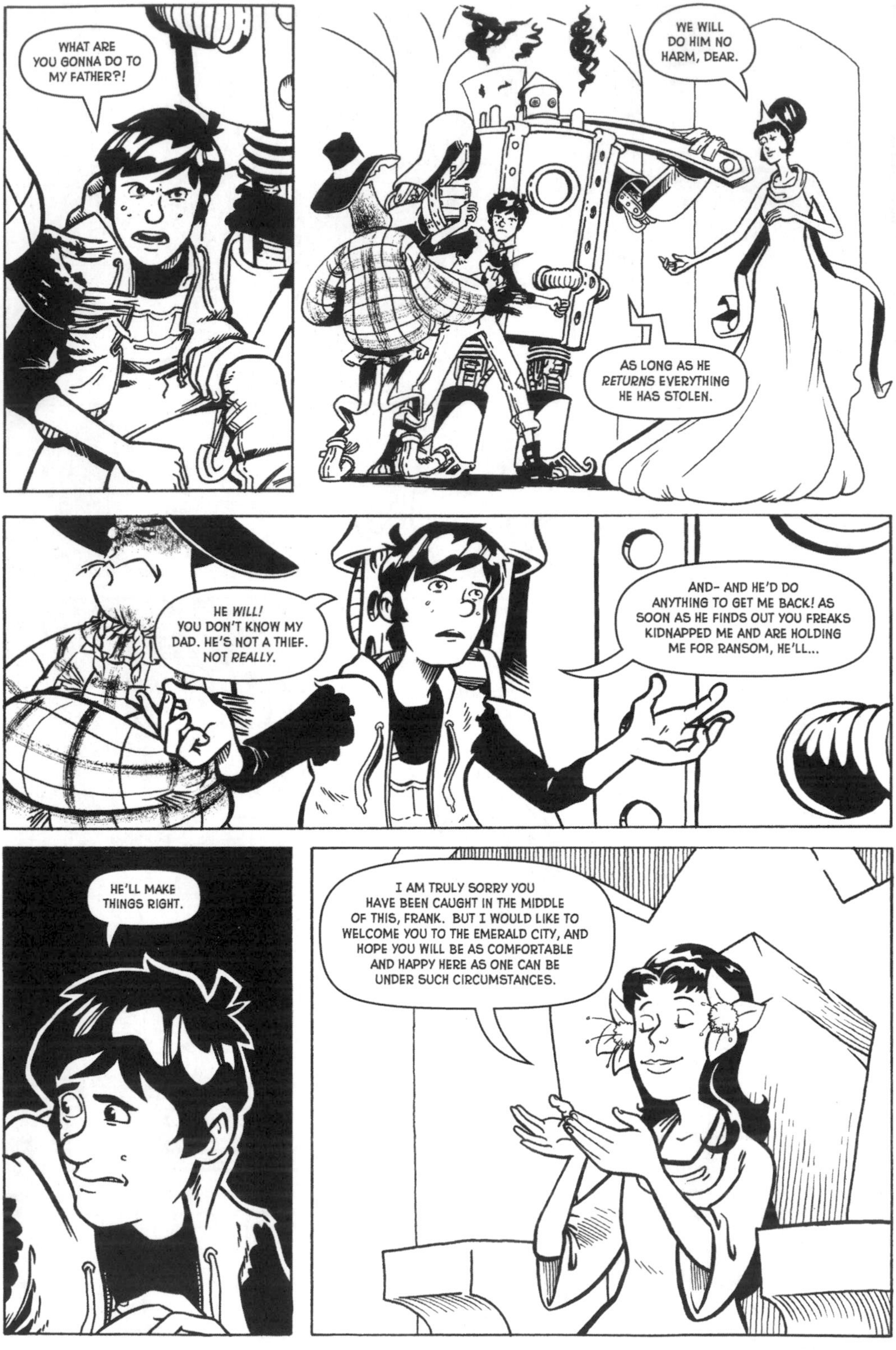
WHAT ARE YOU GONNA DO TO MY FATHER?!
WE WILL DO HIM NO HARM, DEAR.
AS LONG AS HE *RETURNS* EVERYTHING HE HAS STOLEN.
HE *WILL!* YOU DON'T KNOW MY DAD. HE'S NOT A THIEF. NOT *REALLY*.
AND- AND HE'D DO ANYTHING TO GET ME BACK! AS SOON AS HE FINDS OUT YOU FREAKS KIDNAPPED ME AND ARE HOLDING ME FOR RANSOM, HE'LL...
HE'LL MAKE THINGS RIGHT.
I AM TRULY SORRY YOU HAVE BEEN CAUGHT IN THE MIDDLE OF THIS, FRANK. BUT I WOULD LIKE TO WELCOME YOU TO THE EMERALD CITY, AND HOPE YOU WILL BE AS COMFORTABLE AND HAPPY HERE AS ONE CAN BE UNDER SUCH CIRCUMSTANCES.

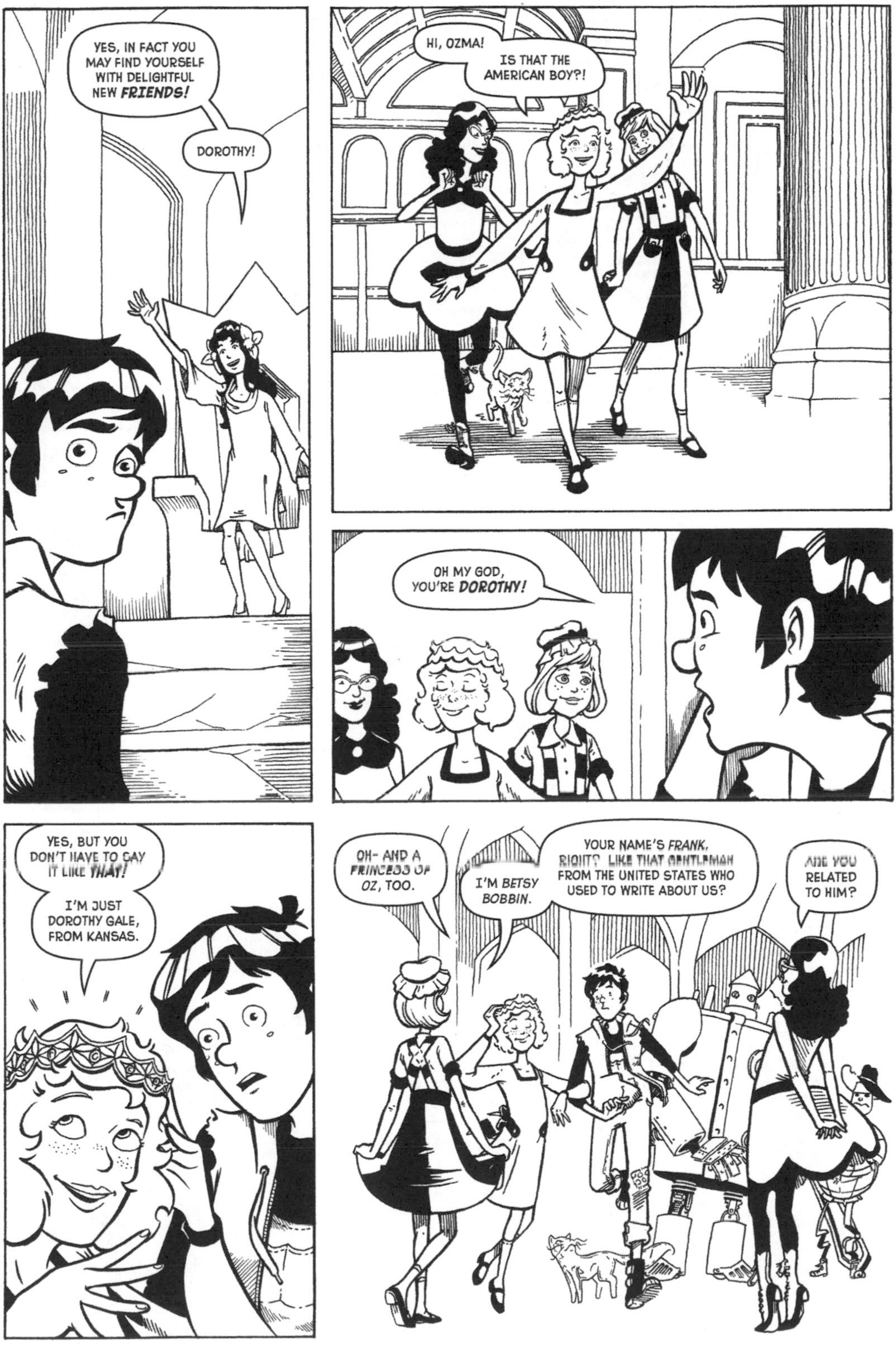
YES, IN FACT YOU MAY FIND YOURSELF WITH DELIGHTFUL NEW **FRIENDS!**
DOROTHY!
HI, OZMA!
IS THAT THE AMERICAN BOY?!
OH MY GOD, YOU'RE **DOROTHY!**
YES, BUT YOU DON'T HAVE TO SAY IT LIKE *THAT!*
I'M JUST DOROTHY GALE, FROM KANSAS.
OH- AND A PRINCESS OF OZ, TOO.
I'M *BETSY BOBBIN.*
YOUR NAME'S *FRANK,* RIGHT? LIKE THAT GENTLEMAN FROM THE UNITED STATES WHO USED TO WRITE ABOUT US?
ARE YOU RELATED TO HIM?

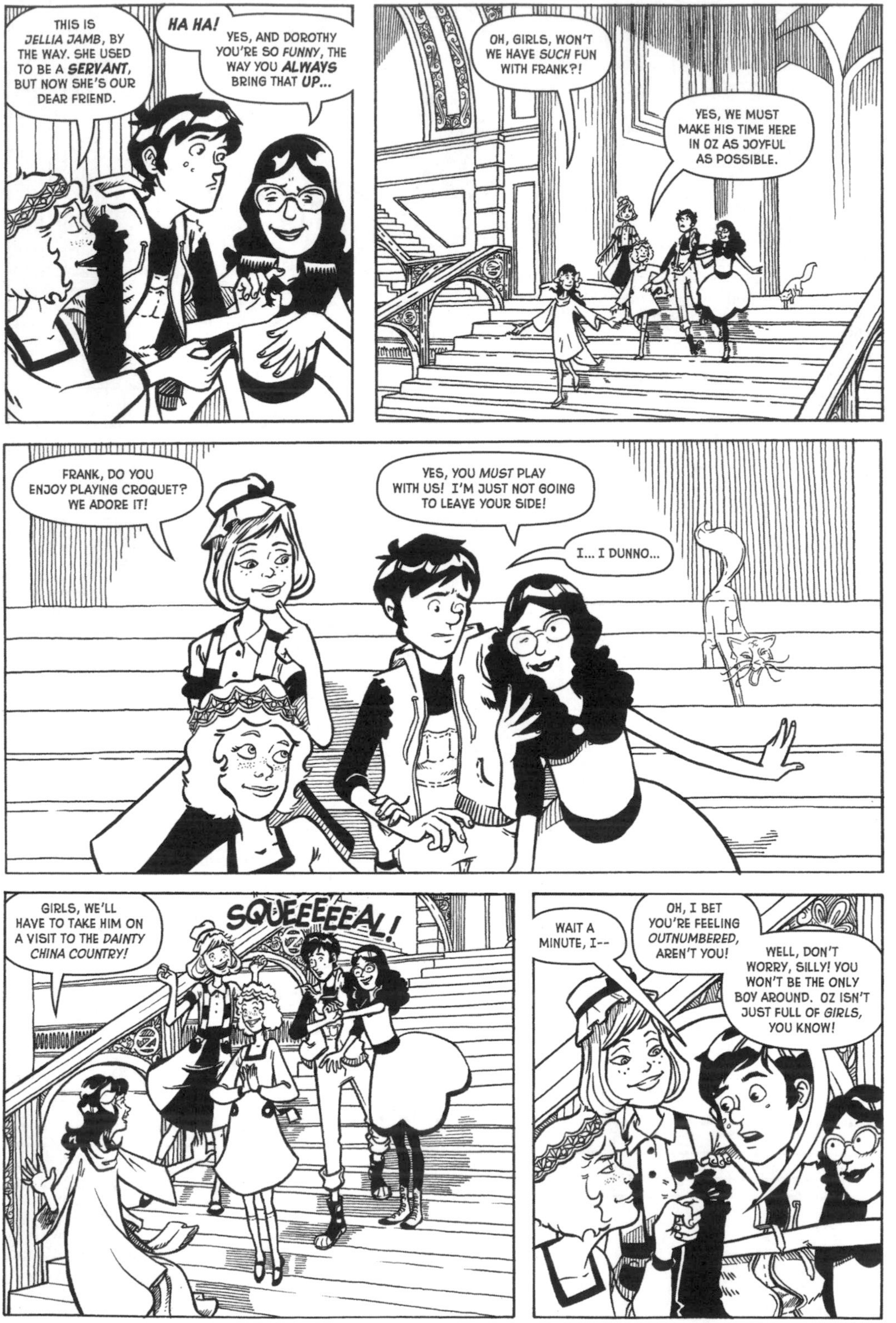
THIS IS *JELLIA JAMB*, BY THE WAY. SHE USED TO BE A ***SERVANT***, BUT NOW SHE'S OUR DEAR FRIEND.
HA HA!
YES, AND DOROTHY YOU'RE SO *FUNNY*, THE WAY YOU ***ALWAYS*** BRING THAT ***UP...***
OH, GIRLS, WON'T WE HAVE *SUCH* FUN WITH FRANK?!
YES, WE MUST MAKE HIS TIME HERE IN OZ AS JOYFUL AS POSSIBLE.
FRANK, DO *YOU* ENJOY PLAYING CROQUET? WE ADORE IT!
YES, *YOU MUST* PLAY WITH US! I'M JUST NOT GOING TO LEAVE YOUR SIDE!
I... I DUNNO...
GIRLS, WE'LL HAVE TO TAKE HIM ON A VISIT TO THE *DAINTY CHINA COUNTRY!*
SQUEEEEEEAL!
WAIT A MINUTE, I--
OH, I BET YOU'RE FEELING *OUTNUMBERED*, AREN'T YOU!
WELL, DON'T WORRY, SILLY! YOU WON'T BE THE ONLY BOY AROUND. OZ ISN'T JUST FULL OF *GIRLS*, YOU KNOW!

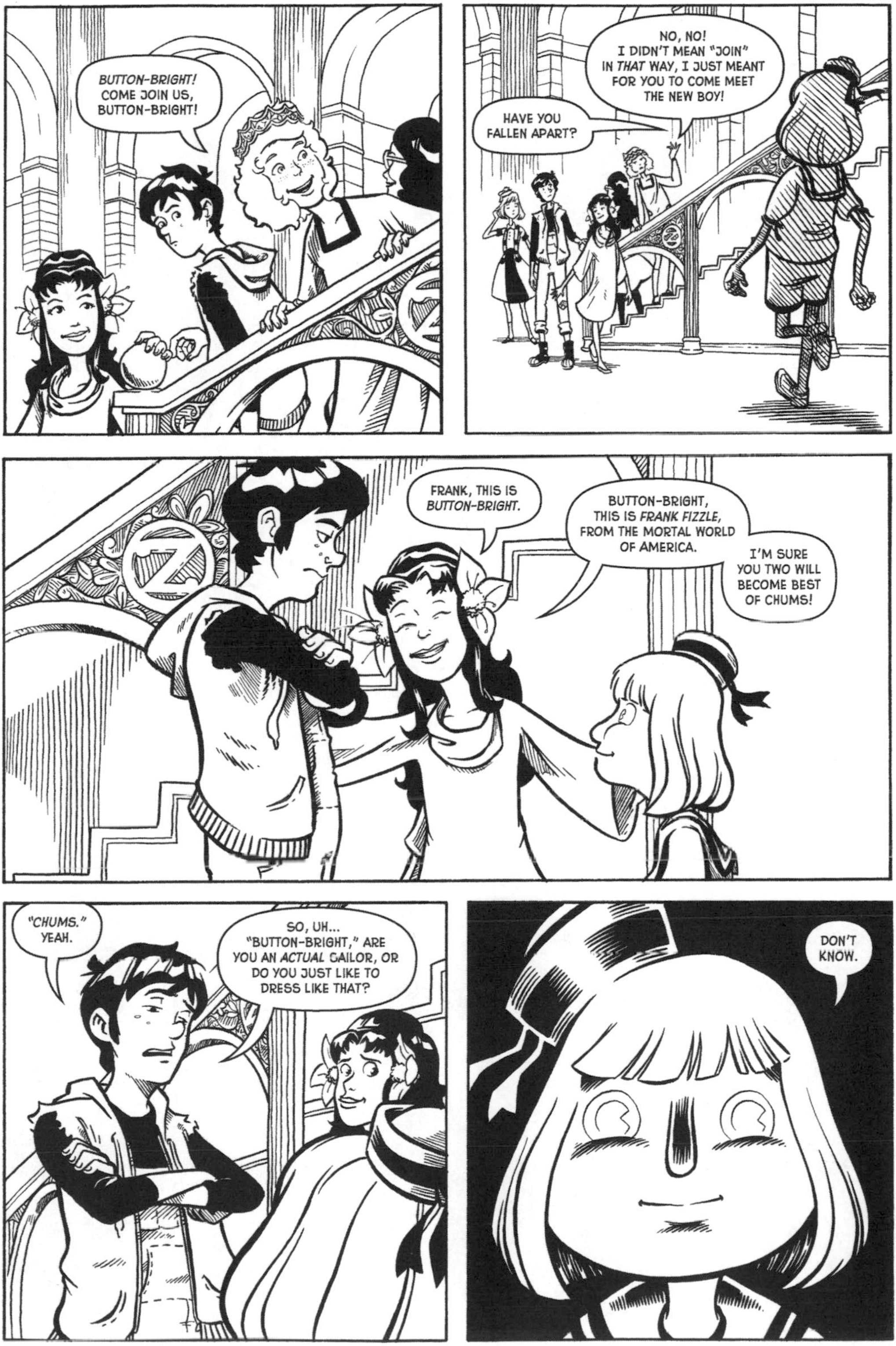
BUTTON-BRIGHT! COME JOIN US, BUTTON-BRIGHT!
HAVE YOU FALLEN APART?
NO, NO! I DIDN'T MEAN "JOIN" IN THAT WAY, I JUST MEANT FOR YOU TO COME MEET THE NEW BOY!
FRANK, THIS IS BUTTON-BRIGHT.
BUTTON-BRIGHT, THIS IS FRANK FIZZLE, FROM THE MORTAL WORLD OF AMERICA.
I'M SURE YOU TWO WILL BECOME BEST OF CHUMS!
"CHUMS." YEAH.
SO, UH... "BUTTON-BRIGHT," ARE YOU AN ACTUAL SAILOR, OR DO YOU JUST LIKE TO DRESS LIKE THAT?
DON'T KNOW.

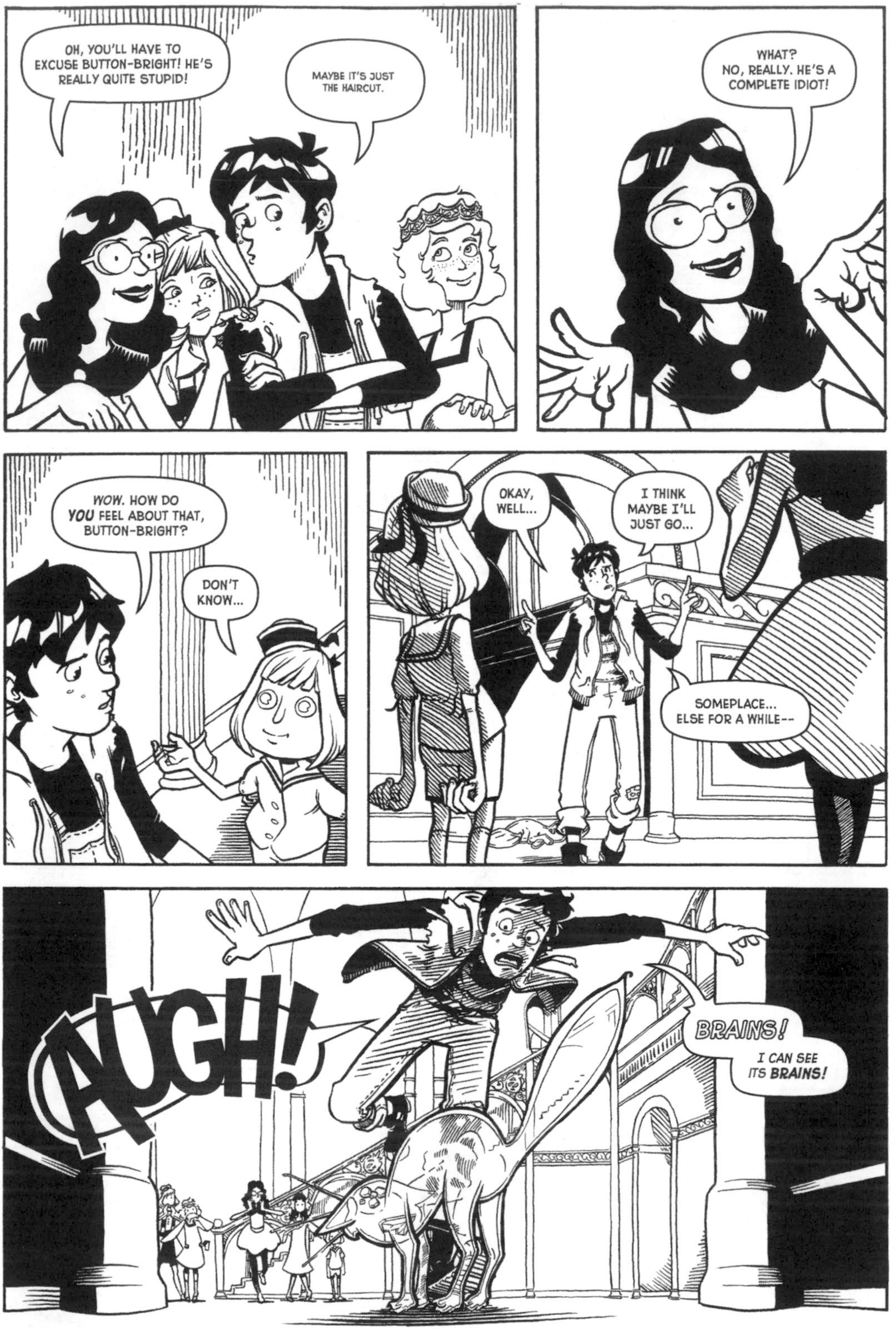
OH, YOU'LL HAVE TO EXCUSE BUTTON-BRIGHT! HE'S REALLY QUITE STUPID!
MAYBE IT'S JUST THE HAIRCUT.
WHAT? NO, REALLY. HE'S A COMPLETE IDIOT!
WOW. HOW DO YOU FEEL ABOUT THAT, BUTTON-BRIGHT?
DON'T KNOW...
OKAY, WELL...
I THINK MAYBE I'LL JUST GO...
SOMEPLACE... ELSE FOR A WHILE--
AUGH!
BRAINS!
I CAN SEE ITS BRAINS!

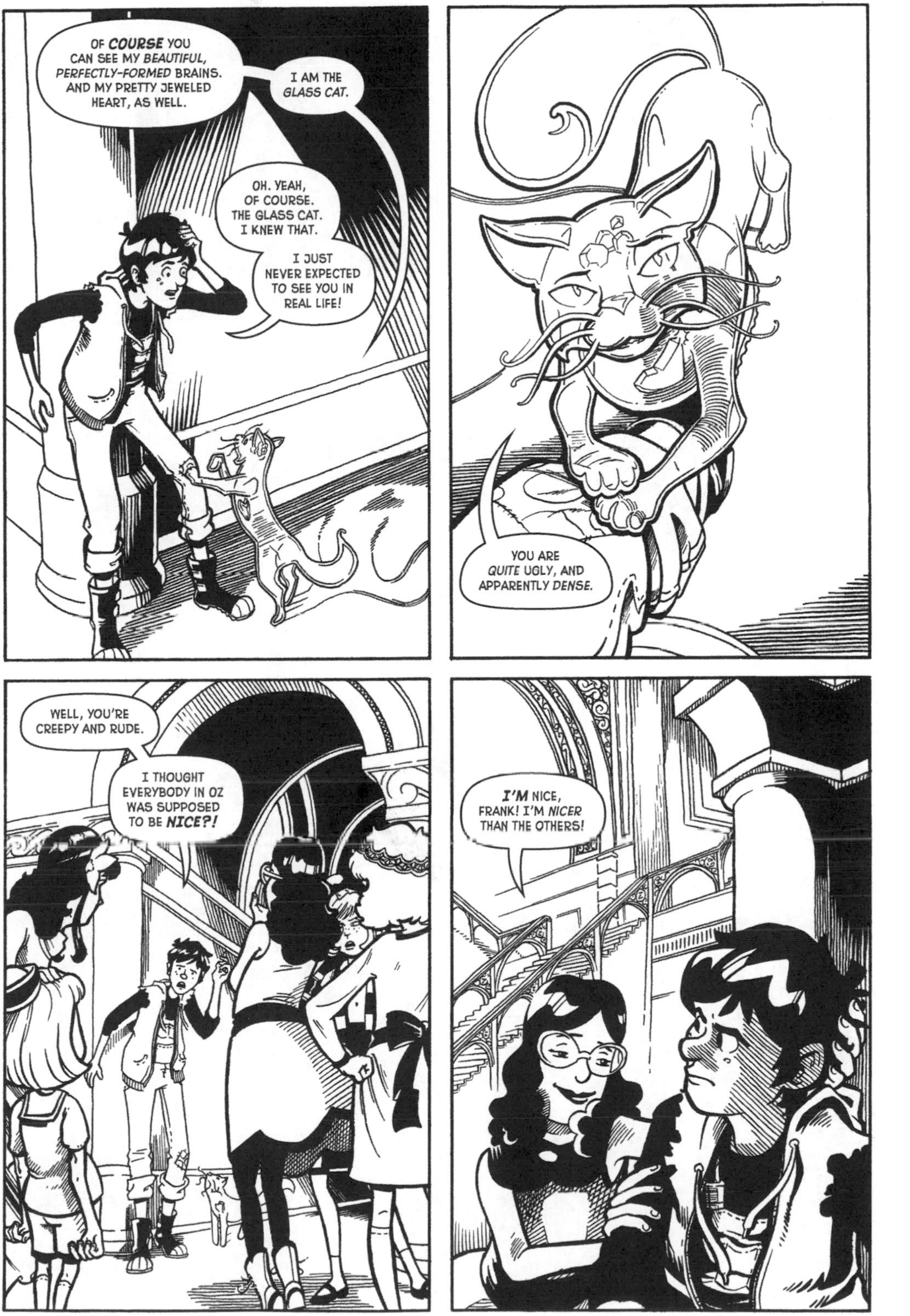
OF **COURSE** YOU CAN SEE MY *BEAUTIFUL, PERFECTLY-FORMED* BRAINS. AND MY PRETTY JEWELED HEART, AS WELL.
I AM THE *GLASS CAT.*
OH. YEAH, OF COURSE. THE GLASS CAT. I KNEW THAT.
I JUST NEVER EXPECTED TO SEE YOU IN REAL LIFE!
YOU ARE *QUITE* UGLY, AND APPARENTLY *DENSE.*
WELL, YOU'RE CREEPY AND RUDE.
I THOUGHT EVERYBODY IN OZ WAS SUPPOSED TO BE ***NICE?!***
I'M NICE, FRANK! I'M *NICER* THAN THE OTHERS!

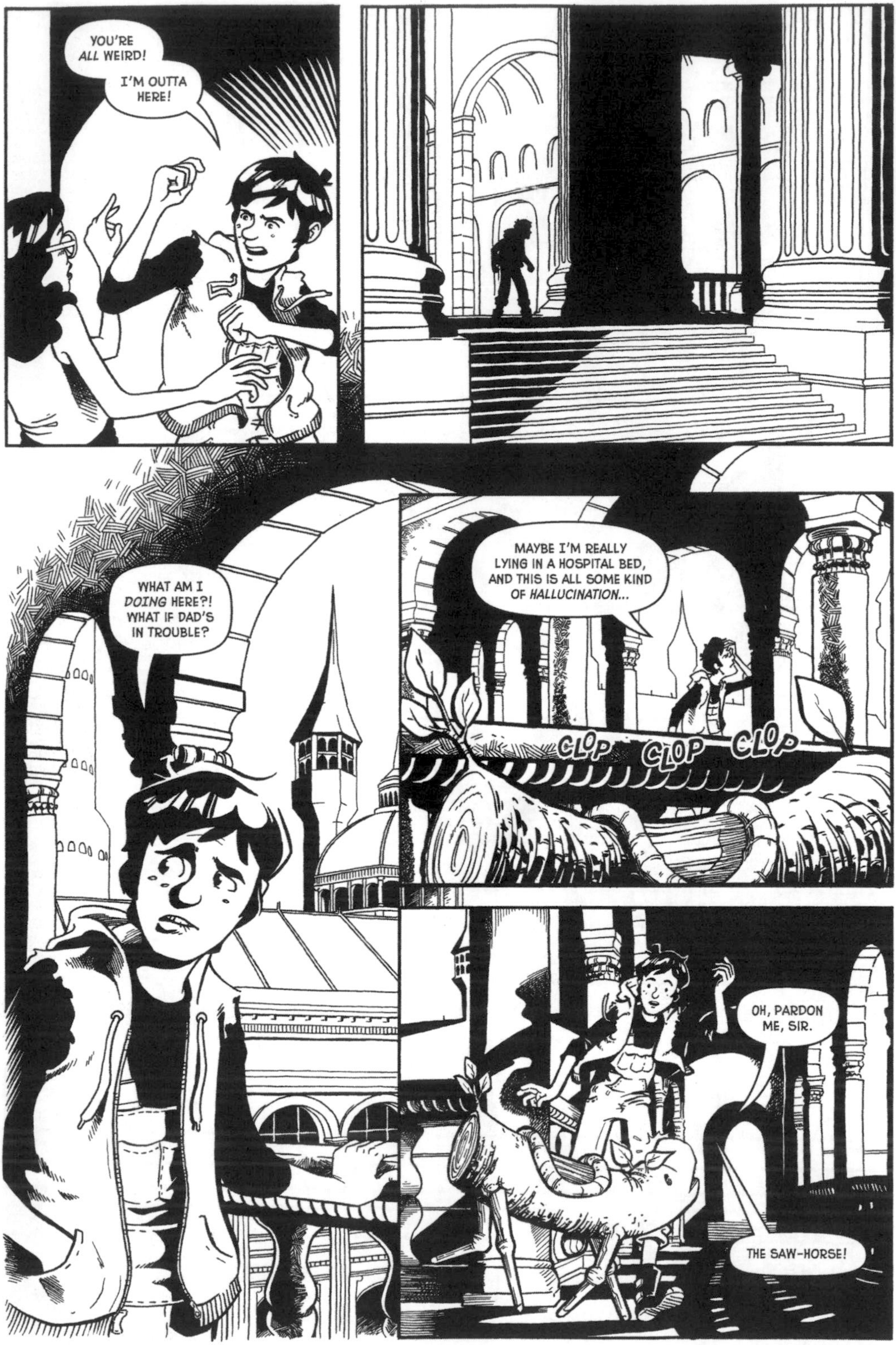

YOU'RE *ALL* WEIRD!
I'M OUTTA HERE!
WHAT AM I *DOING* HERE?! WHAT IF DAD'S IN TROUBLE?
MAYBE I'M REALLY LYING IN A HOSPITAL BED, AND THIS IS ALL SOME KIND OF *HALLUCINATION*...
CLOP CLOP CLOP
OH, PARDON ME, SIR.
THE SAW-HORSE!

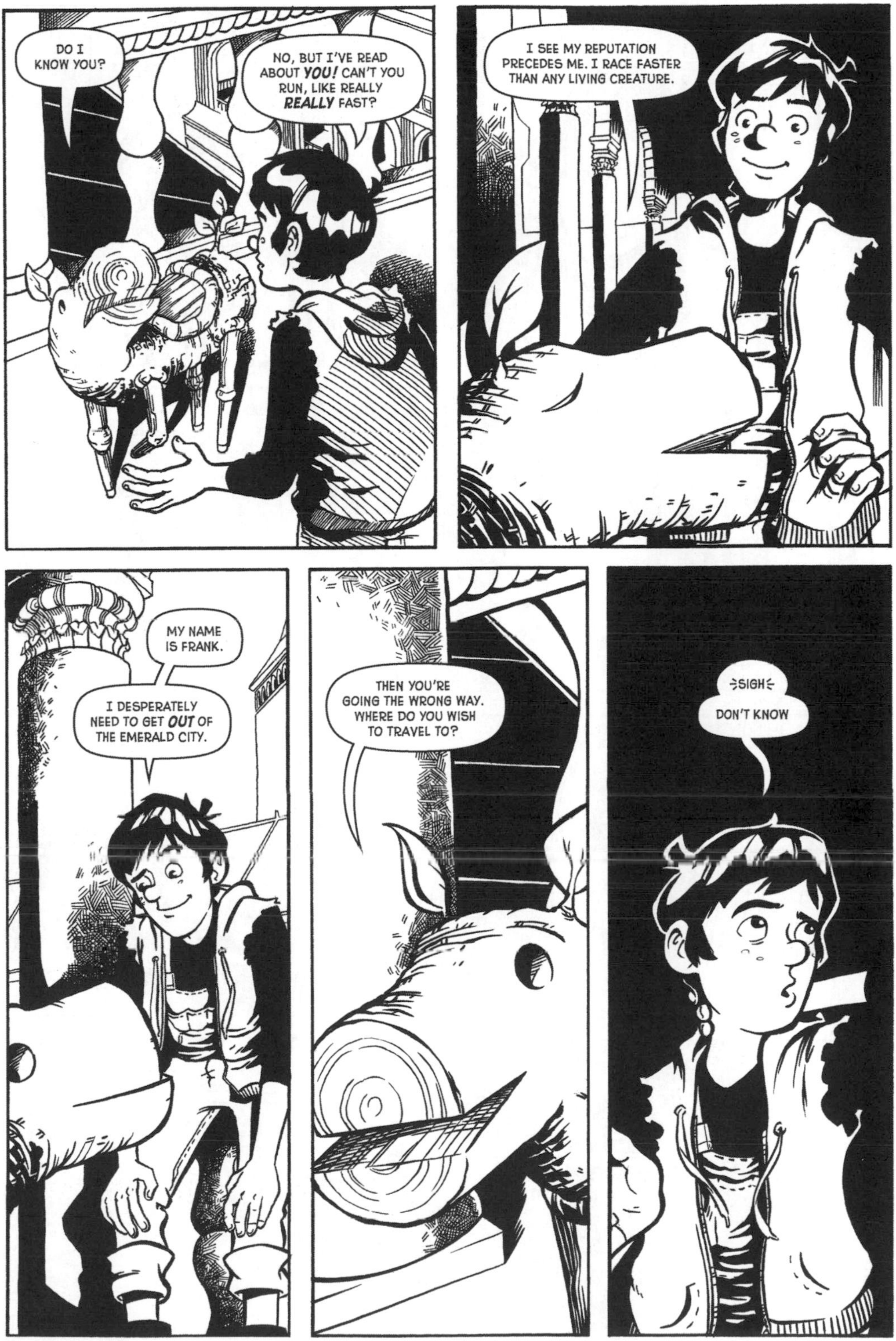
DO I KNOW YOU?
NO, BUT I'VE READ ABOUT *YOU!* CAN'T YOU RUN, LIKE REALLY *REALLY* FAST?
I SEE MY REPUTATION PRECEDES ME. I RACE FASTER THAN ANY LIVING CREATURE.
MY NAME IS FRANK.
I DESPERATELY NEED TO GET *OUT* OF THE EMERALD CITY.
THEN YOU'RE GOING THE WRONG WAY. WHERE DO YOU WISH TO TRAVEL TO?
SIGH
DON'T KNOW

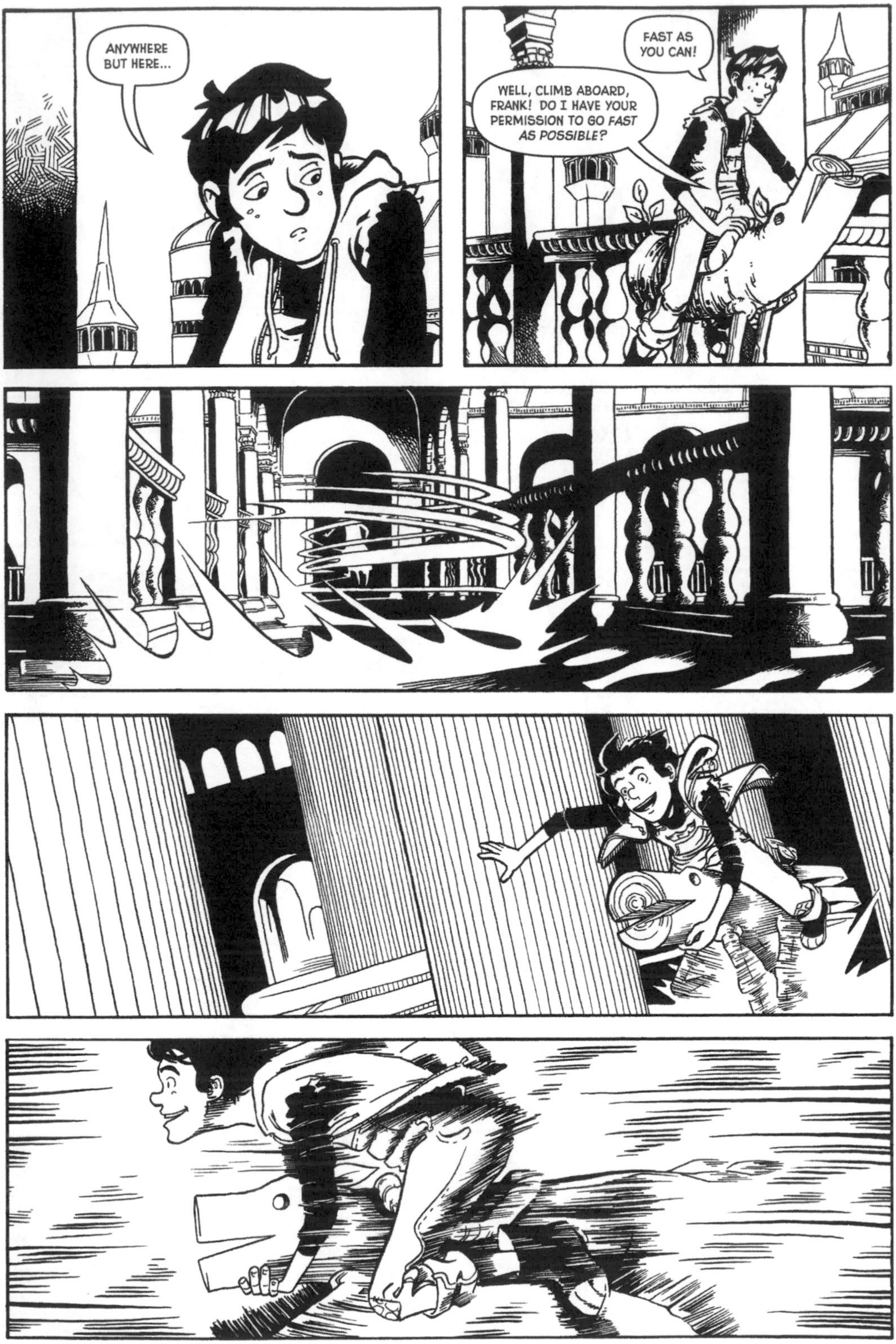
ANYWHERE BUT HERE...
FAST AS YOU CAN!
WELL, CLIMB ABOARD, FRANK! DO I HAVE YOUR PERMISSION TO GO *FAST AS POSSIBLE?*

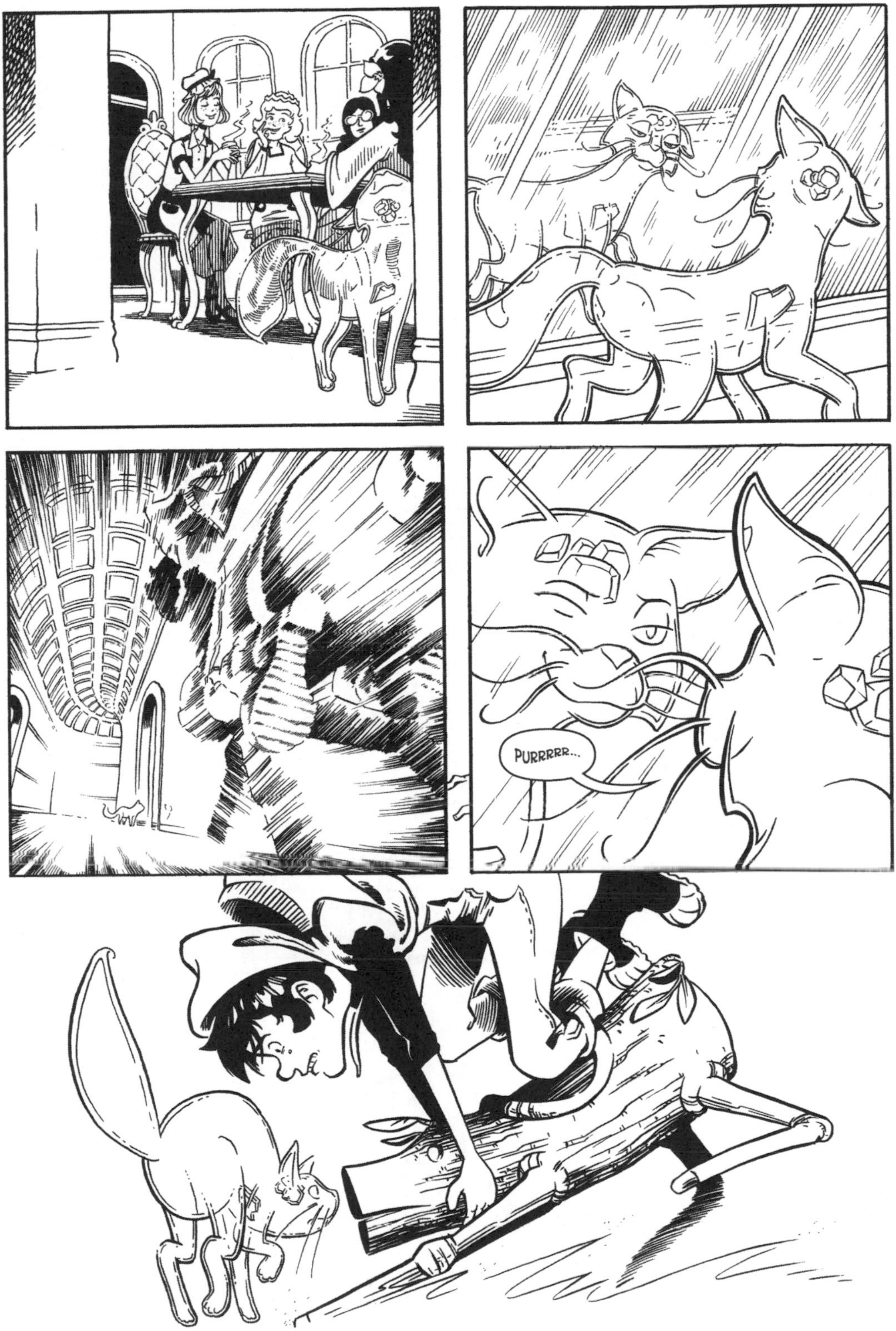
PURRRRR...

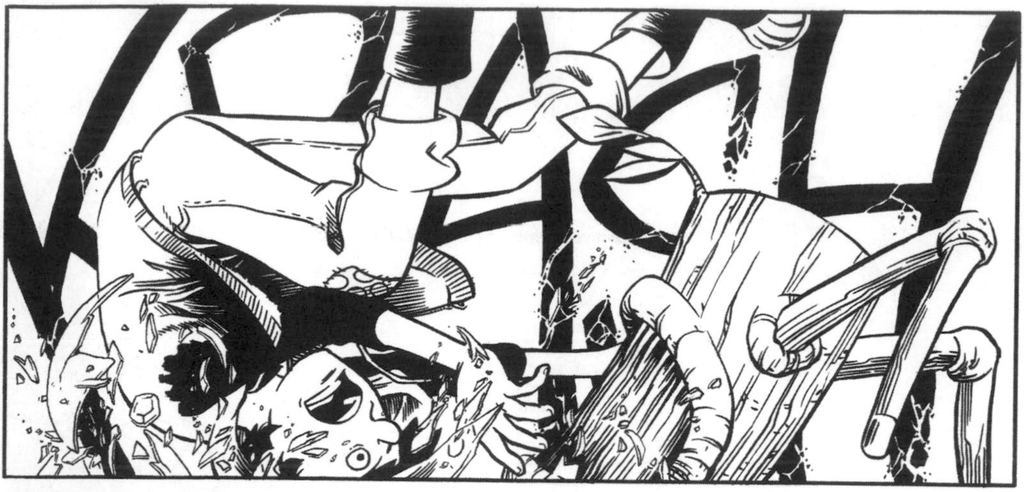

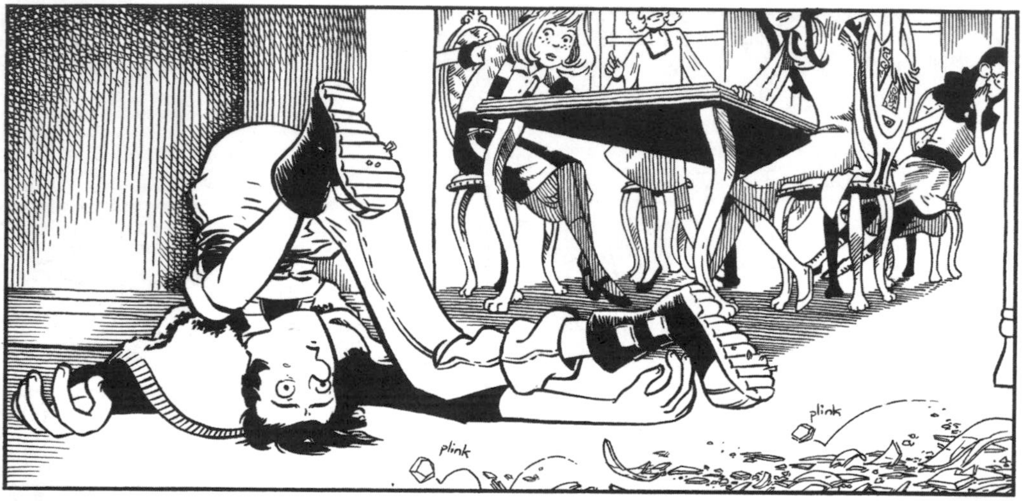
plink
plink

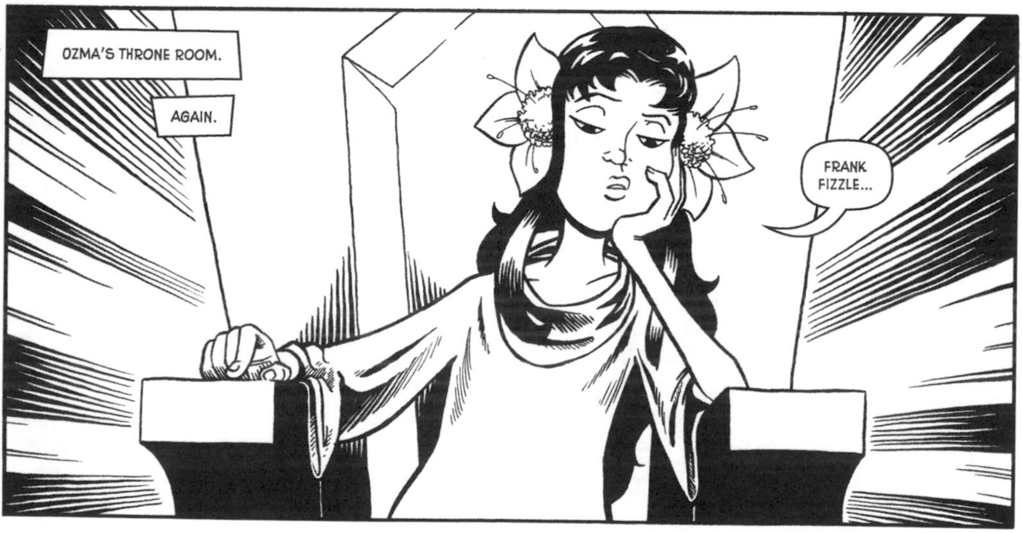
OZMA'S THRONE ROOM.
AGAIN.
FRANK FIZZLE...

WE ARE DISAPPOINTED IN YOUR DESTRUCTIVE BEHAVIOR.

I... I'M SO SORRY! I DIDN'T MEAN—

WHETHER YOU MEANT IT OR NOT, YOUR ACTIONS RESULTED IN THE GLASS CAT BEING SHATTERED INTO SO MANY PIECES IT WILL TAKE A LONG TIME TO REPAIR HER COMPLETELY.

THE POOR VAIN CREATURE MAY NEVER BE THE SAME AGAIN.

YOU CALLED US MEAN AND WEIRD, TOO!

WE'RE THE NICEST GIRLS I KNOW!

SINCE THIS *OBVIOUSLY* ISN'T WORKING OUT HERE IN THE PALACE, AT MY SUGGESTION OZMA IS PUTTING YOU IN THE CUSTODY OF *NICK CHOPPER* FOR THE REMAINDER OF YOUR STAY HERE IN OZ.

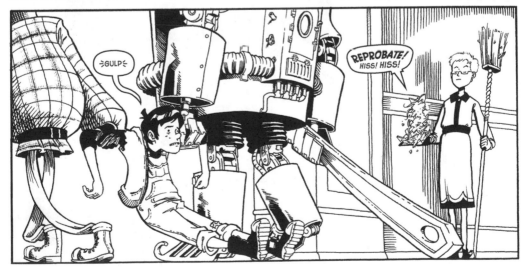

≍GULP≍

REPROBATE! HISS! HISS!

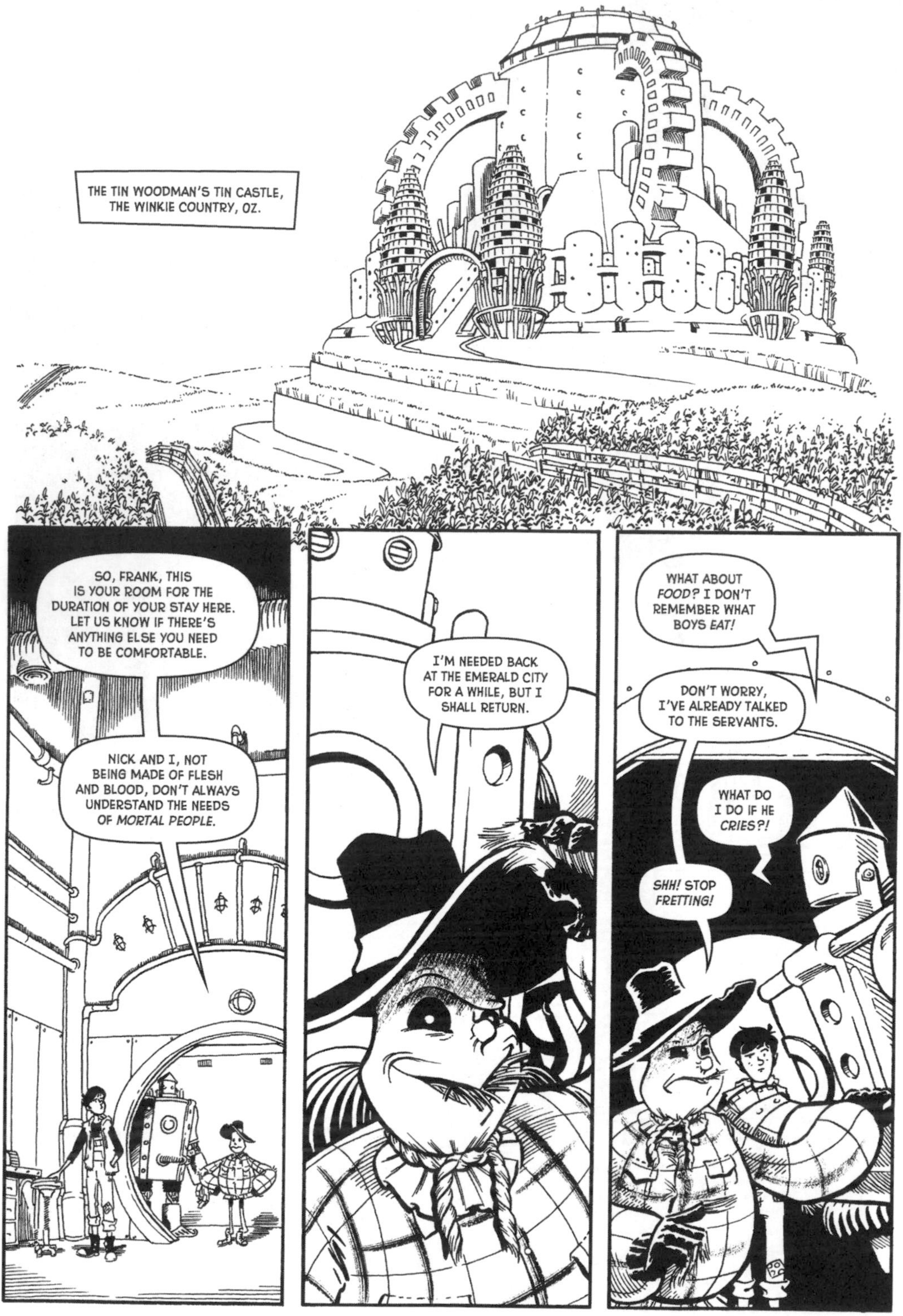
THE TIN WOODMAN'S TIN CASTLE, THE WINKIE COUNTRY, OZ.
SO, FRANK, THIS IS YOUR ROOM FOR THE DURATION OF YOUR STAY HERE. LET US KNOW IF THERE'S ANYTHING ELSE YOU NEED TO BE COMFORTABLE.
NICK AND I, NOT BEING MADE OF FLESH AND BLOOD, DON'T ALWAYS UNDERSTAND THE NEEDS OF *MORTAL PEOPLE*.
I'M NEEDED BACK AT THE EMERALD CITY FOR A WHILE, BUT I SHALL RETURN.
WHAT ABOUT *FOOD?* I DON'T REMEMBER WHAT BOYS *EAT!*
DON'T WORRY, I'VE ALREADY TALKED TO THE SERVANTS.
WHAT DO I DO IF HE *CRIES?!*
SHH! STOP *FRETTING!*

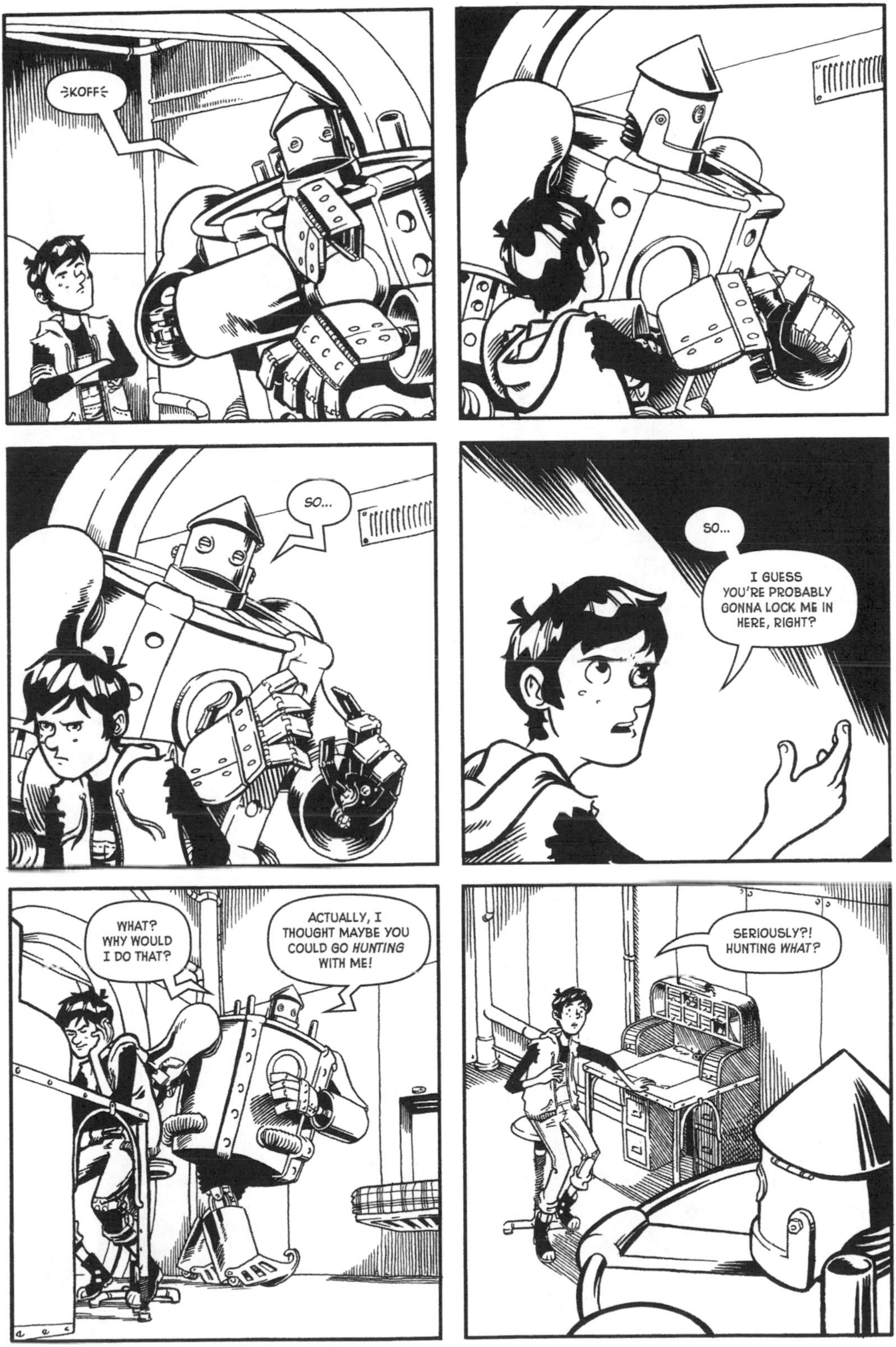
KOFF
SO...
SO...
I GUESS YOU'RE PROBABLY GONNA LOCK ME IN HERE, RIGHT?
WHAT? WHY WOULD I DO THAT?
ACTUALLY, I THOUGHT MAYBE YOU COULD GO *HUNTING* WITH ME!
SERIOUSLY?! HUNTING *WHAT?*

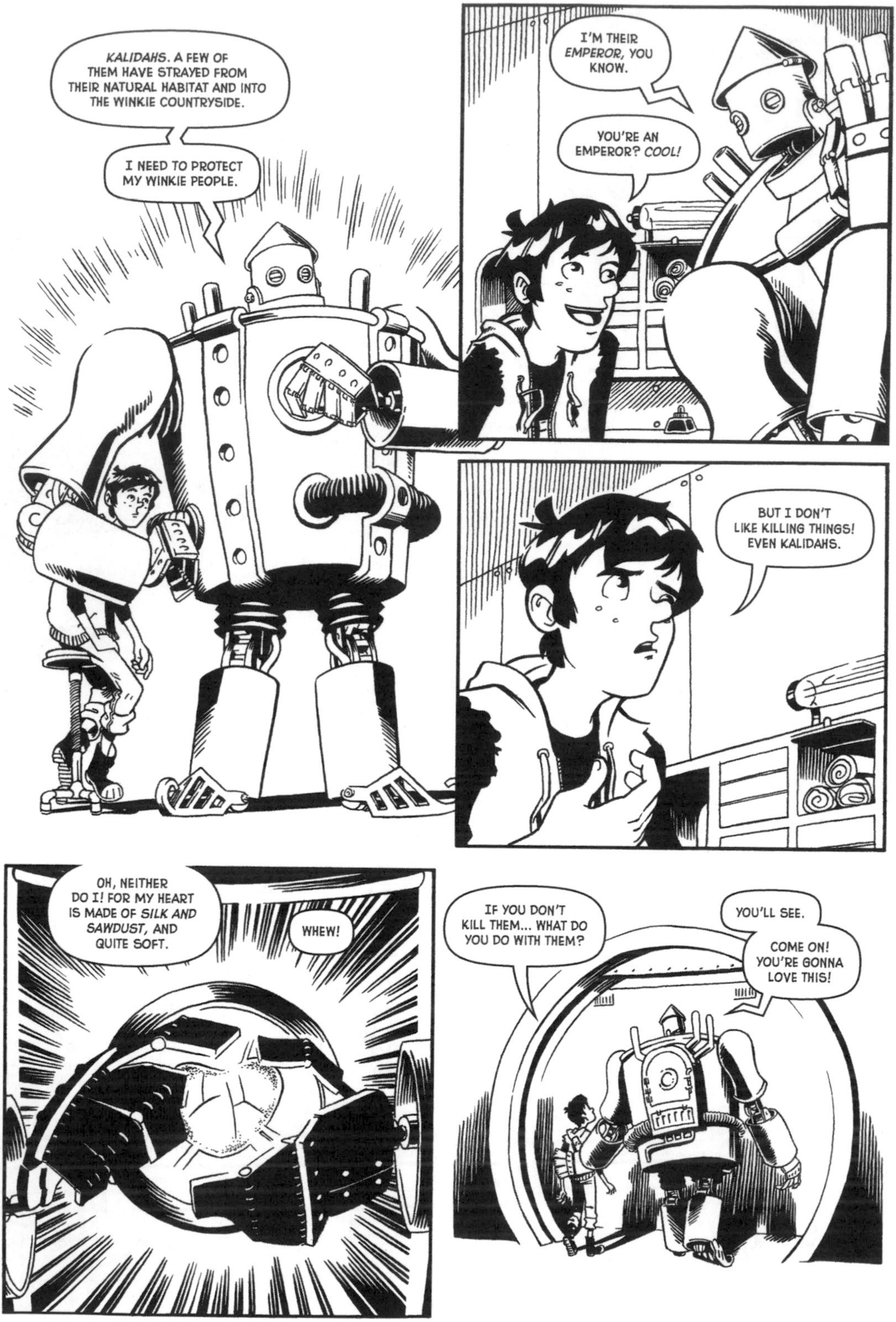
KALIDAHS. A FEW OF THEM HAVE STRAYED FROM THEIR NATURAL HABITAT AND INTO THE WINKIE COUNTRYSIDE.
I NEED TO PROTECT MY WINKIE PEOPLE.
I'M THEIR EMPEROR, YOU KNOW.
YOU'RE AN EMPEROR? COOL!
BUT I DON'T LIKE KILLING THINGS! EVEN KALIDAHS.
OH, NEITHER DO I! FOR MY HEART IS MADE OF SILK AND SAWDUST, AND QUITE SOFT.
WHEW!
IF YOU DON'T KILL THEM... WHAT DO YOU DO WITH THEM?
YOU'LL SEE.
COME ON! YOU'RE GONNA LOVE THIS!

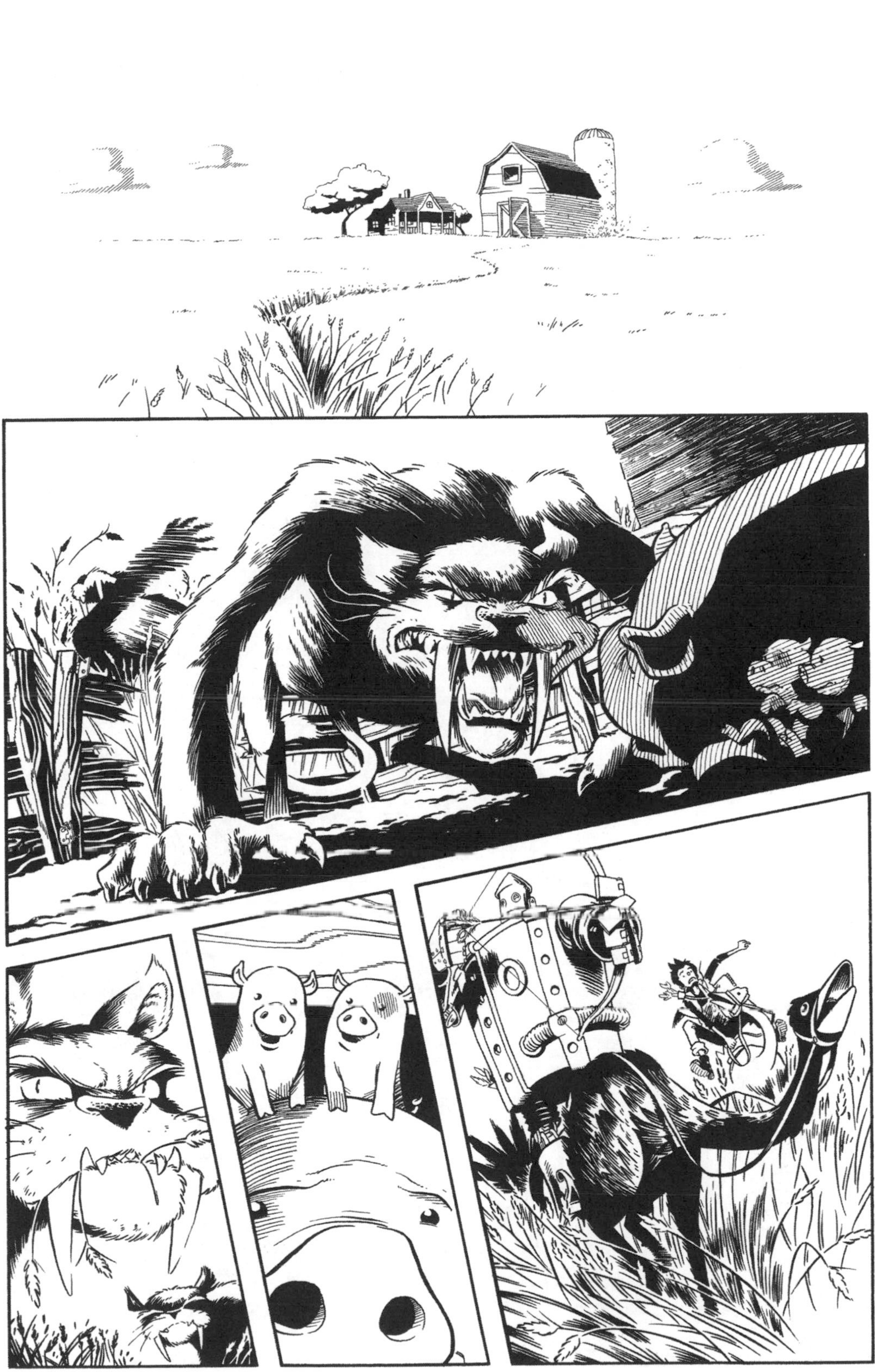

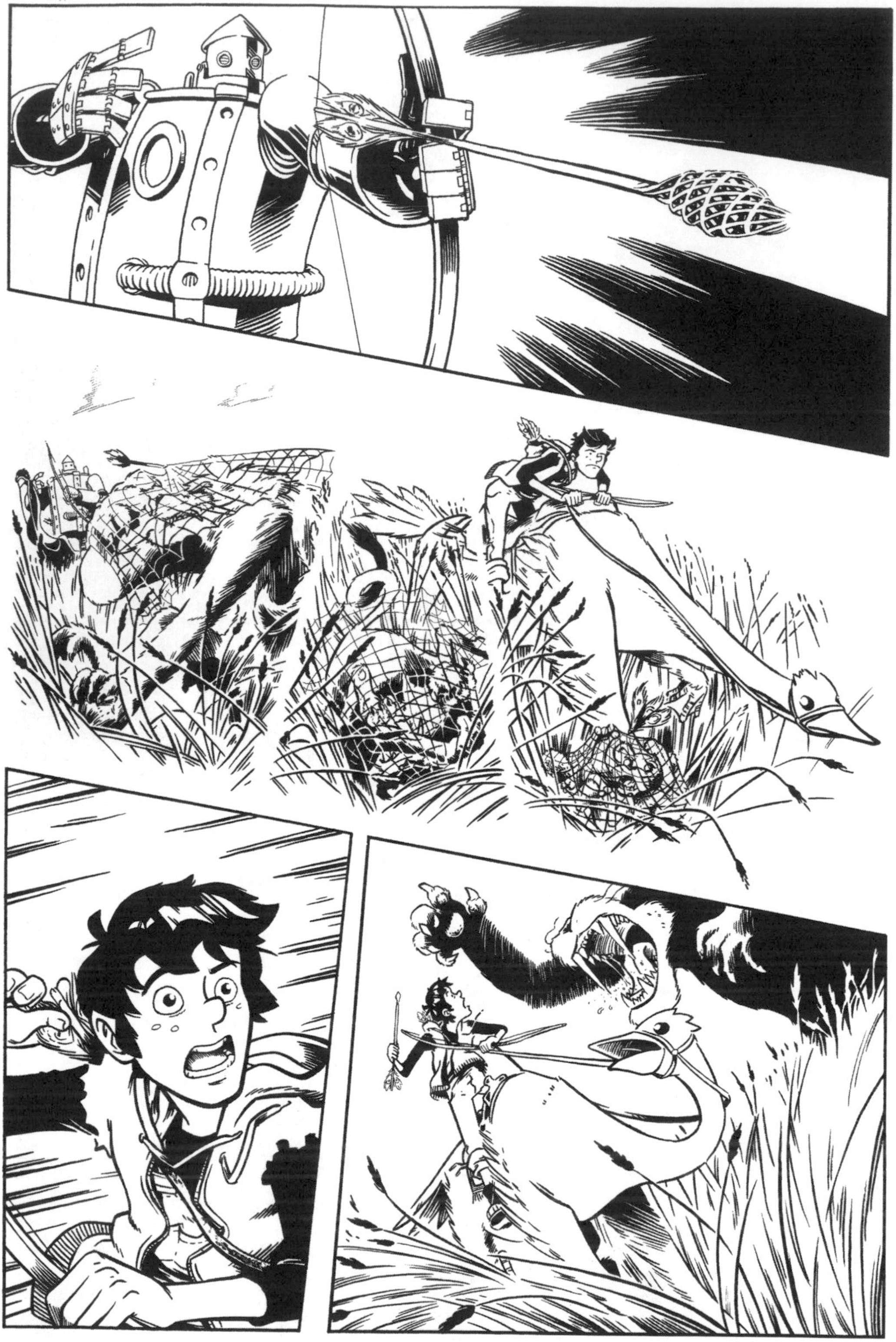

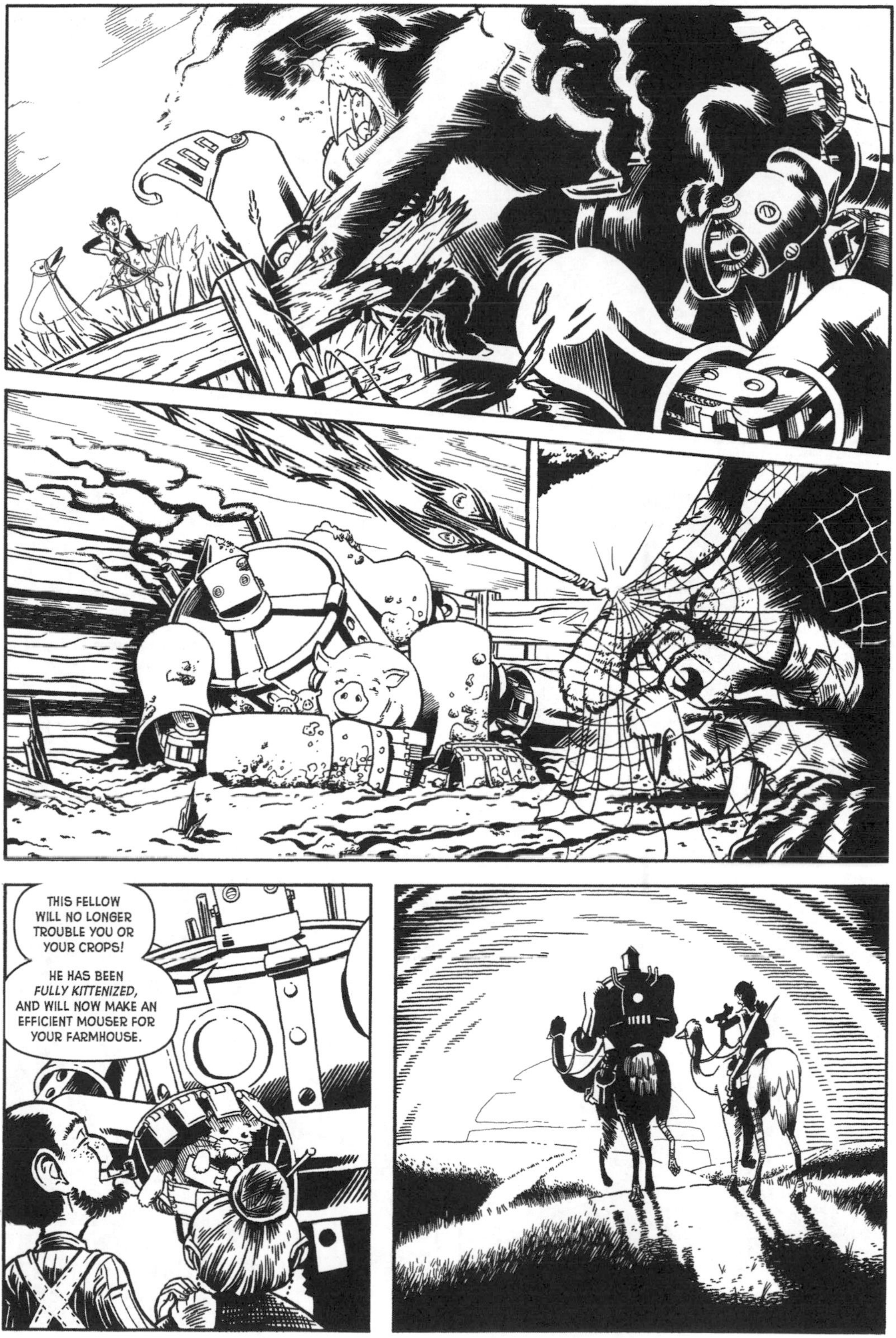
THIS FELLOW WILL NO LONGER TROUBLE YOU OR YOUR CROPS!
HE HAS BEEN *FULLY KITTENIZED,* AND WILL NOW MAKE AN EFFICIENT MOUSER FOR YOUR FARMHOUSE.

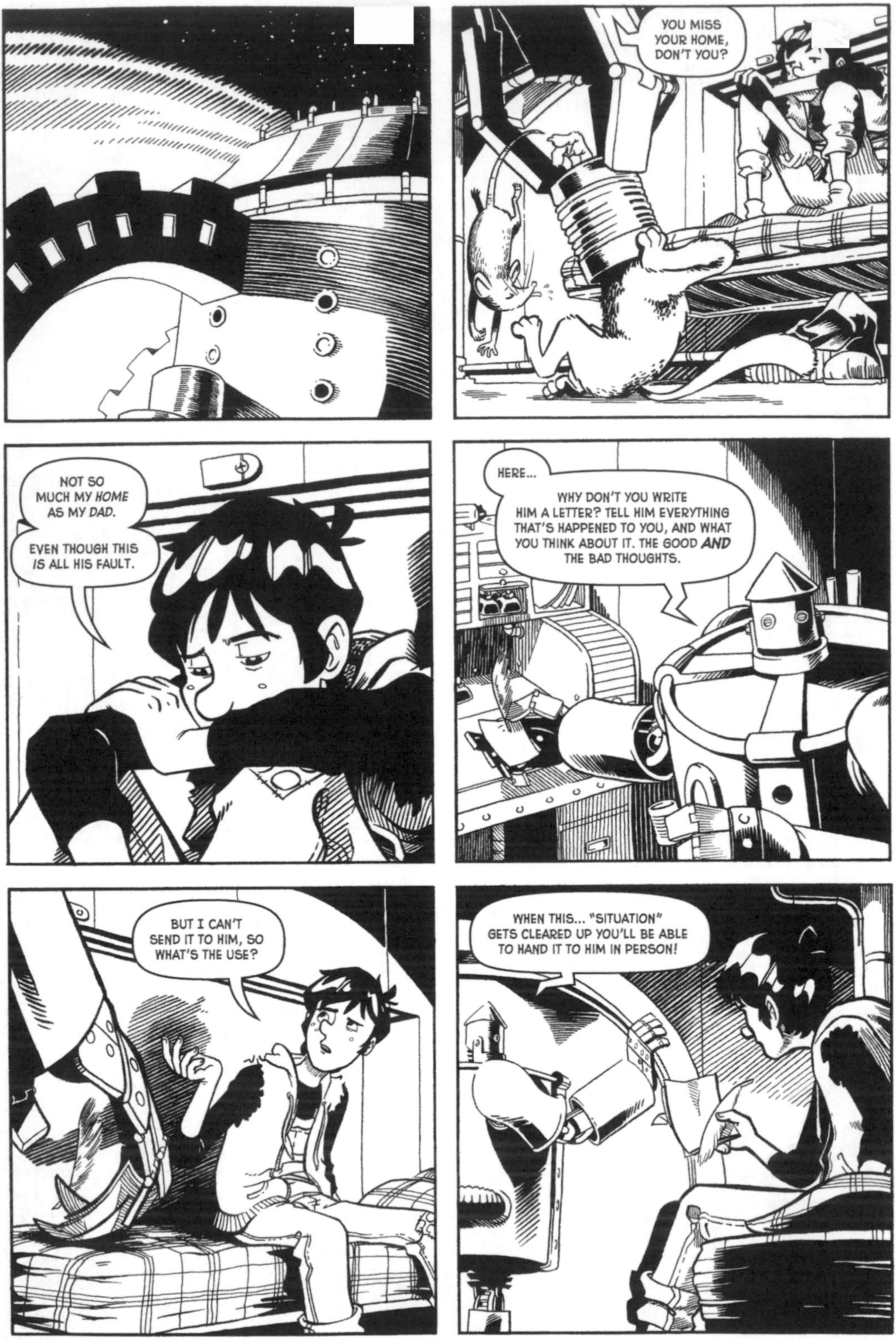
YOU MISS YOUR HOME, DON'T YOU?
NOT SO MUCH MY *HOME* AS MY *DAD*.
EVEN THOUGH THIS *IS* ALL HIS FAULT.
HERE...
WHY DON'T YOU WRITE HIM A LETTER? TELL HIM EVERYTHING THAT'S HAPPENED TO YOU, AND WHAT YOU THINK ABOUT IT. THE GOOD **AND** THE BAD THOUGHTS.
BUT I CAN'T SEND IT TO HIM, SO WHAT'S THE USE?
WHEN THIS... "SITUATION" GETS CLEARED UP YOU'LL BE ABLE TO HAND IT TO HIM IN PERSON!

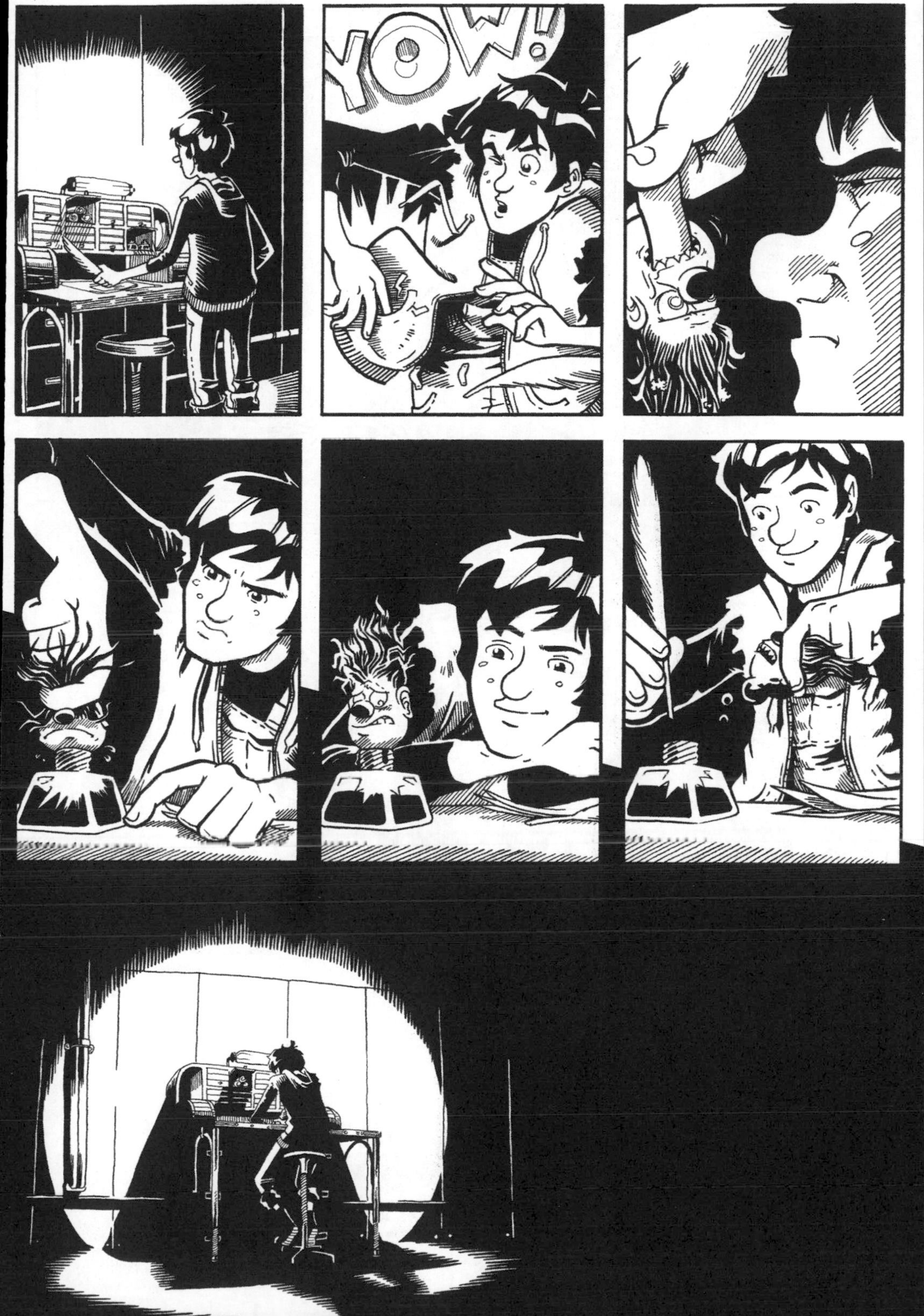
YOW!

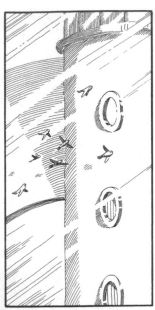

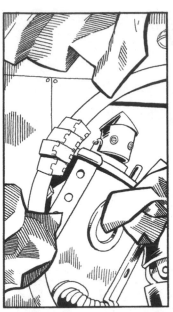

DID YOU TAKE IT?

THE LETTER TO MY DAD IS MISSING! I LEFT IT *RIGHT THERE!*

OH, FRANK, I'M SORRY! I DIDN'T TAKE IT, AND HAVEN'T SEEN IT.

MAYBE YOU MISPLACED IT?

NO!

NO, I'VE LOOKED EVERYWHERE...

IT'S *GONE!*

SOMEBODY STOLE IT...

"Gotta Witch in Here!"

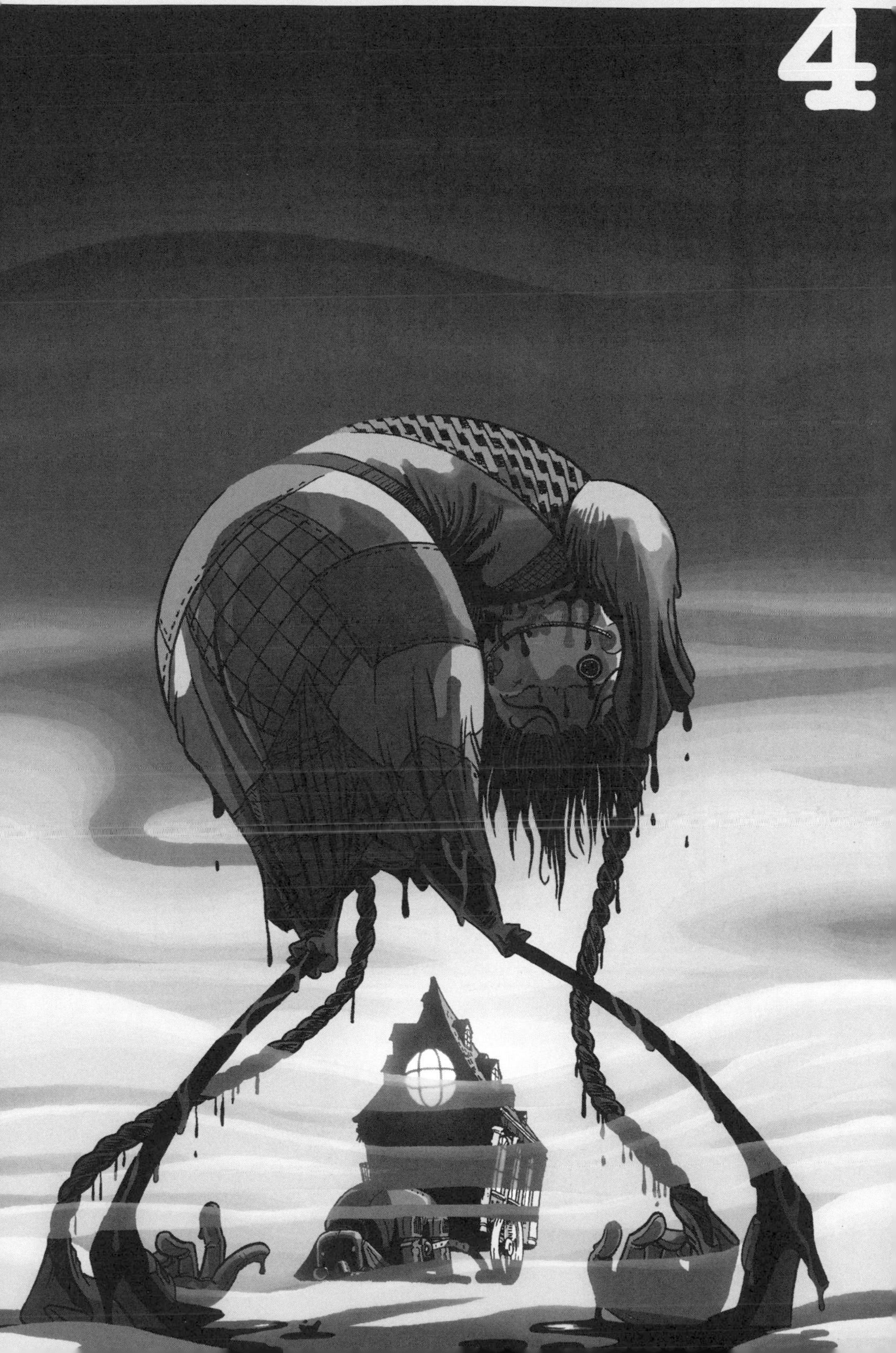
4

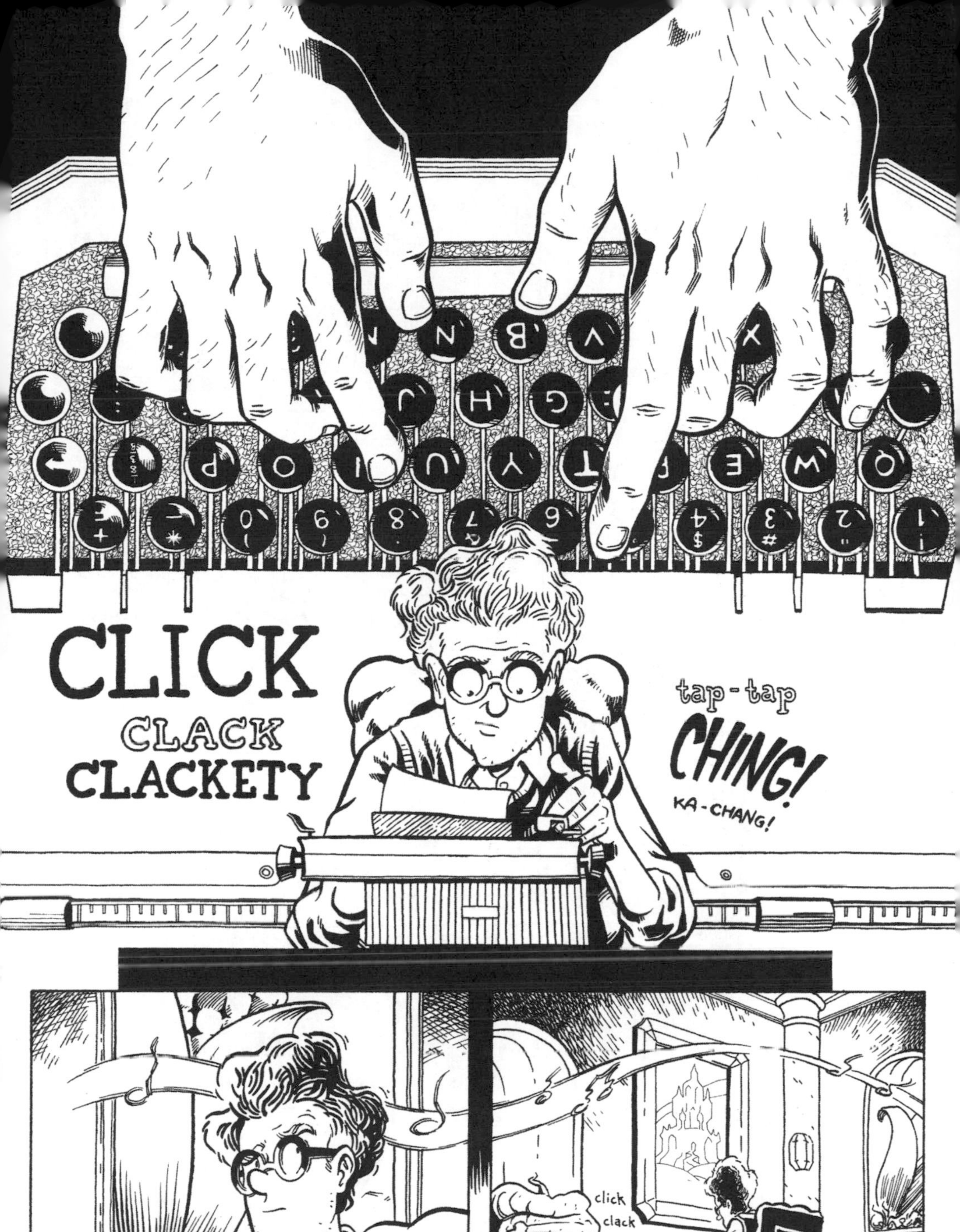
CLICK
CLACK
CLACKETY
tap-tap
CHING!
KA-CHANG!
click
clack
click

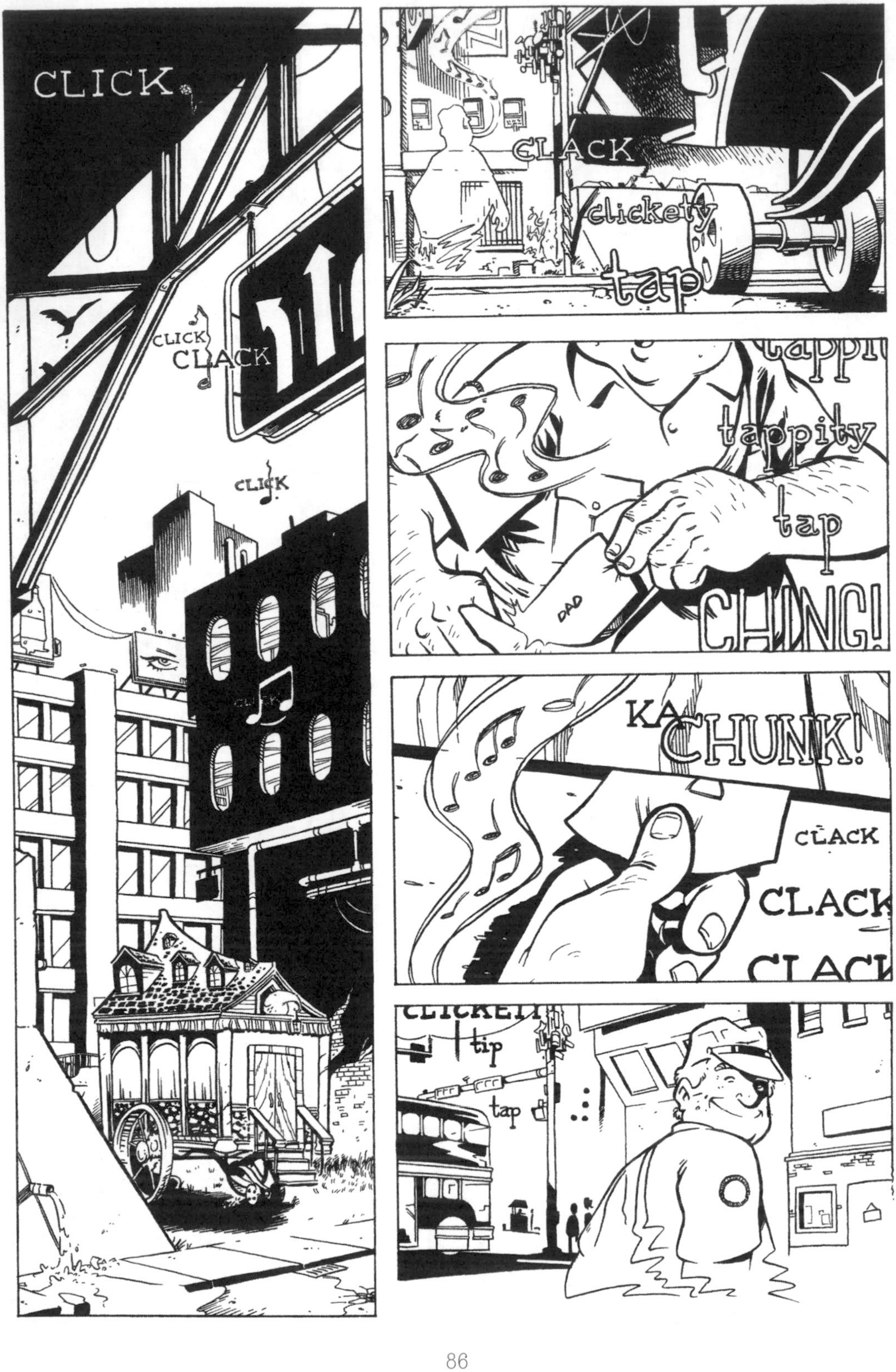

CLICK
CLICK
CLACK
CLICK
CLACK
clickety
tap
tappity
tap
CHING!
DAD
KA CHUNK!
CLACK
CLACK
tip
tap

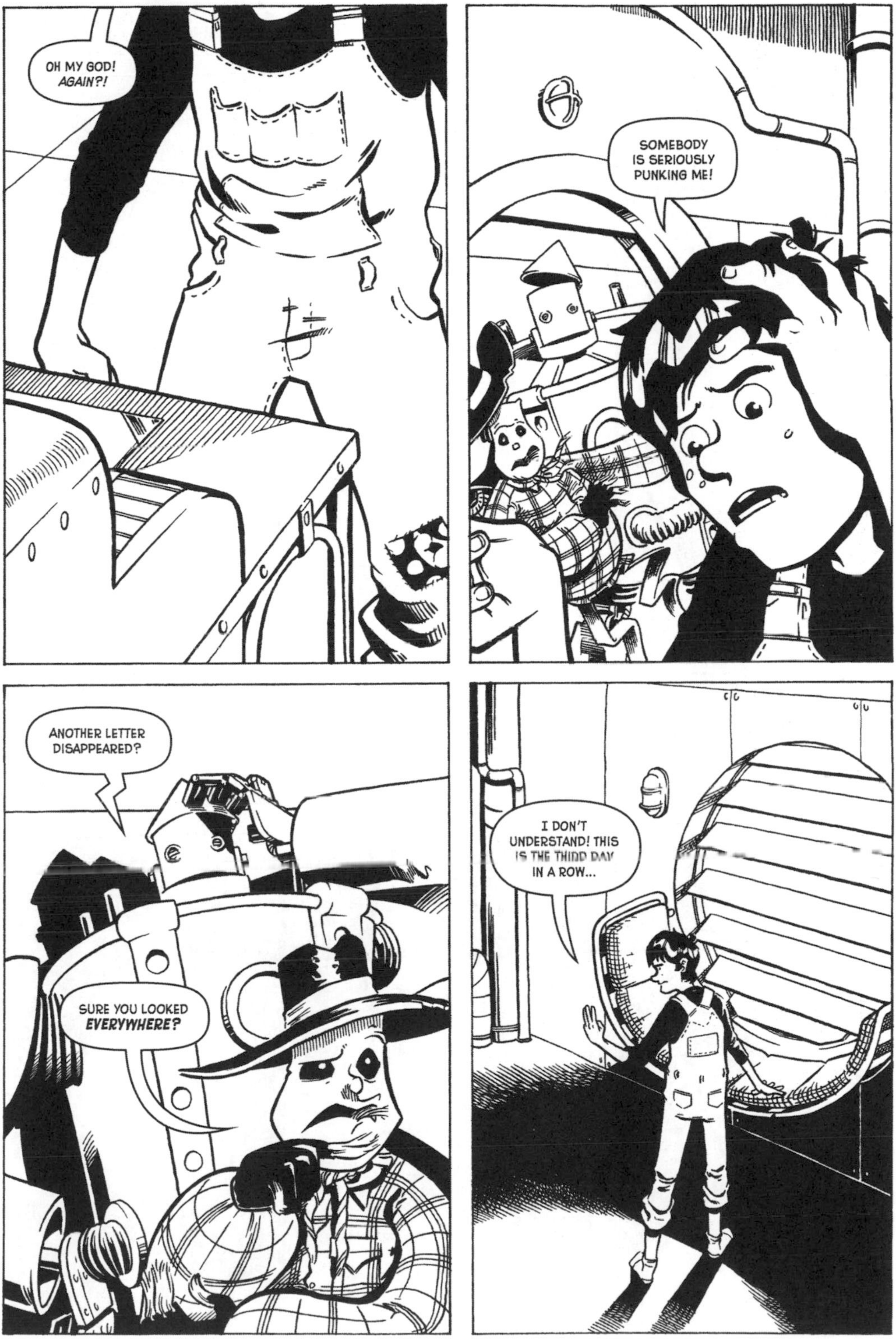
OH MY GOD! *AGAIN?!*
SOMEBODY IS SERIOUSLY PUNKING ME!
ANOTHER LETTER DISAPPEARED?
SURE YOU LOOKED ***EVERYWHERE?***
I DON'T UNDERSTAND! THIS IS THE THIRD DAY IN A ROW...

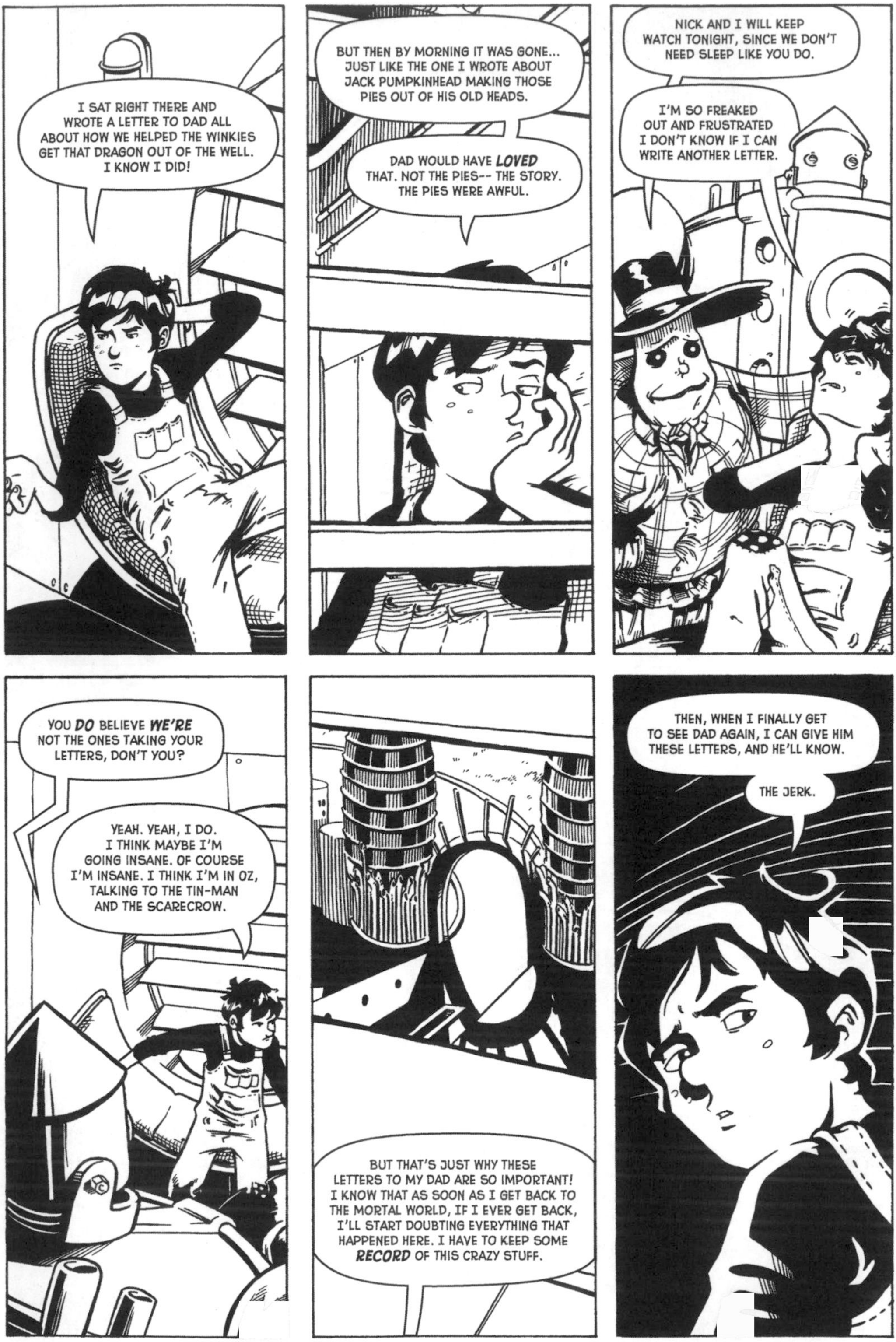
I SAT RIGHT THERE AND WROTE A LETTER TO DAD ALL ABOUT HOW WE HELPED THE WINKIES GET THAT DRAGON OUT OF THE WELL. I KNOW I DID!
BUT THEN BY MORNING IT WAS GONE... JUST LIKE THE ONE I WROTE ABOUT JACK PUMPKINHEAD MAKING THOSE PIES OUT OF HIS OLD HEADS.
DAD WOULD HAVE LOVED THAT. NOT THE PIES-- THE STORY. THE PIES WERE AWFUL.
NICK AND I WILL KEEP WATCH TONIGHT, SINCE WE DON'T NEED SLEEP LIKE YOU DO.
I'M SO FREAKED OUT AND FRUSTRATED I DON'T KNOW IF I CAN WRITE ANOTHER LETTER.
YOU DO BELIEVE WE'RE NOT THE ONES TAKING YOUR LETTERS, DON'T YOU?
YEAH. YEAH, I DO. I THINK MAYBE I'M GOING INSANE. OF COURSE I'M INSANE. I THINK I'M IN OZ, TALKING TO THE TIN-MAN AND THE SCARECROW.
BUT THAT'S JUST WHY THESE LETTERS TO MY DAD ARE SO IMPORTANT! I KNOW THAT AS SOON AS I GET BACK TO THE MORTAL WORLD, IF I EVER GET BACK, I'LL START DOUBTING EVERYTHING THAT HAPPENED HERE. I HAVE TO KEEP SOME RECORD OF THIS CRAZY STUFF.
THEN, WHEN I FINALLY GET TO SEE DAD AGAIN, I CAN GIVE HIM THESE LETTERS, AND HE'LL KNOW.
THE JERK.

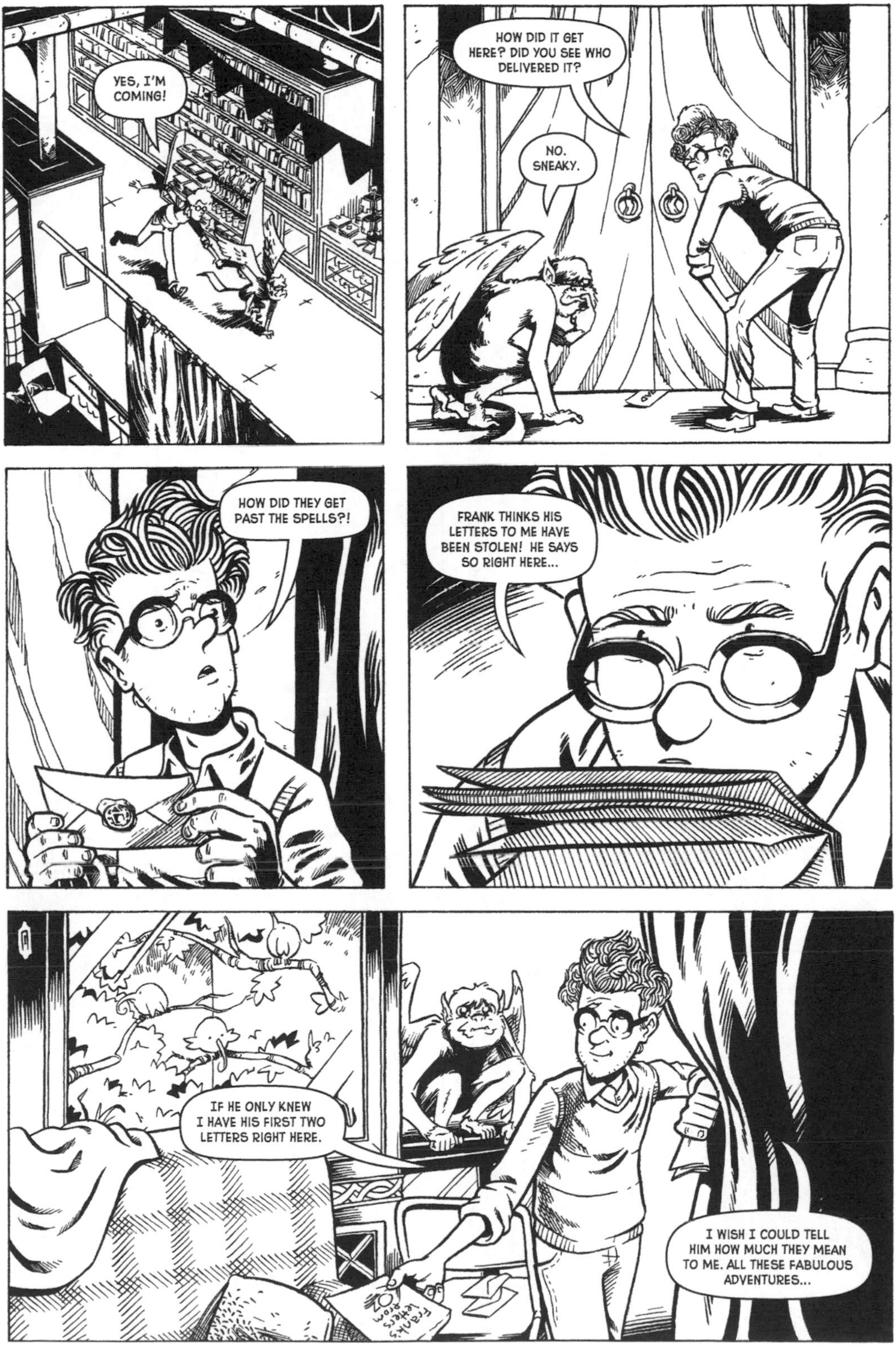
YES, I'M COMING!
HOW DID IT GET HERE? DID YOU SEE WHO DELIVERED IT?
NO. SNEAKY.
HOW DID THEY GET PAST THE SPELLS?!
FRANK THINKS HIS LETTERS TO ME HAVE BEEN STOLEN! HE SAYS SO RIGHT HERE...
IF HE ONLY KNEW I HAVE HIS FIRST TWO LETTERS RIGHT HERE.
Frank's letters from OZ
I WISH I COULD TELL HIM HOW MUCH THEY MEAN TO ME. ALL THESE FABULOUS ADVENTURES...

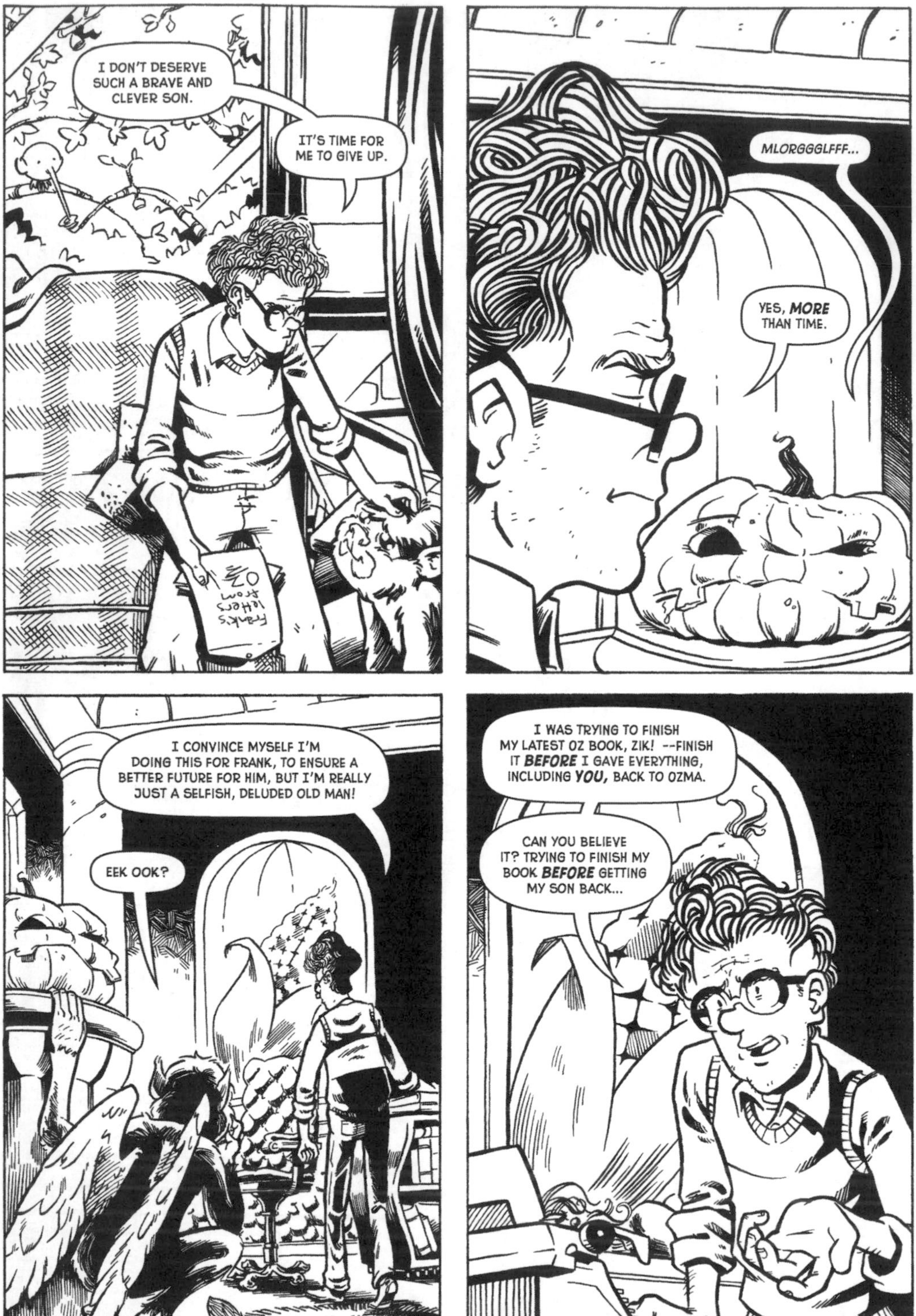
I DON'T DESERVE SUCH A BRAVE AND CLEVER SON.
IT'S TIME FOR ME TO GIVE UP.
Frank's letters from OZ
MLORGGGLFFF...
YES, ***MORE*** THAN TIME.
I CONVINCE MYSELF I'M DOING THIS FOR FRANK, TO ENSURE A BETTER FUTURE FOR HIM, BUT I'M REALLY JUST A SELFISH, DELUDED OLD MAN!
EEK OOK?
I WAS TRYING TO FINISH MY LATEST OZ BOOK, ZIK! --FINISH IT ***BEFORE*** I GAVE EVERYTHING, INCLUDING ***YOU,*** BACK TO OZMA.
CAN YOU BELIEVE IT? TRYING TO FINISH MY BOOK ***BEFORE*** GETTING MY SON BACK...

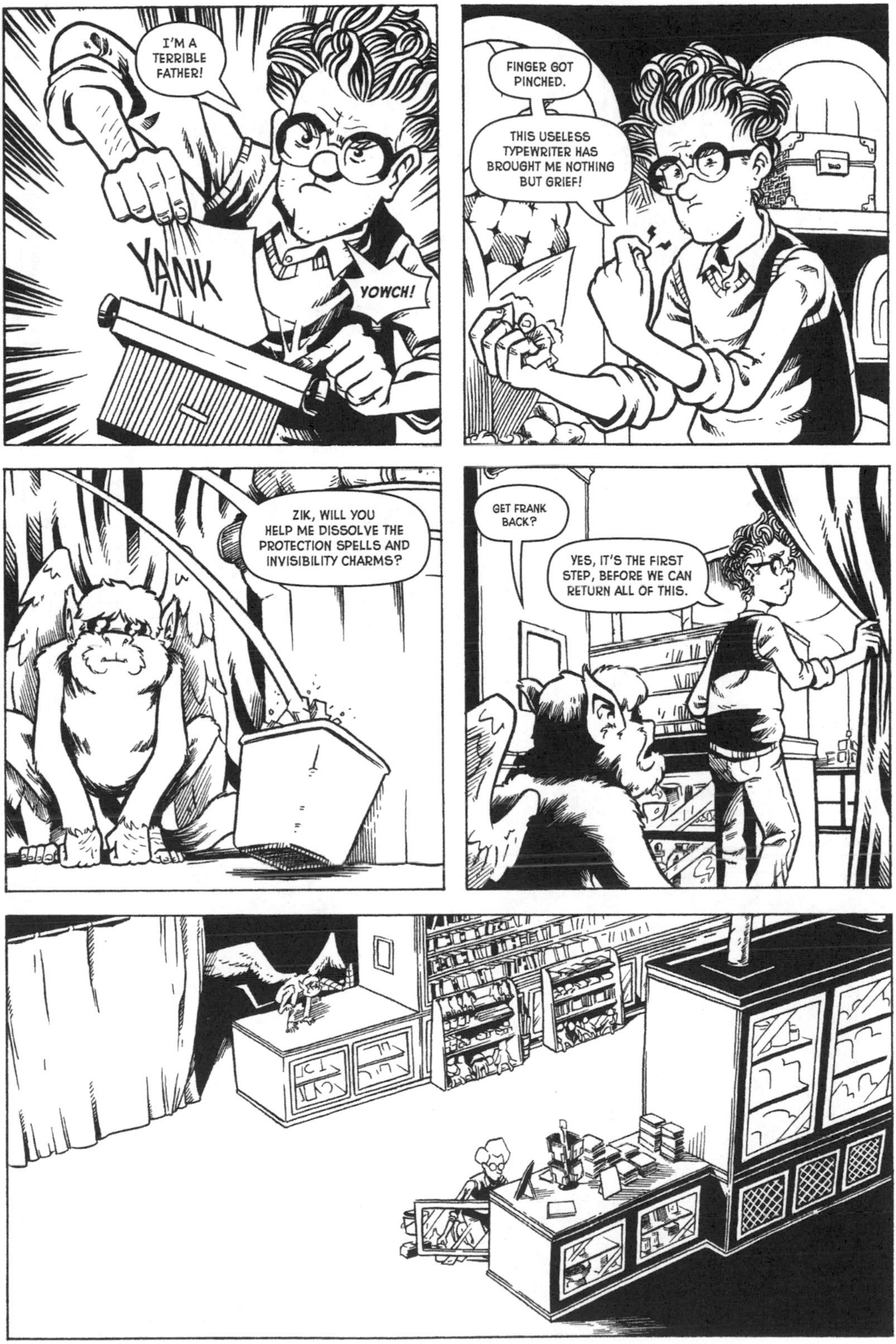
I'M A TERRIBLE FATHER!
YANK
YOWCH!
FINGER GOT PINCHED.
THIS USELESS TYPEWRITER HAS BROUGHT ME NOTHING BUT GRIEF!
ZIK, WILL YOU HELP ME DISSOLVE THE PROTECTION SPELLS AND INVISIBILITY CHARMS?
GET FRANK BACK?
YES, IT'S THE FIRST STEP, BEFORE WE CAN RETURN ALL OF THIS.

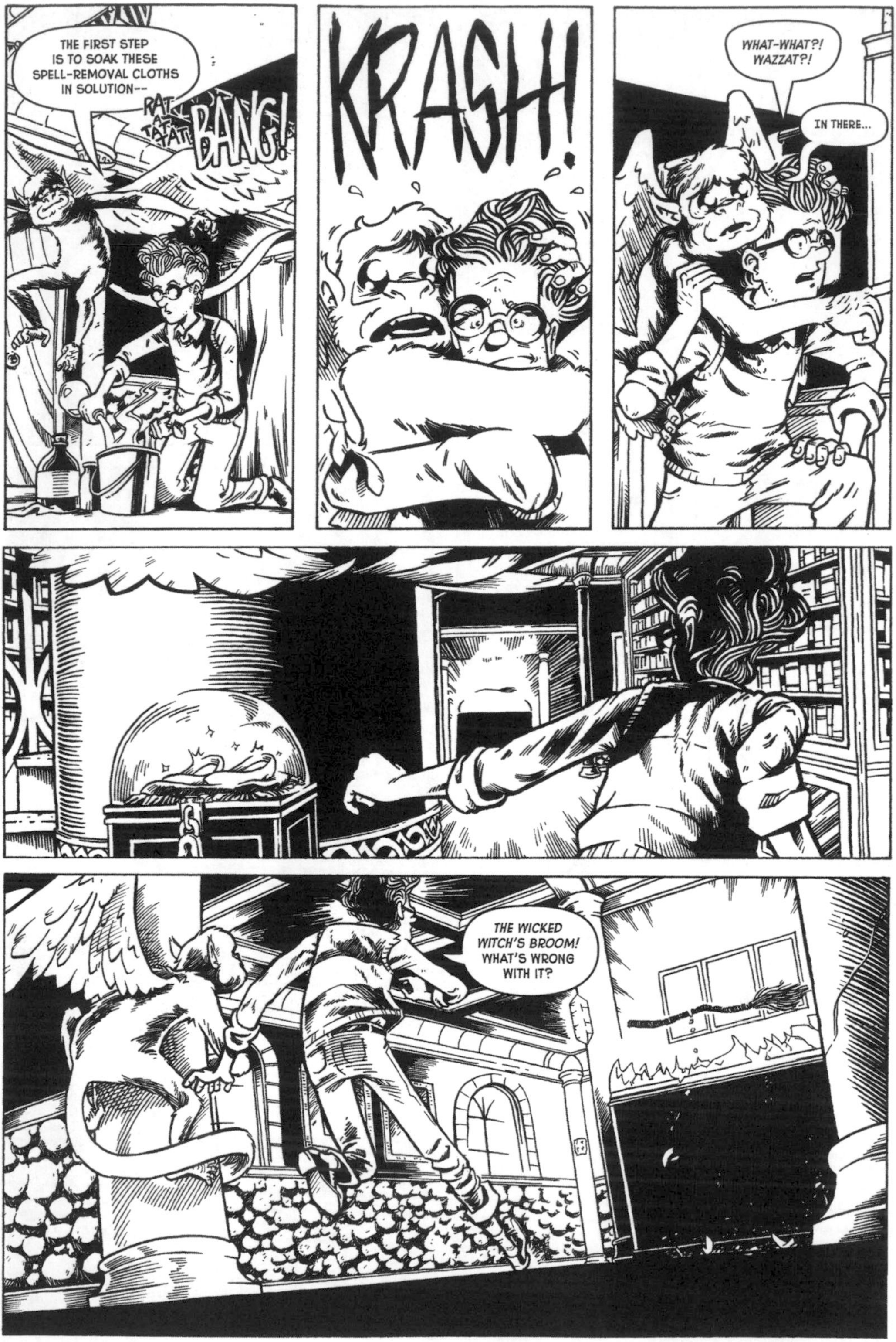
THE FIRST STEP IS TO SOAK THESE SPELL-REMOVAL CLOTHS IN SOLUTION--
RAT A TAT TAT!
BANG!
KRASH!
WHAT-WHAT?! WAZZAT?!
IN THERE...
THE WICKED WITCH'S BROOM! WHAT'S WRONG WITH IT?

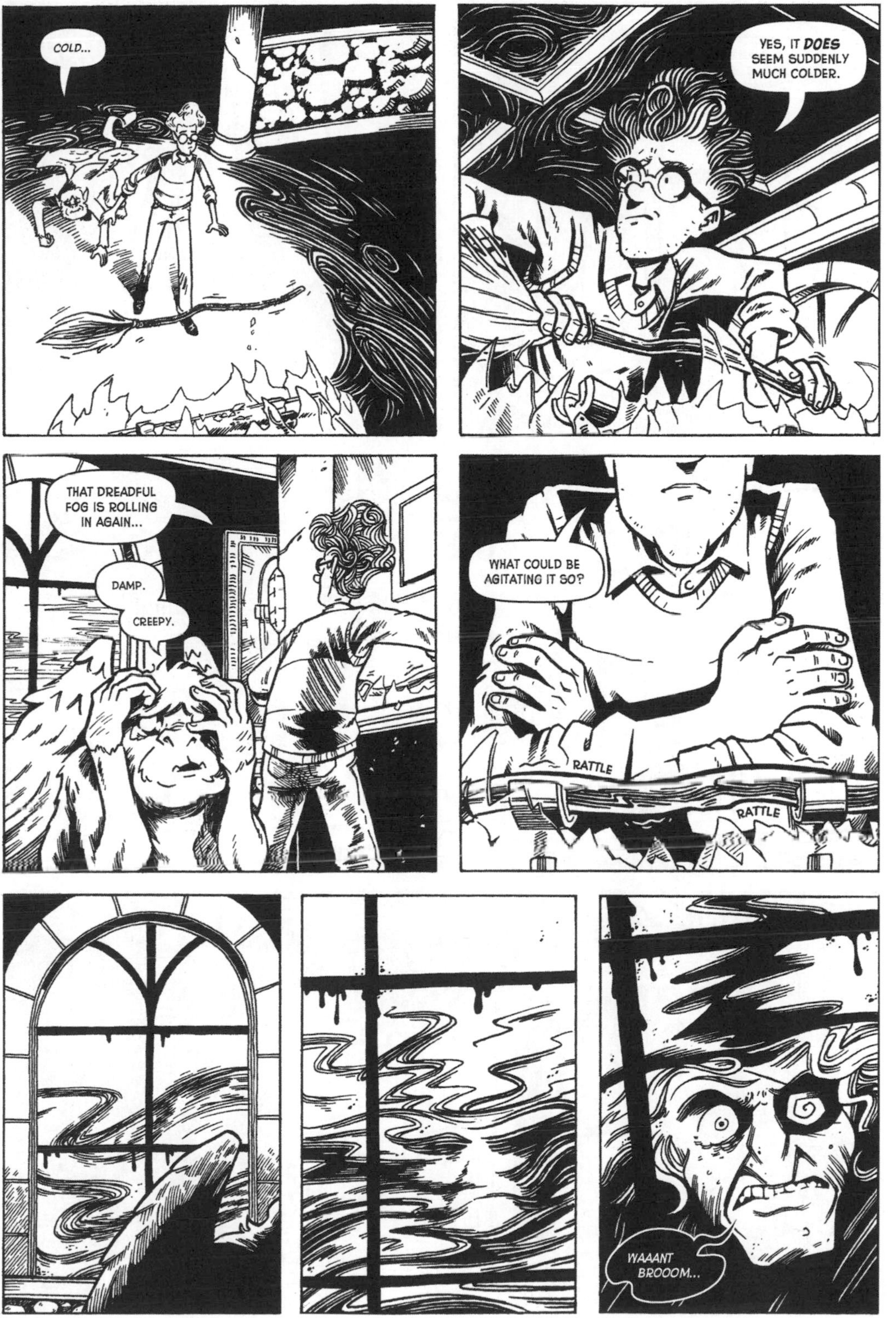
COLD...
YES, IT **DOES** SEEM SUDDENLY MUCH COLDER.
THAT DREADFUL FOG IS ROLLING IN AGAIN...
DAMP.
CREEPY.
WHAT COULD BE AGITATING IT SO?
RATTLE
RATTLE
WAAANT BROOOM...

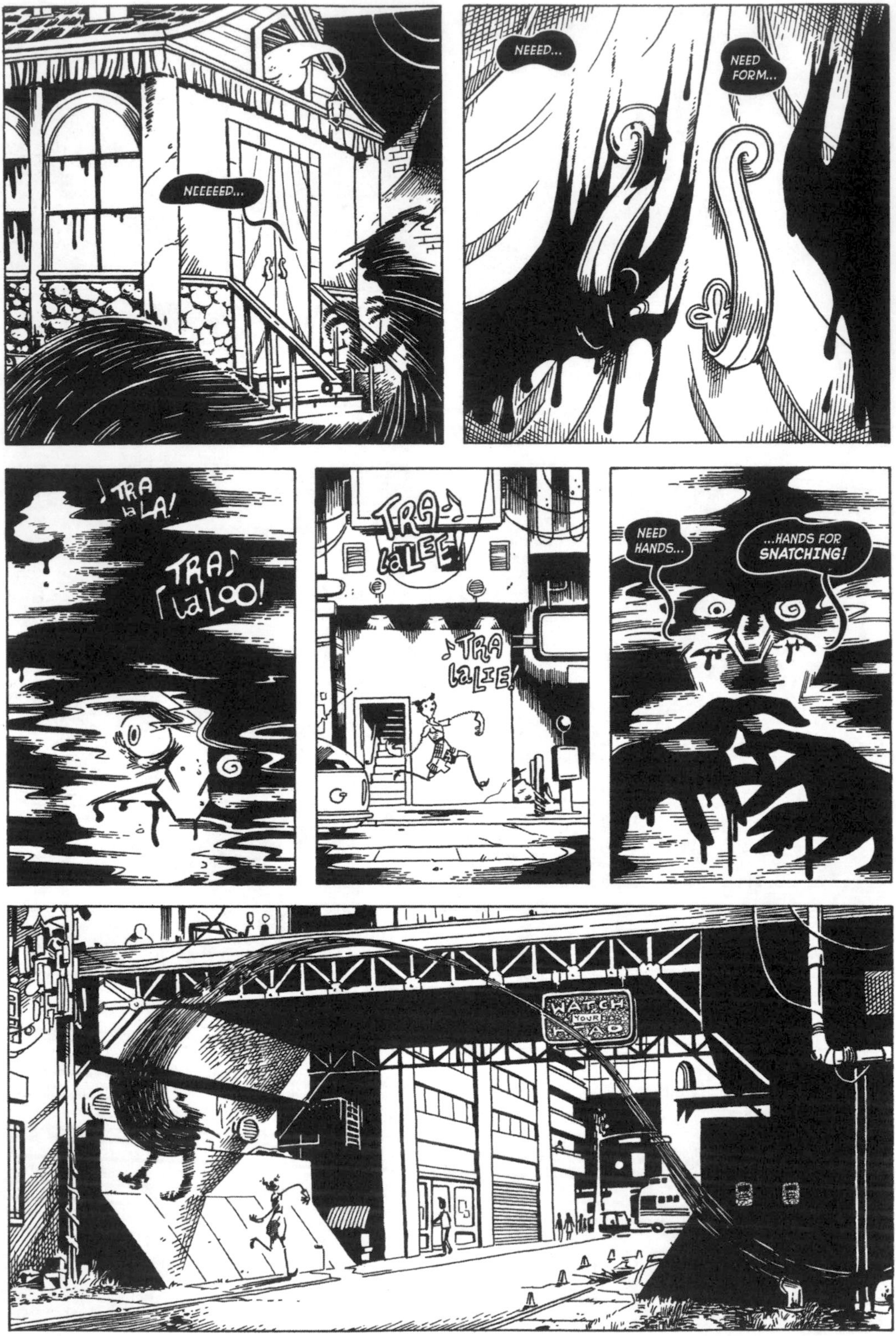
NEEEEED...
NEEED...
NEED FORM...
TRA la LA!
TRA la LOO!
TRA LA LEE!
TRA la LIE!
NEED HANDS...
...HANDS FOR **SNATCHING!**
WATCH
YOUR

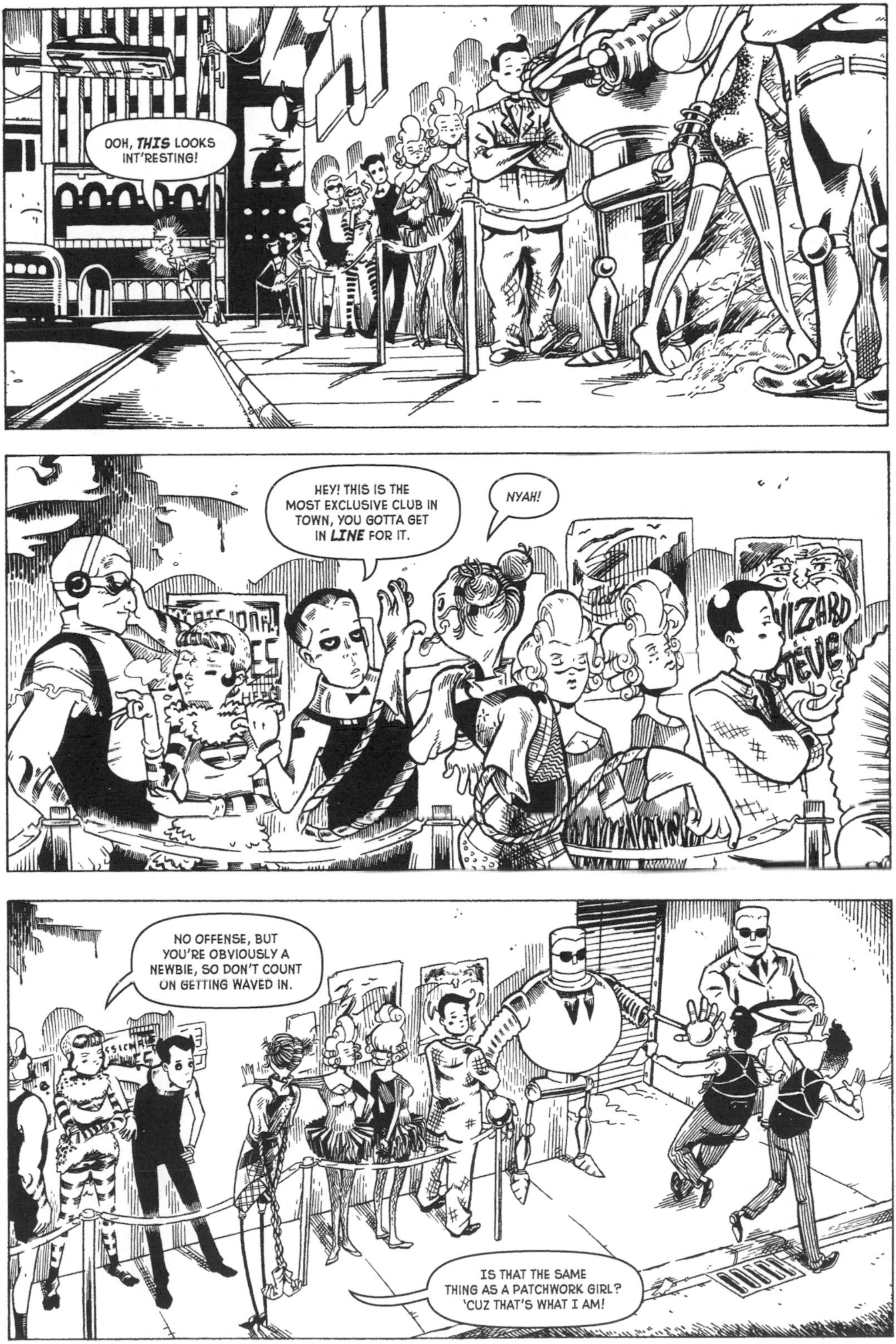
OOH, **THIS** LOOKS INT'RESTING!
HEY! THIS IS THE MOST EXCLUSIVE CLUB IN TOWN, YOU GOTTA GET IN **LINE** FOR IT.
NYAH!
NO OFFENSE, BUT YOU'RE OBVIOUSLY A NEWBIE, SO DON'T COUNT ON GETTING WAVED IN.
IS THAT THE SAME THING AS A PATCHWORK GIRL? 'CUZ THAT'S WHAT I AM!

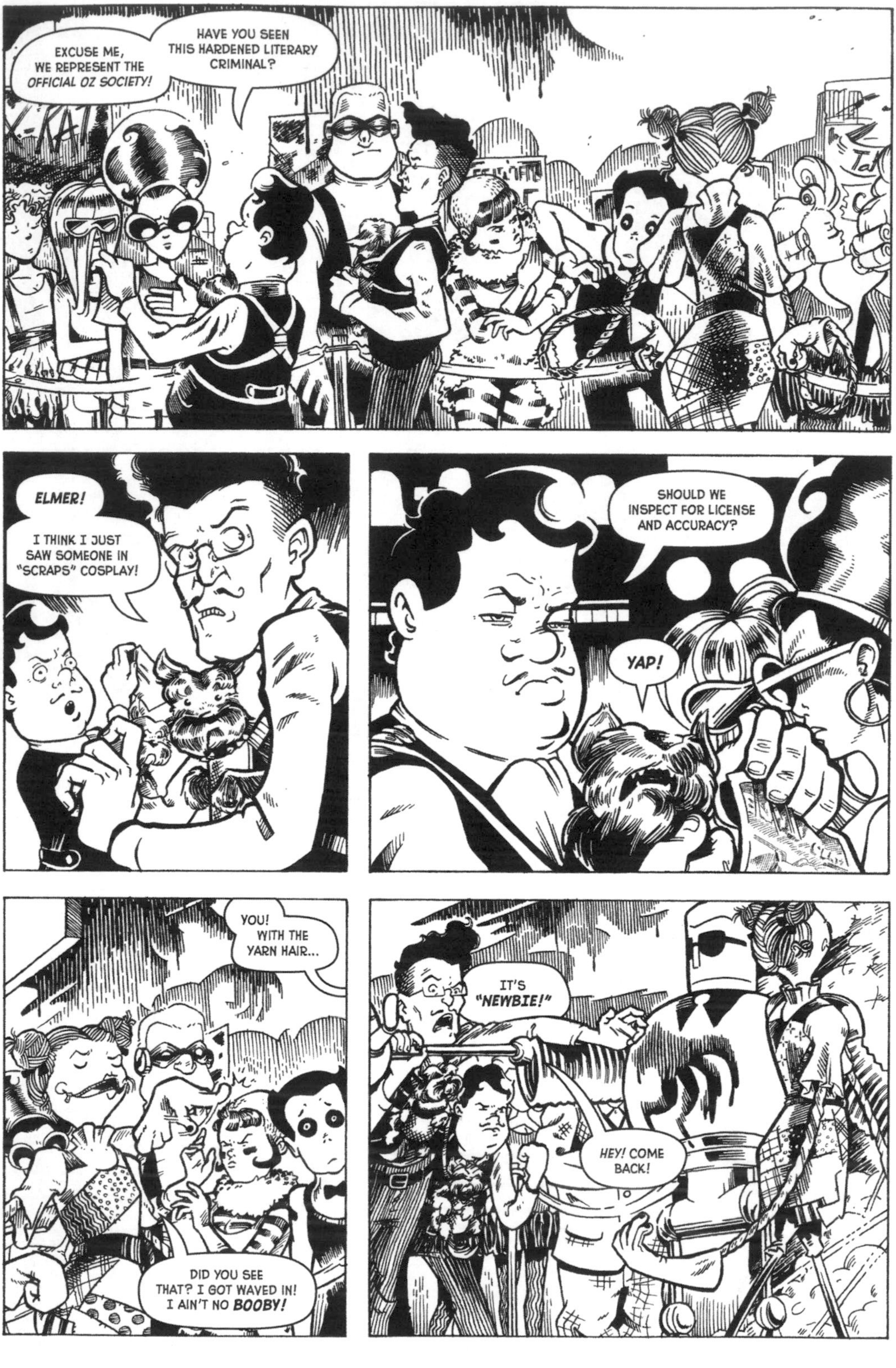
EXCUSE ME, WE REPRESENT THE *OFFICIAL OZ SOCIETY!*
HAVE YOU SEEN THIS HARDENED LITERARY CRIMINAL?
ELMER!
I THINK I JUST SAW SOMEONE IN "SCRAPS" COSPLAY!
SHOULD WE INSPECT FOR LICENSE AND ACCURACY?
YAP!
YOU! WITH THE YARN HAIR...
DID YOU SEE THAT? I GOT WAVED IN! I AIN'T NO ***BOOBY!***
IT'S ***"NEWBIE!"***
HEY! COME BACK!

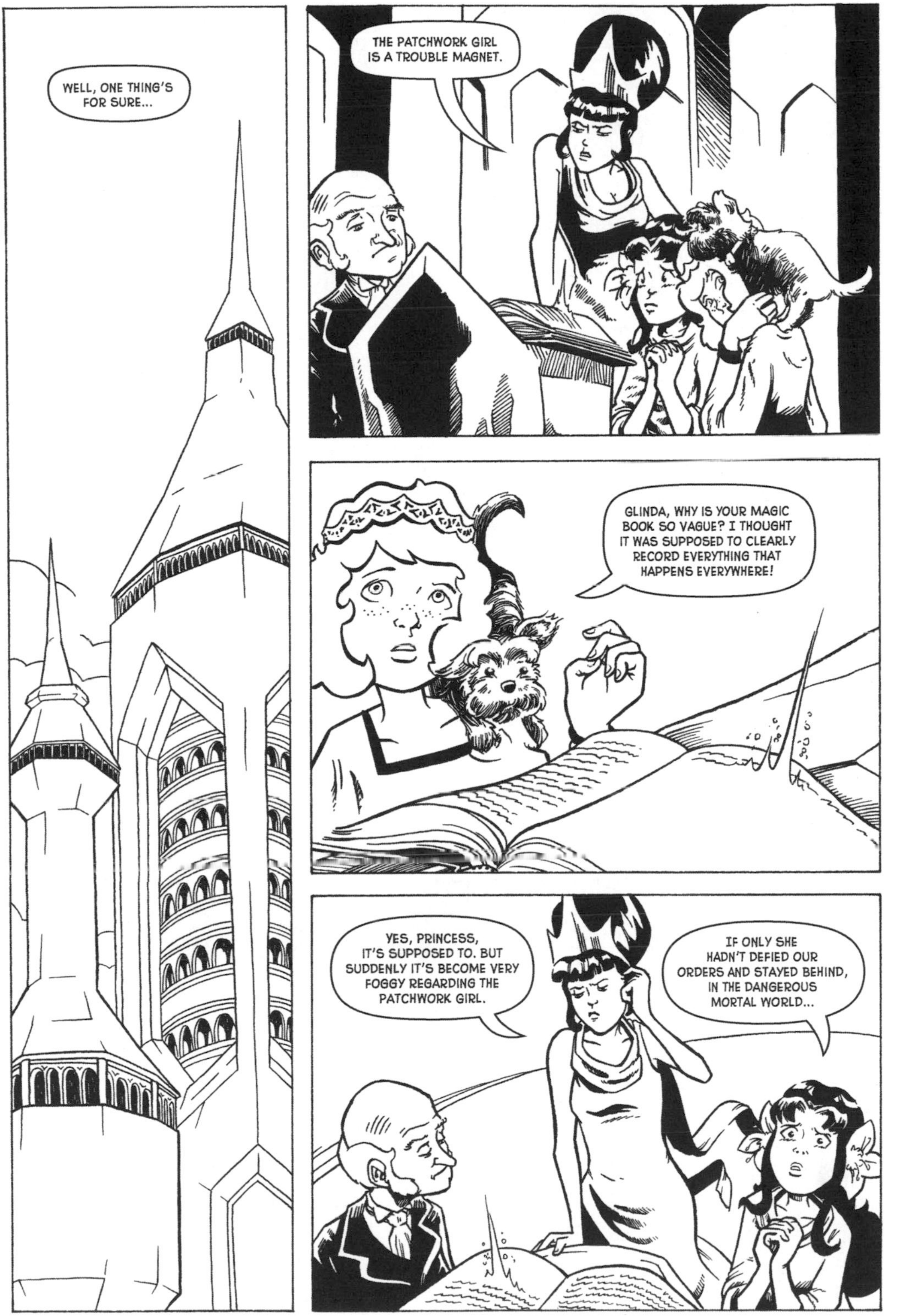
WELL, ONE THING'S FOR SURE...
THE PATCHWORK GIRL IS A TROUBLE MAGNET.
GLINDA, WHY IS YOUR MAGIC BOOK SO VAGUE? I THOUGHT IT WAS SUPPOSED TO CLEARLY RECORD EVERYTHING THAT HAPPENS EVERYWHERE!
YES, PRINCESS, IT'S SUPPOSED TO. BUT SUDDENLY IT'S BECOME VERY FOGGY REGARDING THE PATCHWORK GIRL.
IF ONLY SHE HADN'T DEFIED OUR ORDERS AND STAYED BEHIND, IN THE DANGEROUS MORTAL WORLD...

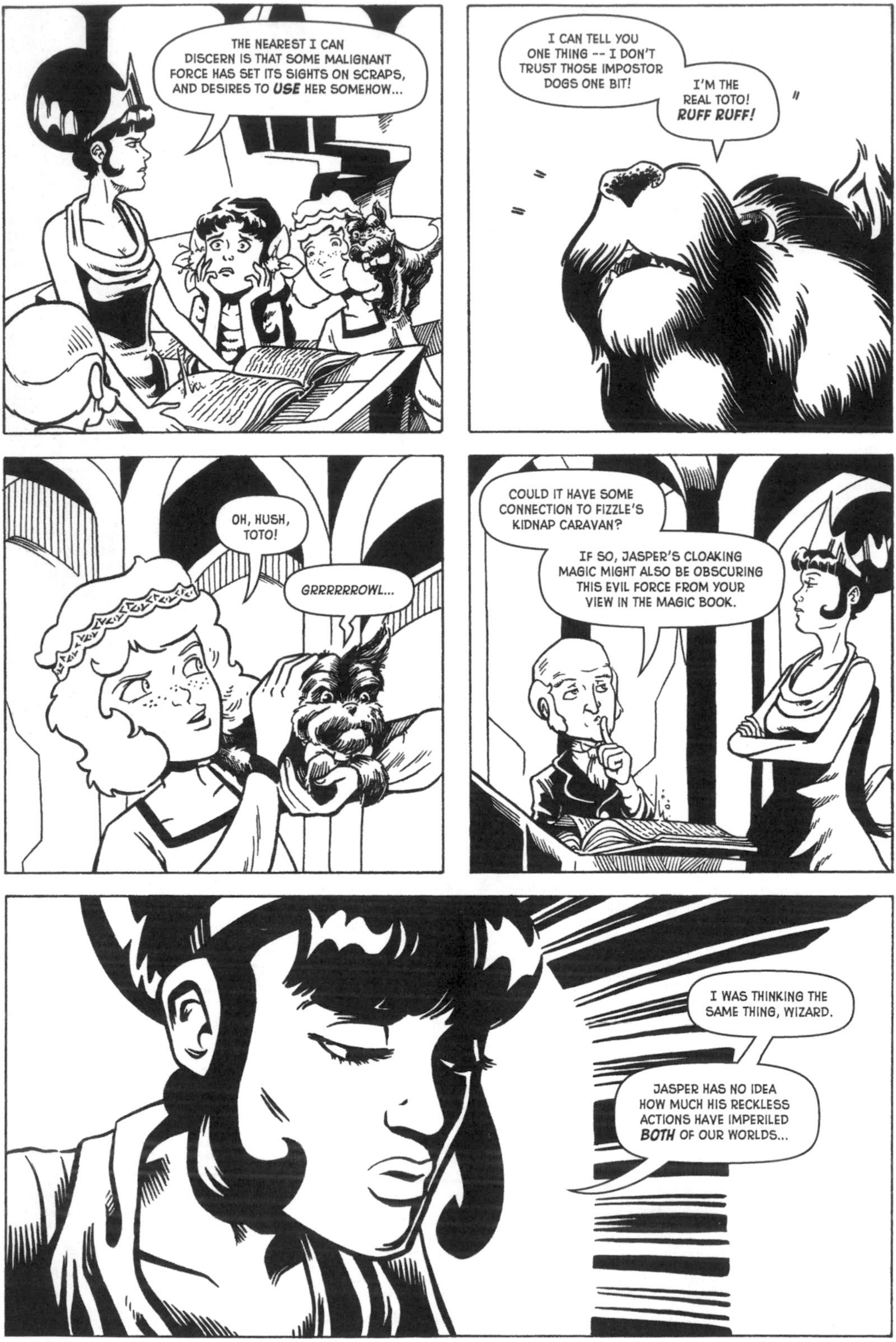
THE NEAREST I CAN DISCERN IS THAT SOME MALIGNANT FORCE HAS SET ITS SIGHTS ON SCRAPS, AND DESIRES TO **USE** HER SOMEHOW...
I CAN TELL YOU ONE THING -- I DON'T TRUST THOSE IMPOSTOR DOGS ONE BIT!
I'M THE REAL TOTO! **RUFF RUFF!**
OH, HUSH, TOTO!
GRRRRRROWL...
COULD IT HAVE SOME CONNECTION TO FIZZLE'S KIDNAP CARAVAN?
IF SO, JASPER'S CLOAKING MAGIC MIGHT ALSO BE OBSCURING THIS EVIL FORCE FROM YOUR VIEW IN THE MAGIC BOOK.
I WAS THINKING THE SAME THING, WIZARD.
JASPER HAS NO IDEA HOW MUCH HIS RECKLESS ACTIONS HAVE IMPERILED **BOTH** OF OUR WORLDS...

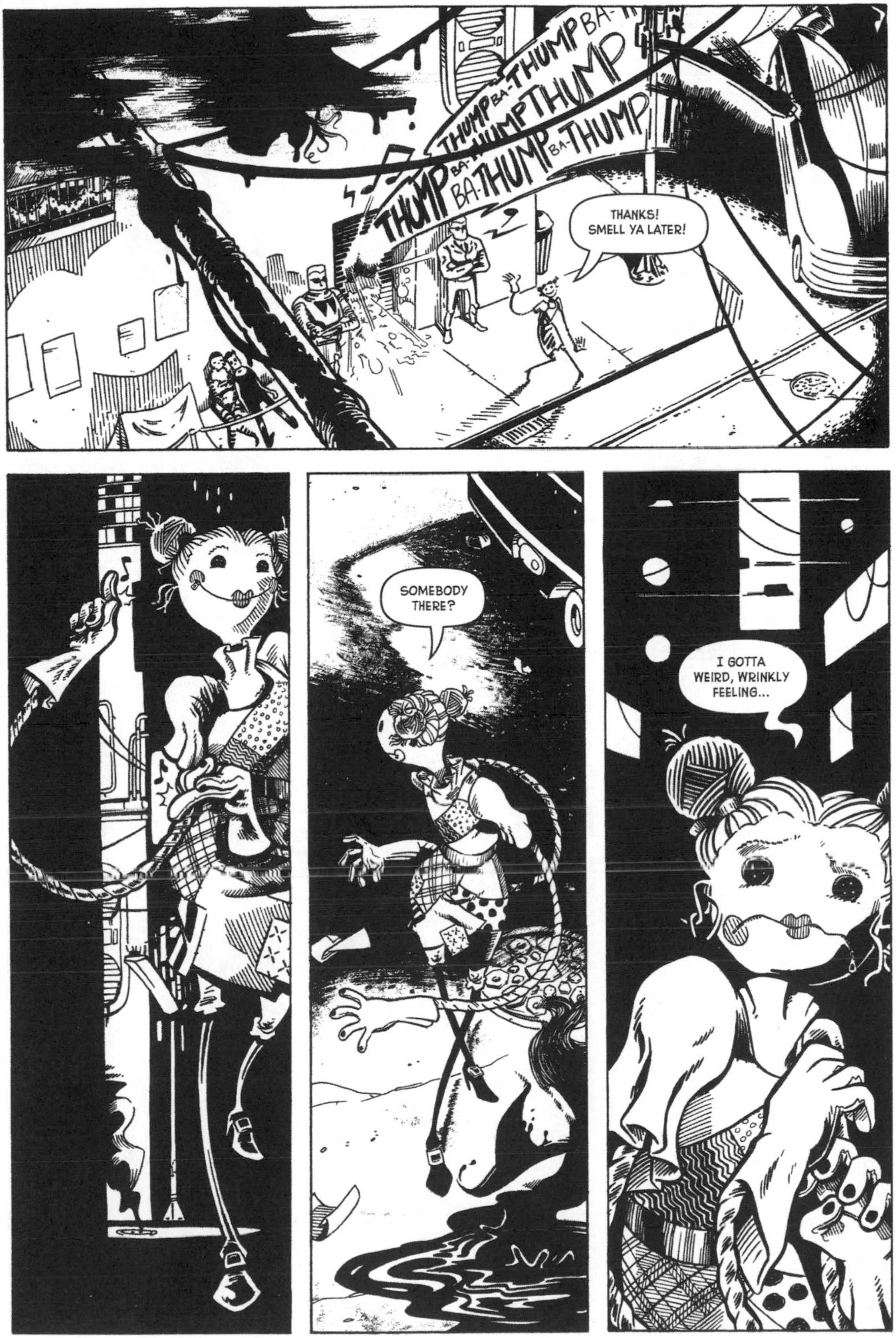
THUMP BA-THUMP
THUMP BA-THUMP
THUMP BA-THUMP BA-THUMP
THANKS! SMELL YA LATER!
SOMEBODY THERE?
I GOTTA WEIRD, WRINKLY FEELING...

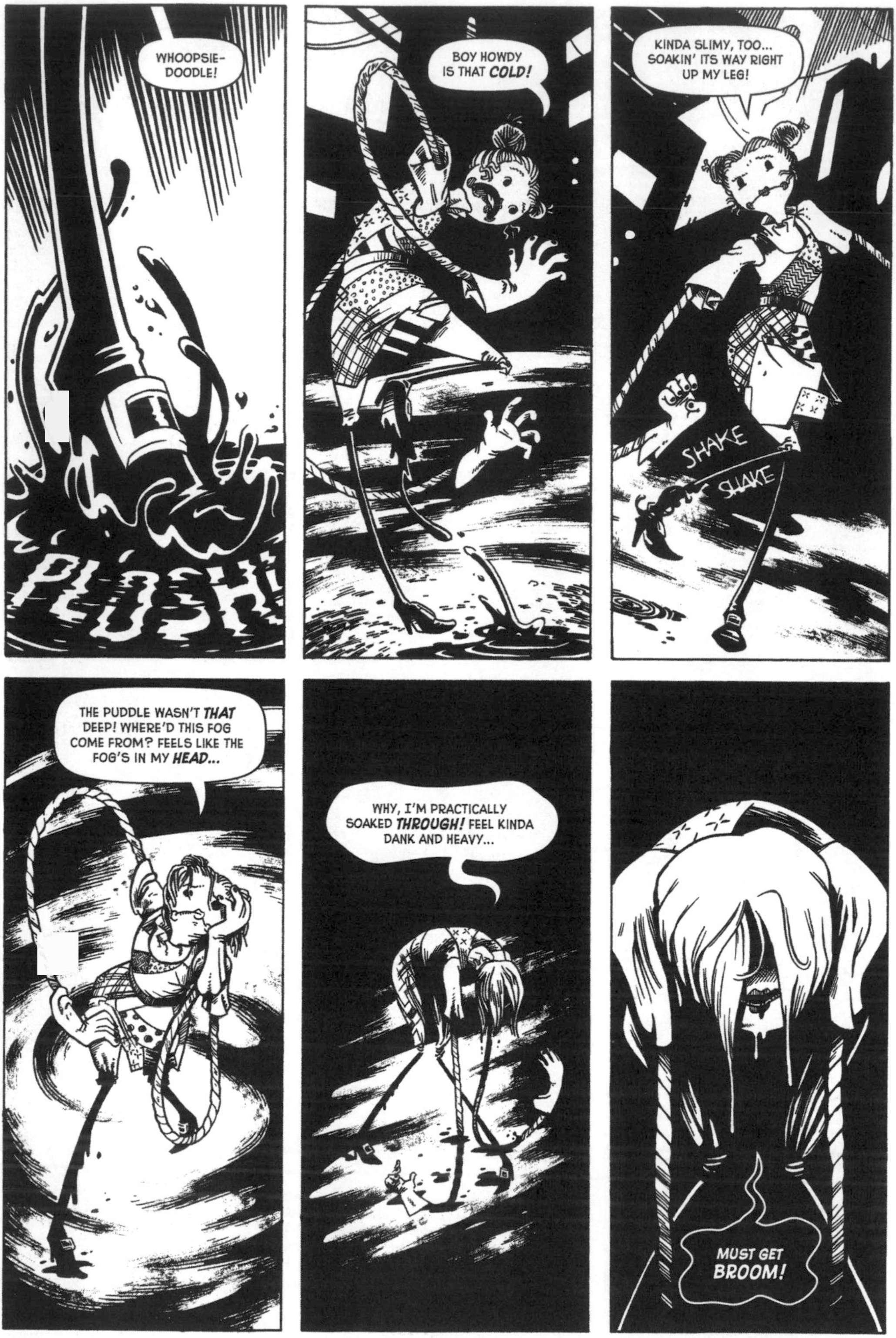
WHOOPSIE-DOODLE!
PLOSH!
BOY HOWDY IS THAT COLD!
KINDA SLIMY, TOO... SOAKIN' ITS WAY RIGHT UP MY LEG!
SHAKE
SHAKE
THE PUDDLE WASN'T THAT DEEP! WHERE'D THIS FOG COME FROM? FEELS LIKE THE FOG'S IN MY HEAD...
WHY, I'M PRACTICALLY SOAKED THROUGH! FEEL KINDA DANK AND HEAVY...
MUST GET BROOM!

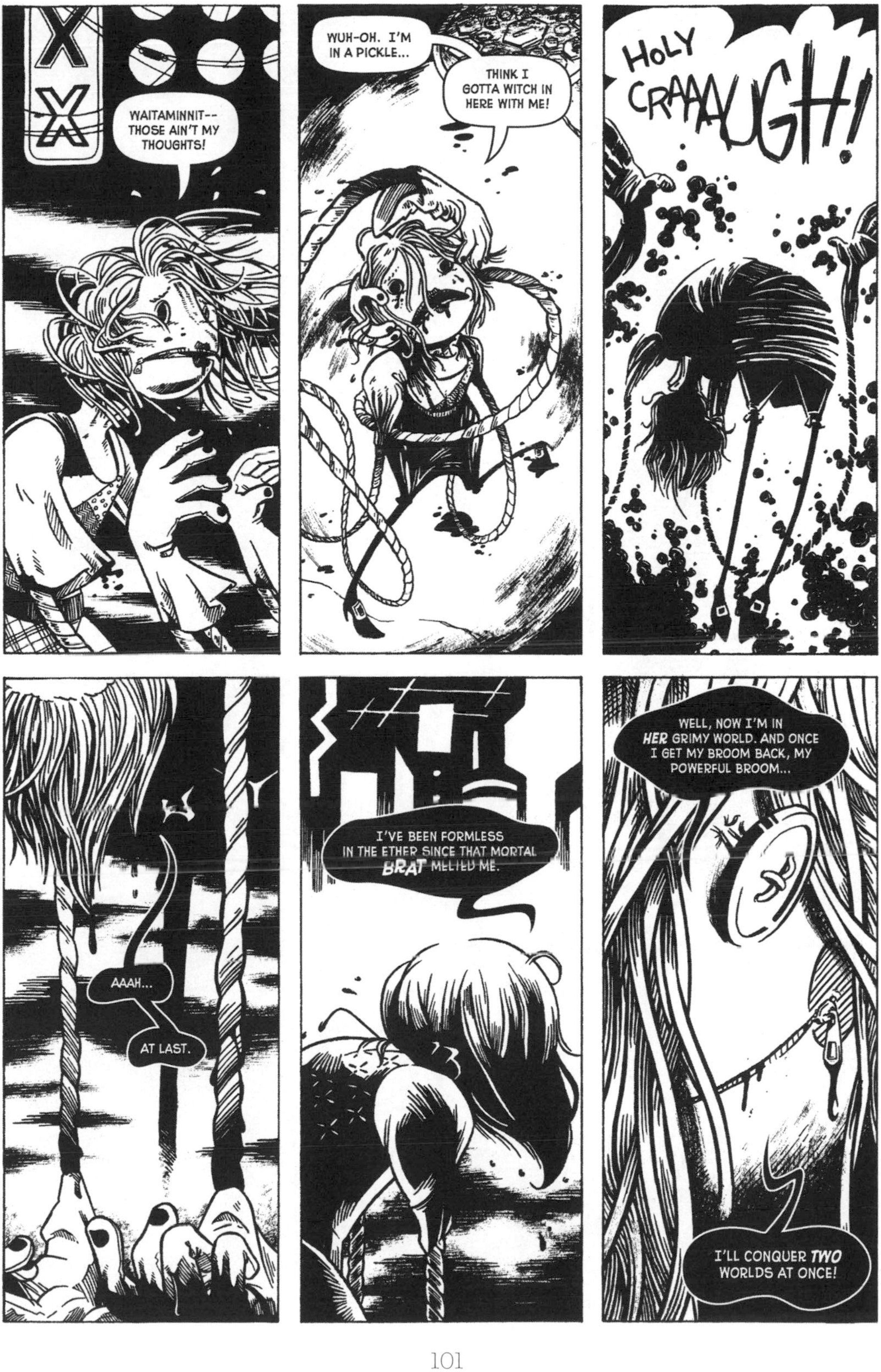
WAITAMINNIT-- THOSE AIN'T MY THOUGHTS!
WUH-OH. I'M IN A PICKLE...
THINK I GOTTA WITCH IN HERE WITH ME!
HOLY CRAAAAUGH!
AAAH...
AT LAST.
I'VE BEEN FORMLESS IN THE ETHER SINCE THAT MORTAL BRAT MELTED ME.
WELL, NOW I'M IN HER GRIMY WORLD. AND ONCE I GET MY BROOM BACK, MY POWERFUL BROOM...
I'LL CONQUER TWO WORLDS AT ONCE!

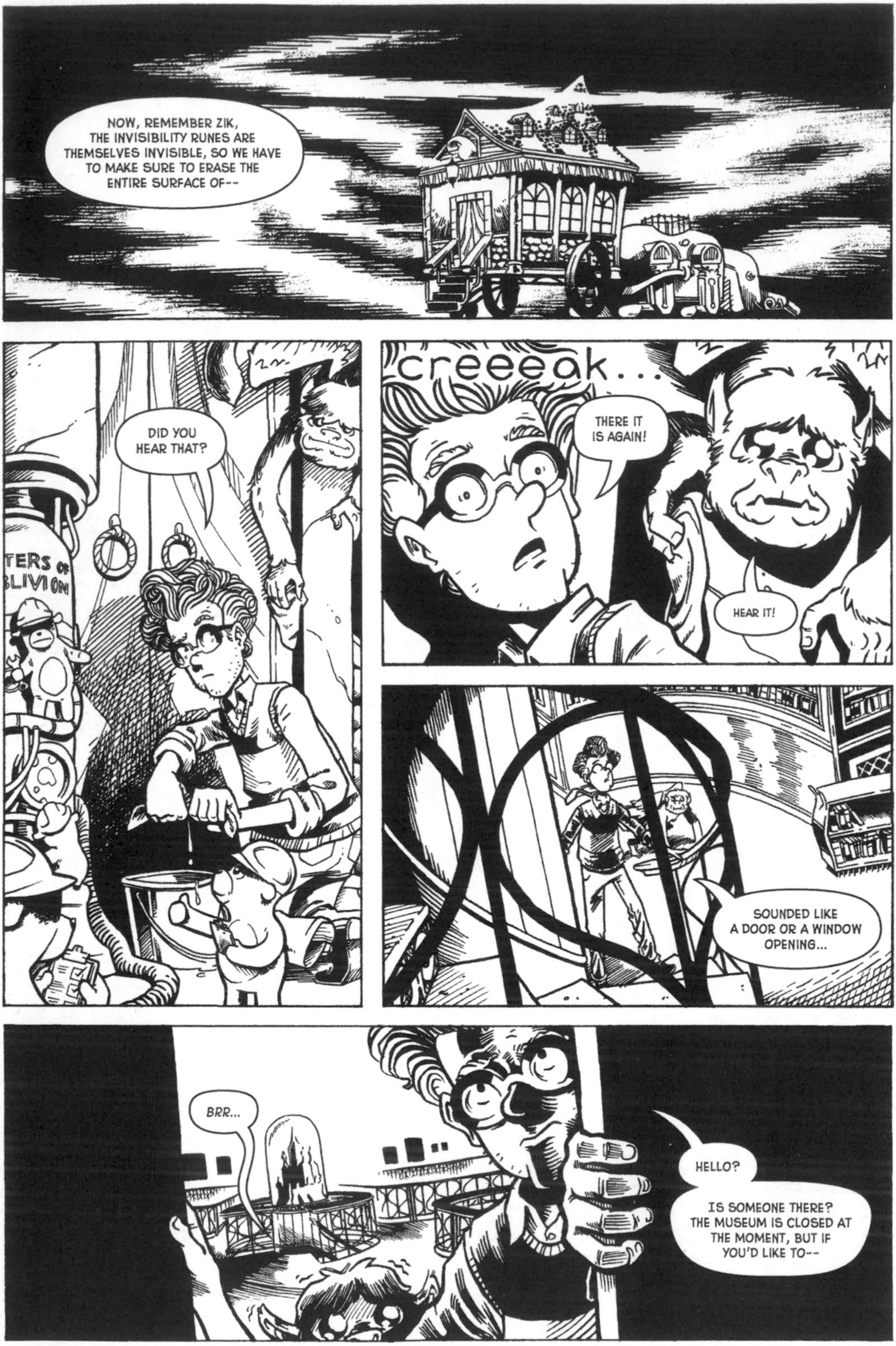
NOW, REMEMBER ZIK, THE INVISIBILITY RUNES ARE THEMSELVES INVISIBLE, SO WE HAVE TO MAKE SURE TO ERASE THE ENTIRE SURFACE OF--
DID YOU HEAR THAT?
creeeak...
THERE IT IS AGAIN!
HEAR IT!
SOUNDED LIKE A DOOR OR A WINDOW OPENING...
BRR...
HELLO?
IS SOMEONE THERE? THE MUSEUM IS CLOSED AT THE MOMENT, BUT IF YOU'D LIKE TO--

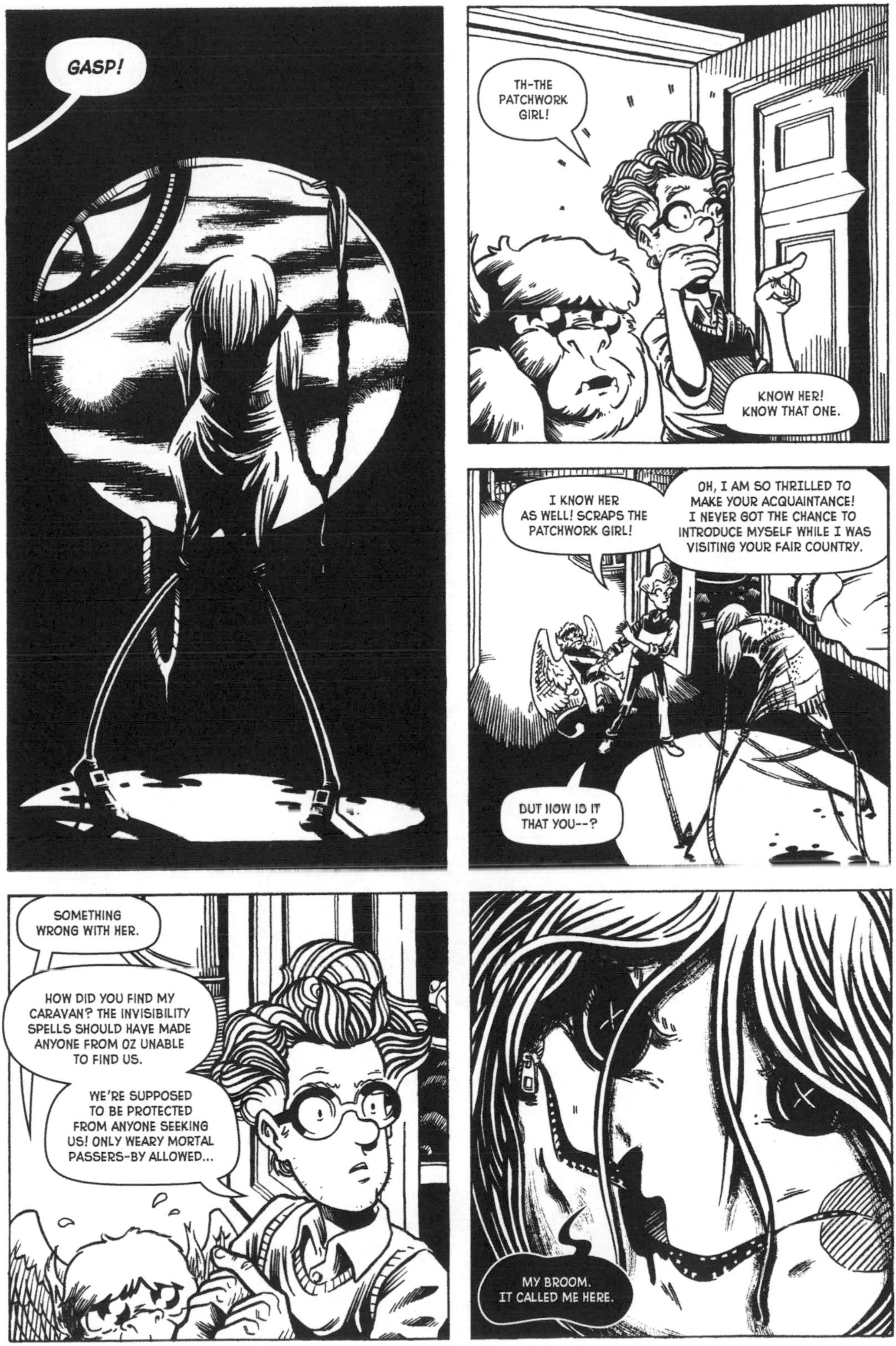
GASP!
TH-THE PATCHWORK GIRL!
KNOW HER! KNOW THAT ONE.
I KNOW HER AS WELL! SCRAPS THE PATCHWORK GIRL!
OH, I AM SO THRILLED TO MAKE YOUR ACQUAINTANCE! I NEVER GOT THE CHANCE TO INTRODUCE MYSELF WHILE I WAS VISITING YOUR FAIR COUNTRY.
BUT HOW IS IT THAT YOU--?
SOMETHING WRONG WITH HER.
HOW DID YOU FIND MY CARAVAN? THE INVISIBILITY SPELLS SHOULD HAVE MADE ANYONE FROM OZ UNABLE TO FIND US.
WE'RE SUPPOSED TO BE PROTECTED FROM ANYONE SEEKING US! ONLY WEARY MORTAL PASSERS-BY ALLOWED...
MY BROOM. IT CALLED ME HERE.

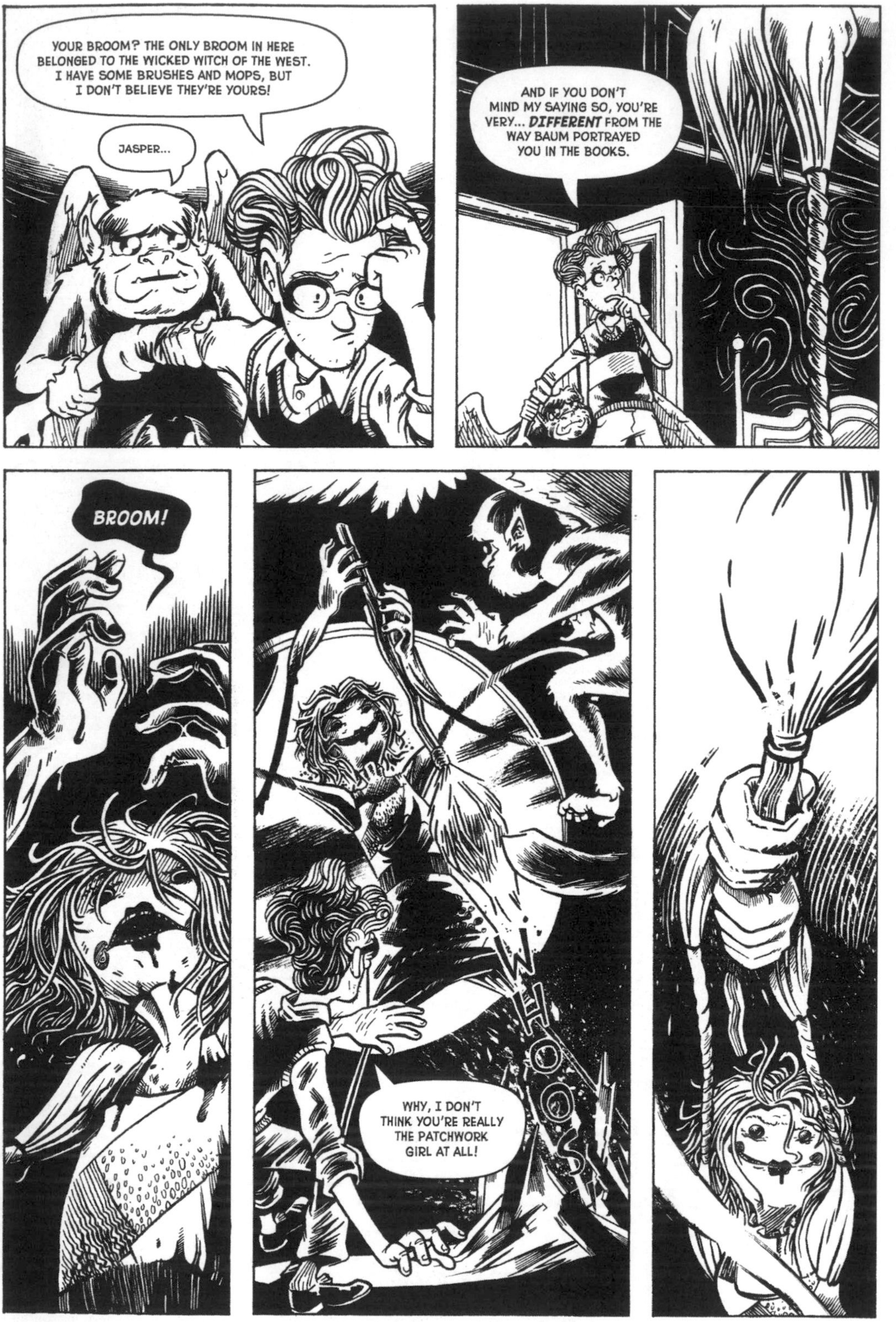
YOUR BROOM? THE ONLY BROOM IN HERE BELONGED TO THE WICKED WITCH OF THE WEST. I HAVE SOME BRUSHES AND MOPS, BUT I DON'T BELIEVE THEY'RE YOURS!
JASPER...
AND IF YOU DON'T MIND MY SAYING SO, YOU'RE VERY... ***DIFFERENT*** FROM THE WAY BAUM PORTRAYED YOU IN THE BOOKS.
BROOM!
WHOOSH
WHY, I DON'T THINK YOU'RE REALLY THE PATCHWORK GIRL AT ALL!

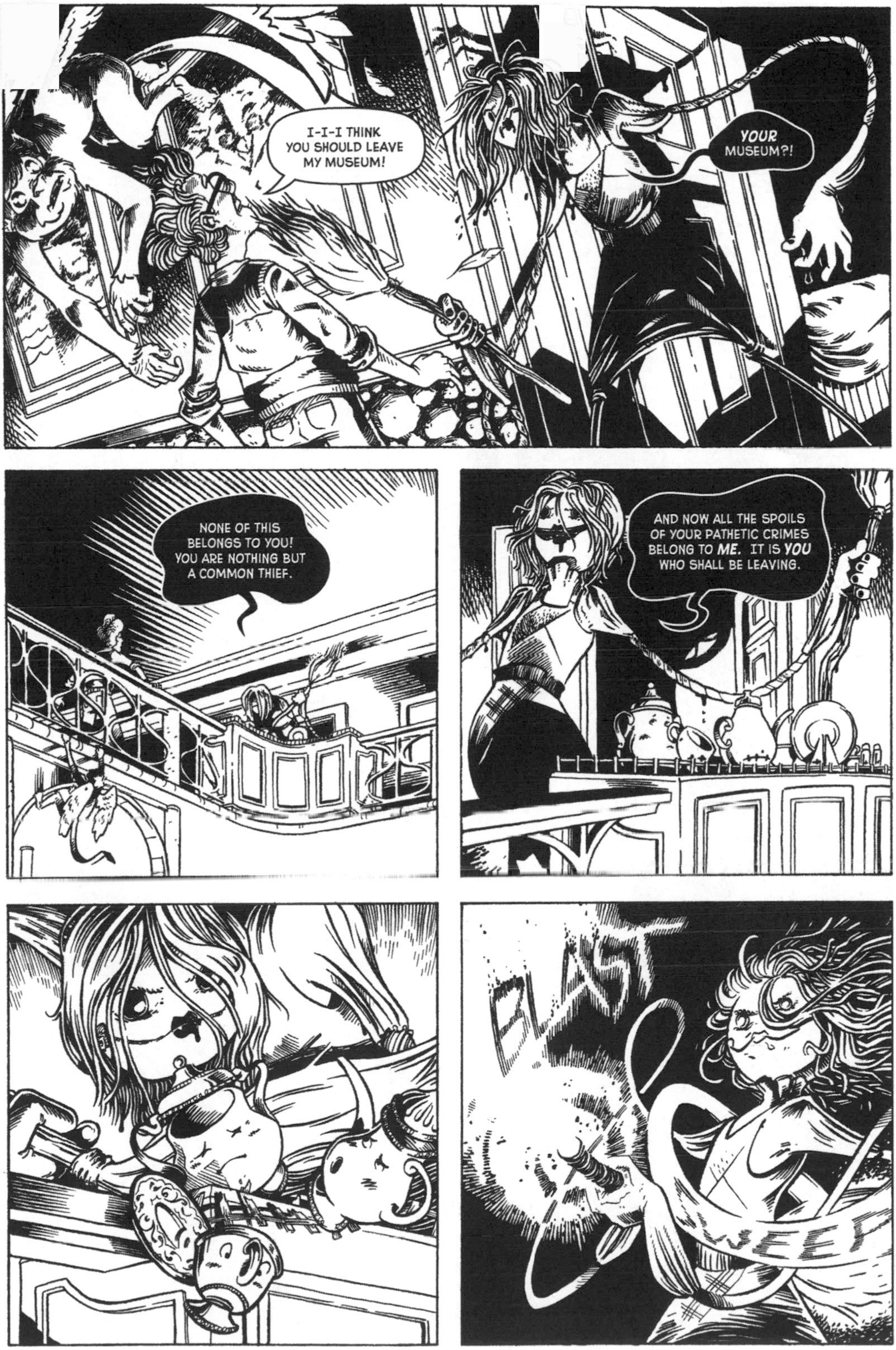
I-I-I THINK YOU SHOULD LEAVE MY MUSEUM!
YOUR MUSEUM?!
NONE OF THIS BELONGS TO YOU! YOU ARE NOTHING BUT A COMMON THIEF.
AND NOW ALL THE SPOILS OF YOUR PATHETIC CRIMES BELONG TO ME. IT IS YOU WHO SHALL BE LEAVING.
BLAST

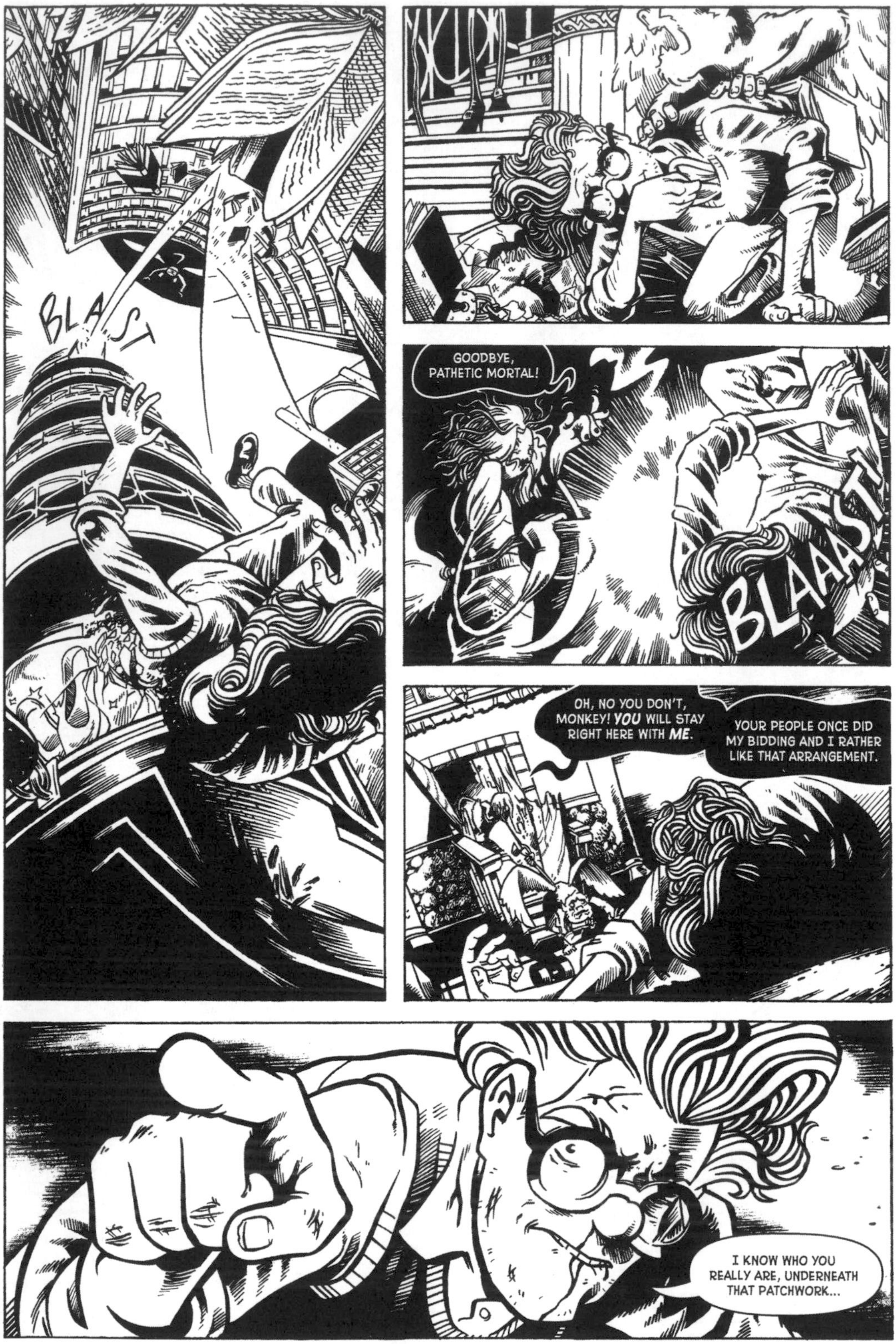
BLAST
GOODBYE, PATHETIC MORTAL!
BLAAAST
OH, NO YOU DON'T, MONKEY! *YOU* WILL STAY RIGHT HERE WITH *ME*.
YOUR PEOPLE ONCE DID MY BIDDING AND I RATHER LIKE THAT ARRANGEMENT.
I KNOW WHO YOU REALLY ARE, UNDERNEATH THAT PATCHWORK...

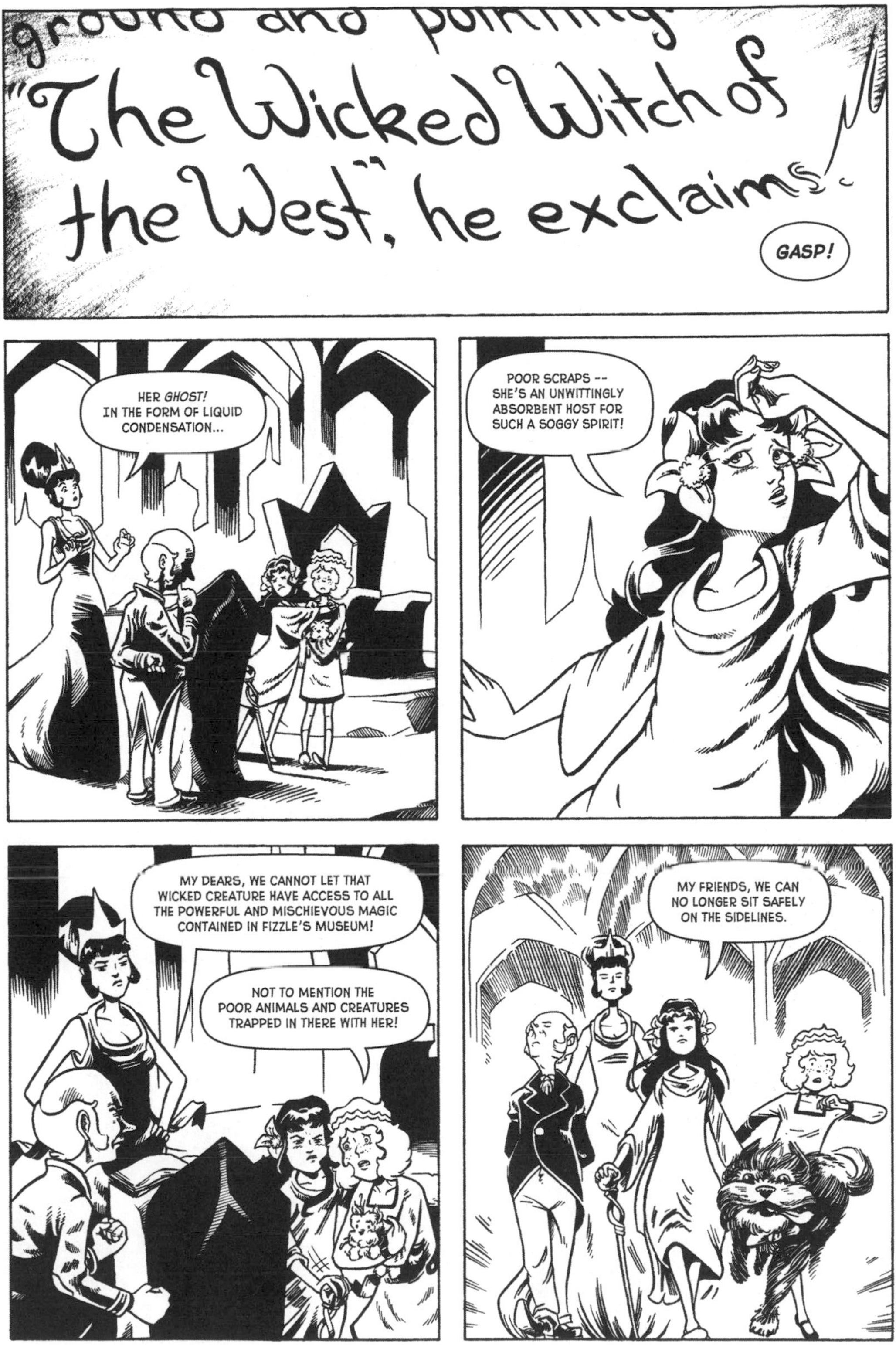
ground and pointing:
"The Wicked Witch of the West", he exclaims!
GASP!
HER GHOST! IN THE FORM OF LIQUID CONDENSATION...
POOR SCRAPS -- SHE'S AN UNWITTINGLY ABSORBENT HOST FOR SUCH A SOGGY SPIRIT!
MY DEARS, WE CANNOT LET THAT WICKED CREATURE HAVE ACCESS TO ALL THE POWERFUL AND MISCHIEVOUS MAGIC CONTAINED IN FIZZLE'S MUSEUM!
NOT TO MENTION THE POOR ANIMALS AND CREATURES TRAPPED IN THERE WITH HER!
MY FRIENDS, WE CAN NO LONGER SIT SAFELY ON THE SIDELINES.

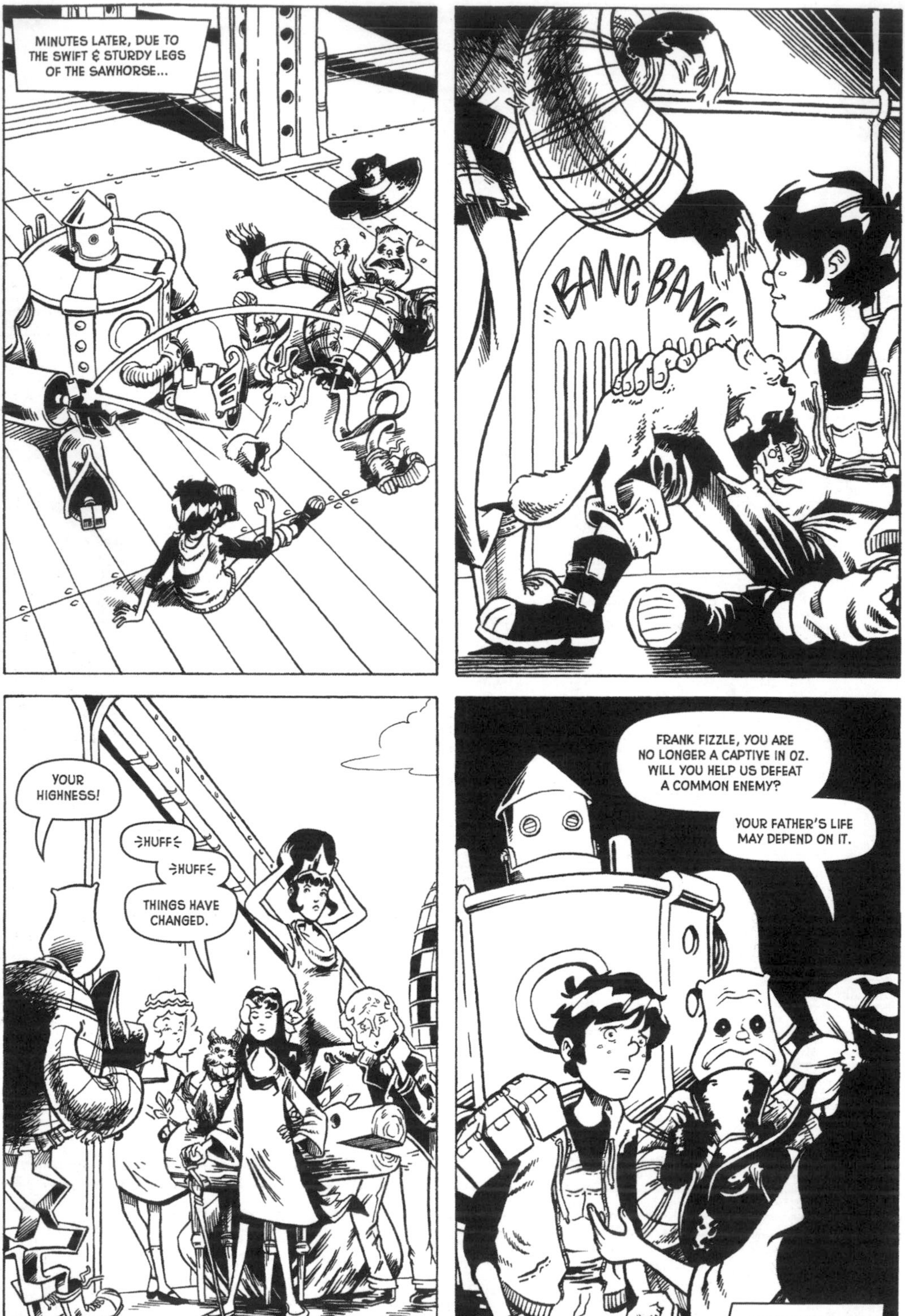
MINUTES LATER, DUE TO THE SWIFT & STURDY LEGS OF THE SAWHORSE...
BANG BANG
YOUR HIGHNESS!
HUFF
HUFF
THINGS HAVE CHANGED.
FRANK FIZZLE, YOU ARE NO LONGER A CAPTIVE IN OZ. WILL YOU HELP US DEFEAT A COMMON ENEMY?
YOUR FATHER'S LIFE MAY DEPEND ON IT.
TO BE CONCLUDED...

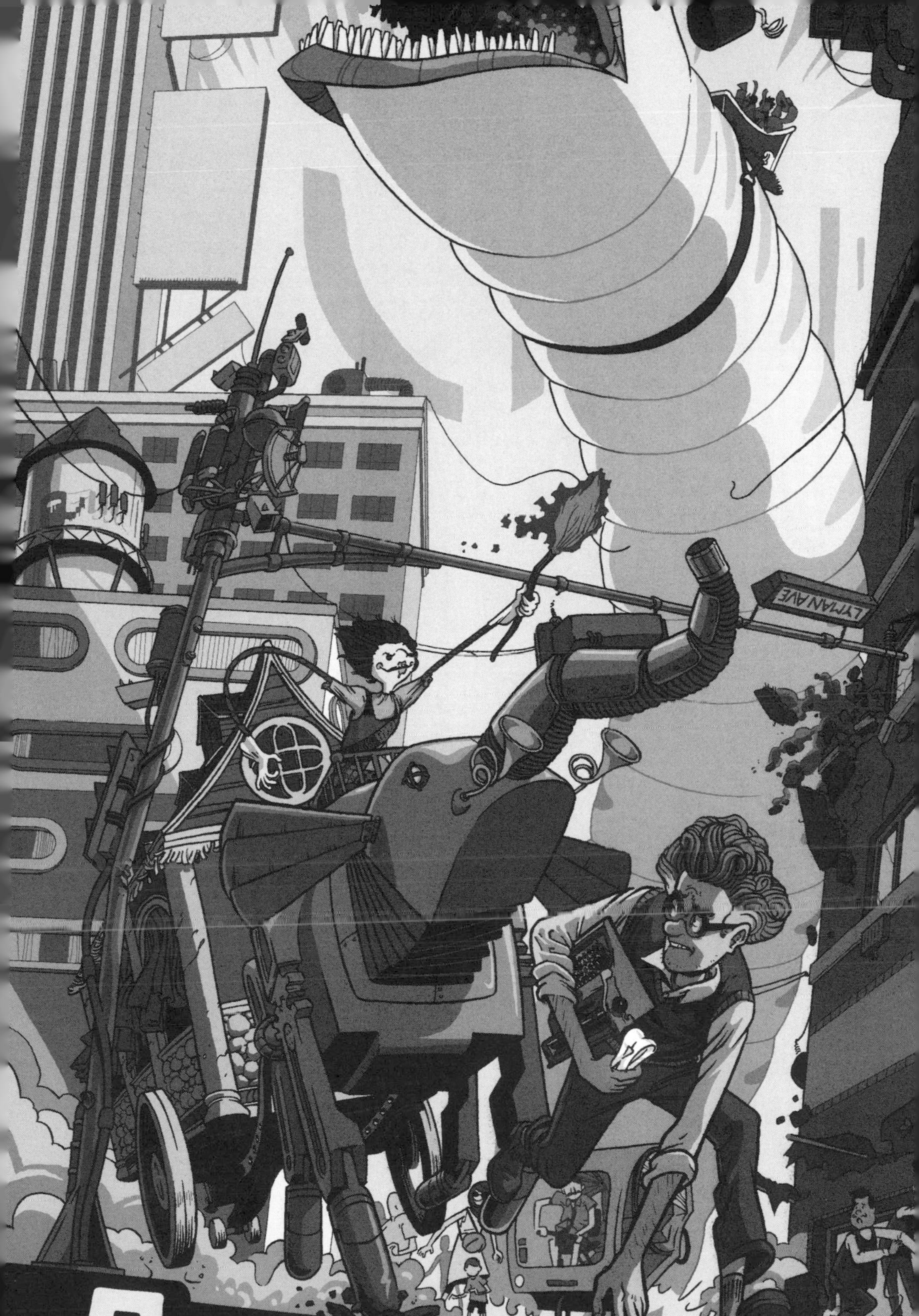
LYMAN AVE

5 “Through the Wringer”

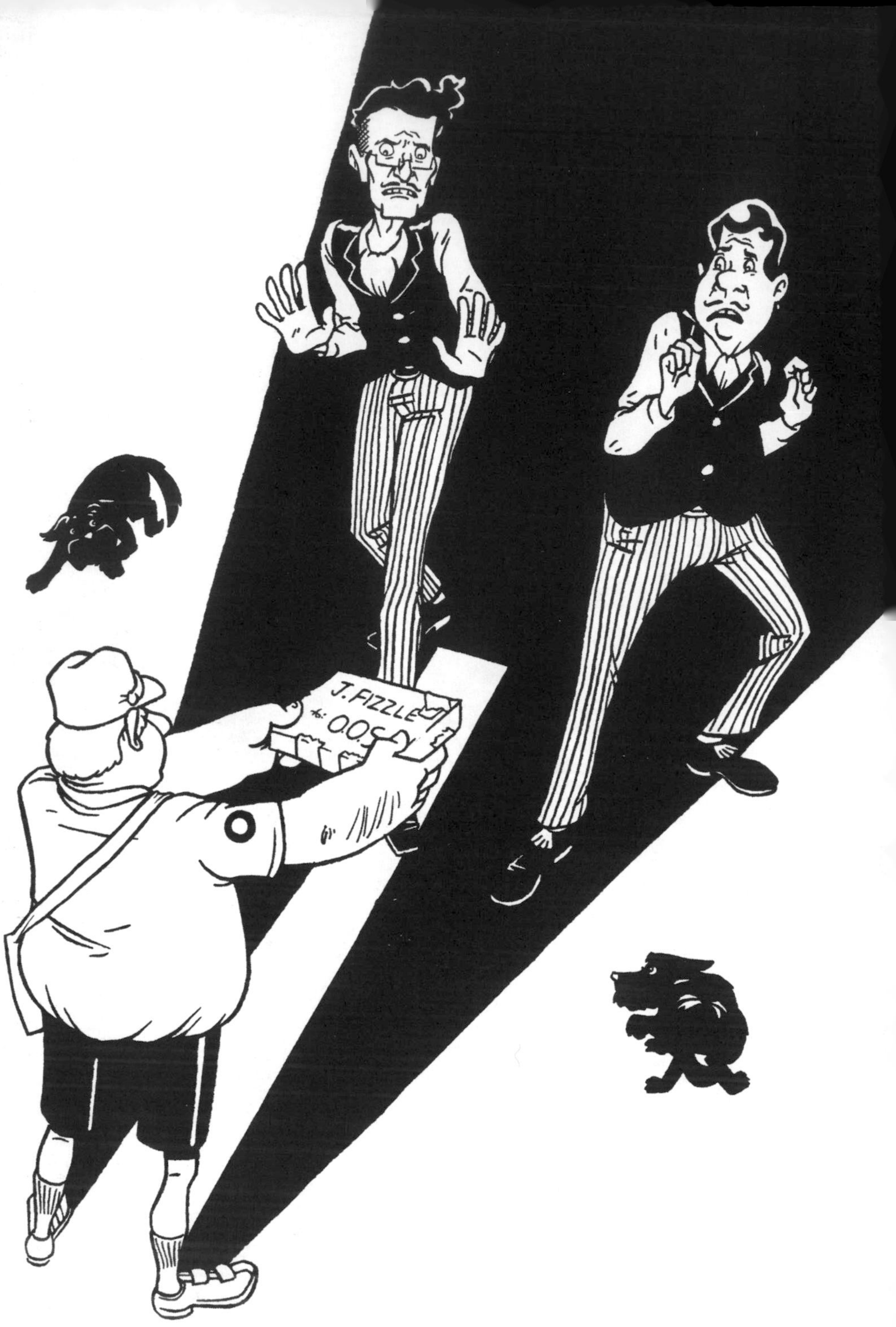
J. FIZZLE

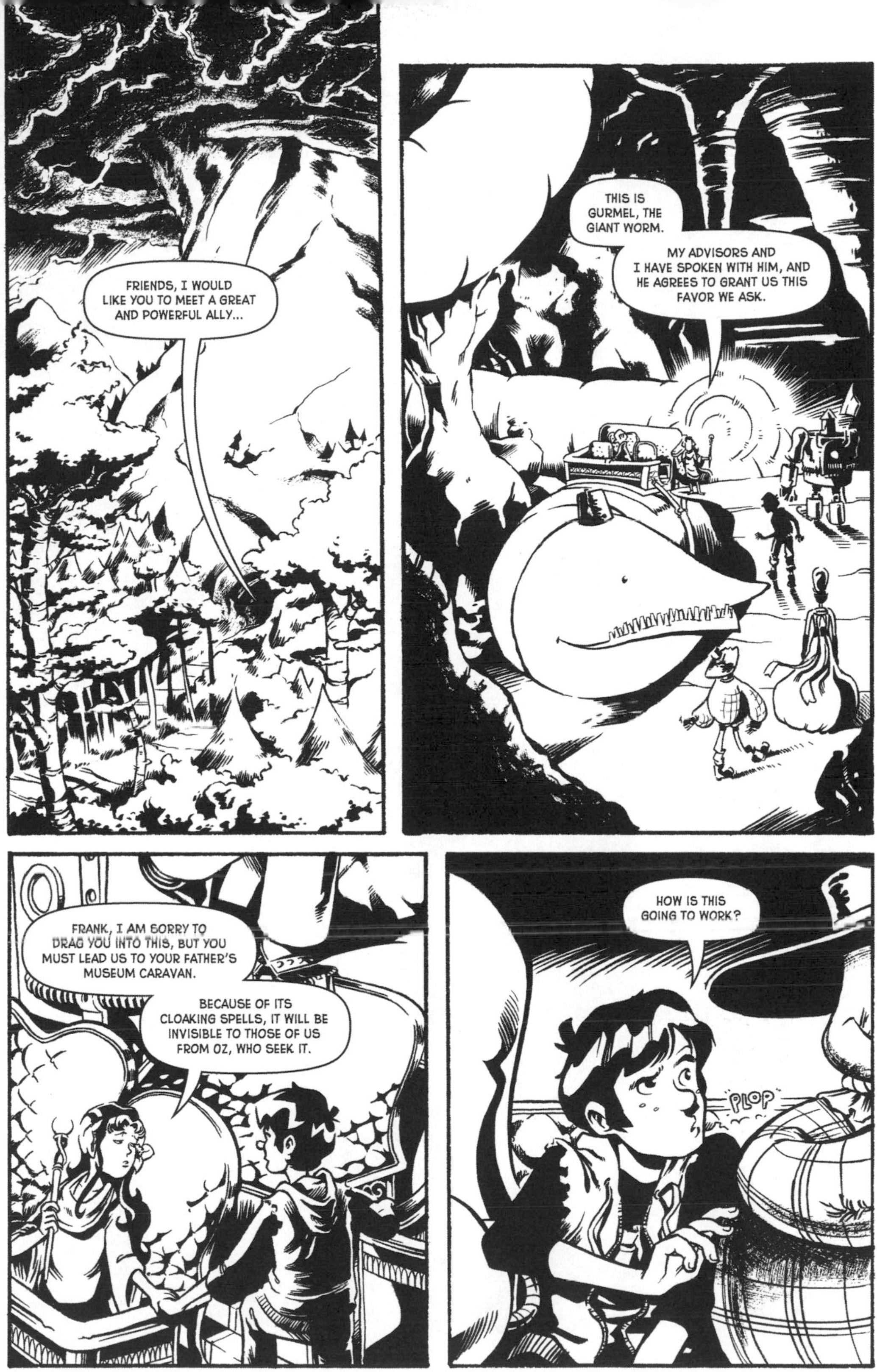

FRIENDS, I WOULD LIKE YOU TO MEET A GREAT AND POWERFUL ALLY...
THIS IS GURMEL, THE GIANT WORM.
MY ADVISORS AND I HAVE SPOKEN WITH HIM, AND HE AGREES TO GRANT US THIS FAVOR WE ASK.
FRANK, I AM SORRY TO DRAG YOU INTO THIS, BUT YOU MUST LEAD US TO YOUR FATHER'S MUSEUM CARAVAN.
BECAUSE OF ITS CLOAKING SPELLS, IT WILL BE INVISIBLE TO THOSE OF US FROM OZ, WHO SEEK IT.
HOW IS THIS GOING TO WORK?
PLOP

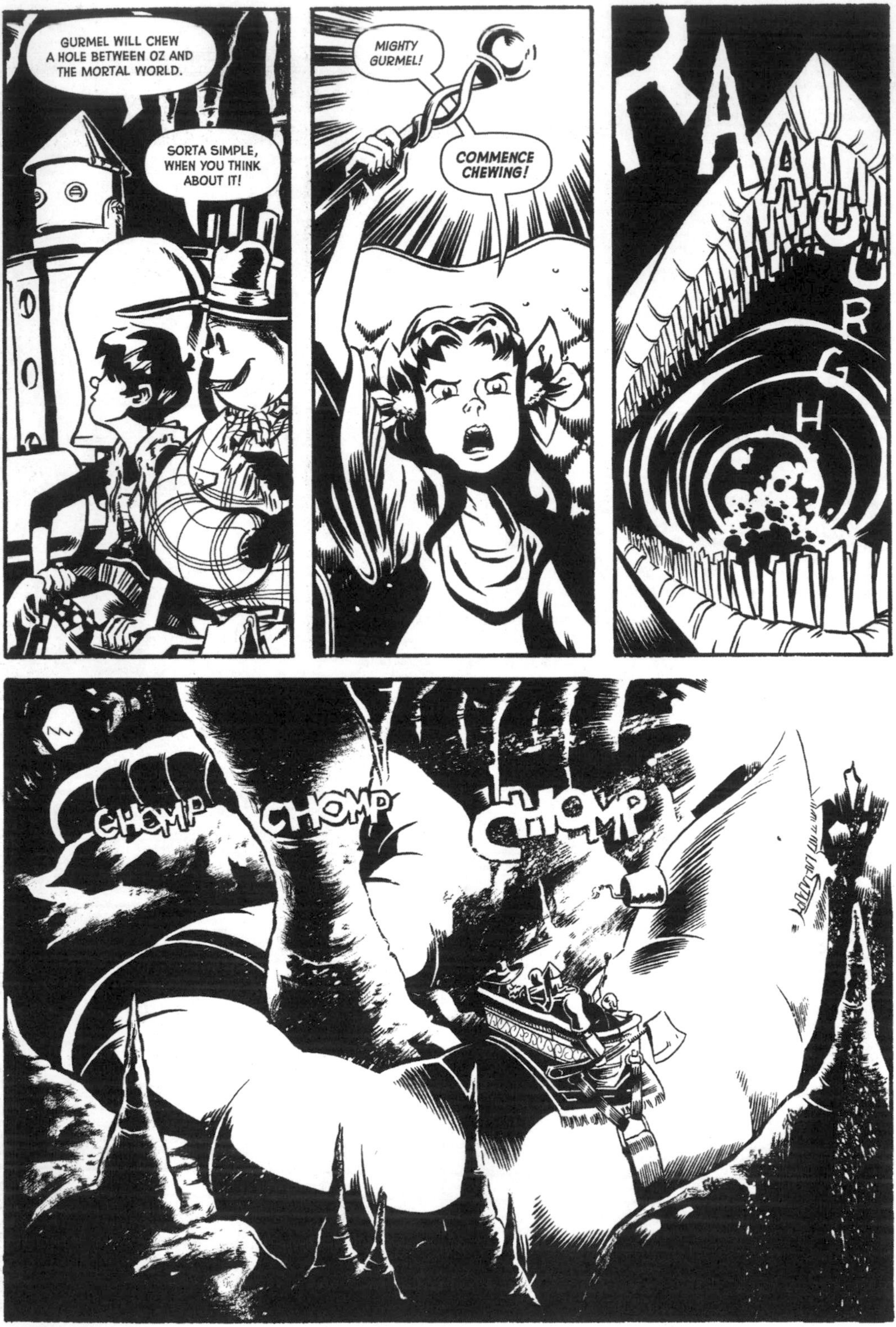
GURMEL WILL CHEW A HOLE BETWEEN OZ AND THE MORTAL WORLD.
SORTA SIMPLE, WHEN YOU THINK ABOUT IT!
MIGHTY GURMEL!
COMMENCE CHEWING!
RAAAURGH
CHOMP
CHOMP
CHOMP

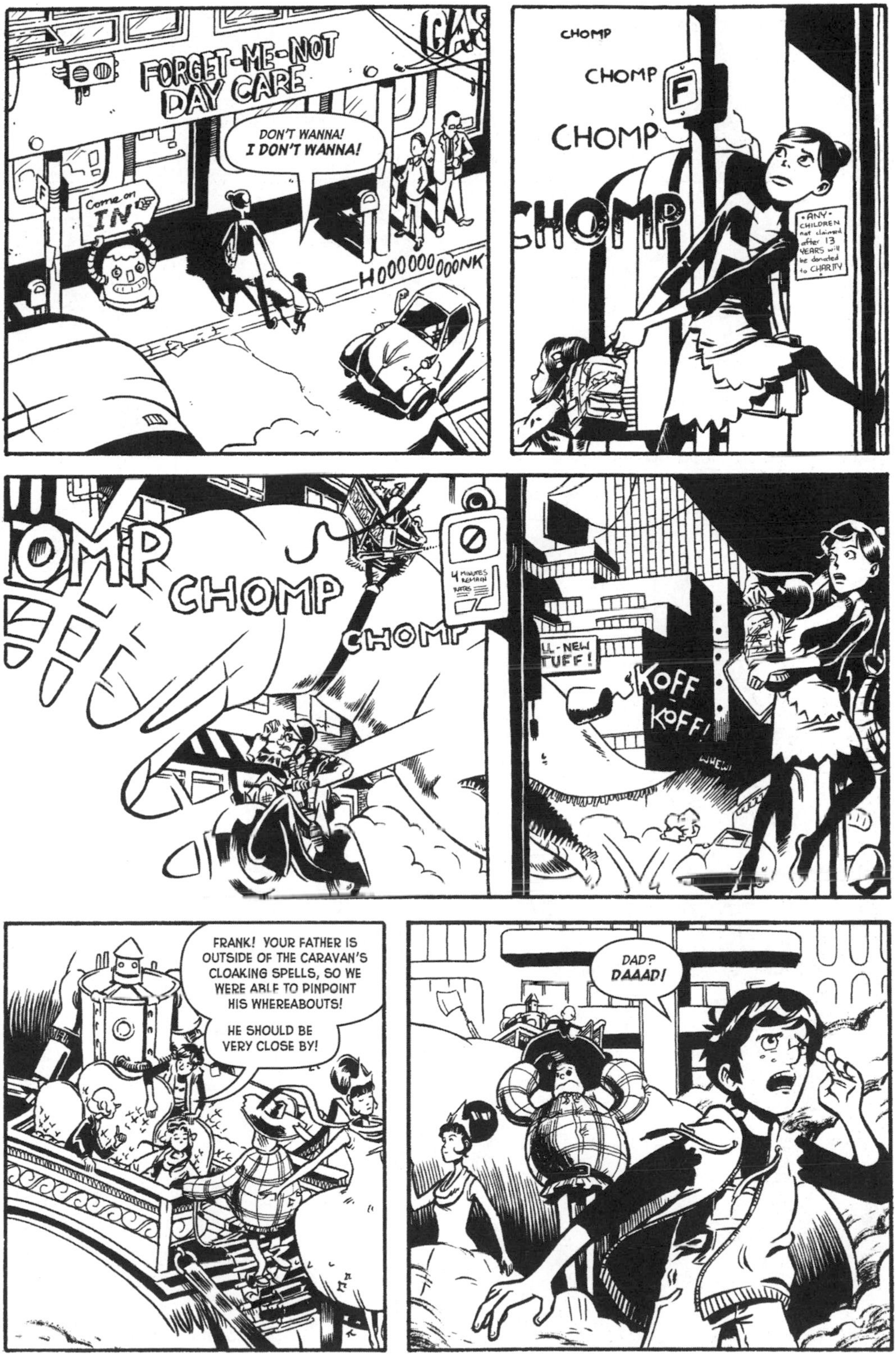

FORGET-ME-NOT DAY CARE
Come on IN
DON'T WANNA! I DON'T WANNA!
HOOOOOOOOOONK
CHOMP
CHOMP
CHOMP
CHOMP
ANY CHILDREN not claimed after 13 YEARS will be donated to CHARITY
OMP
CHOMP
CHOMP
4 MINUTES REMAIN
LL-NEW TUFF!
KOFF KOFF!
WHEW!
FRANK! YOUR FATHER IS OUTSIDE OF THE CARAVAN'S CLOAKING SPELLS, SO WE WERE ABLE TO PINPOINT HIS WHEREABOUTS!
HE SHOULD BE VERY CLOSE BY!
DAD? DAAAD!

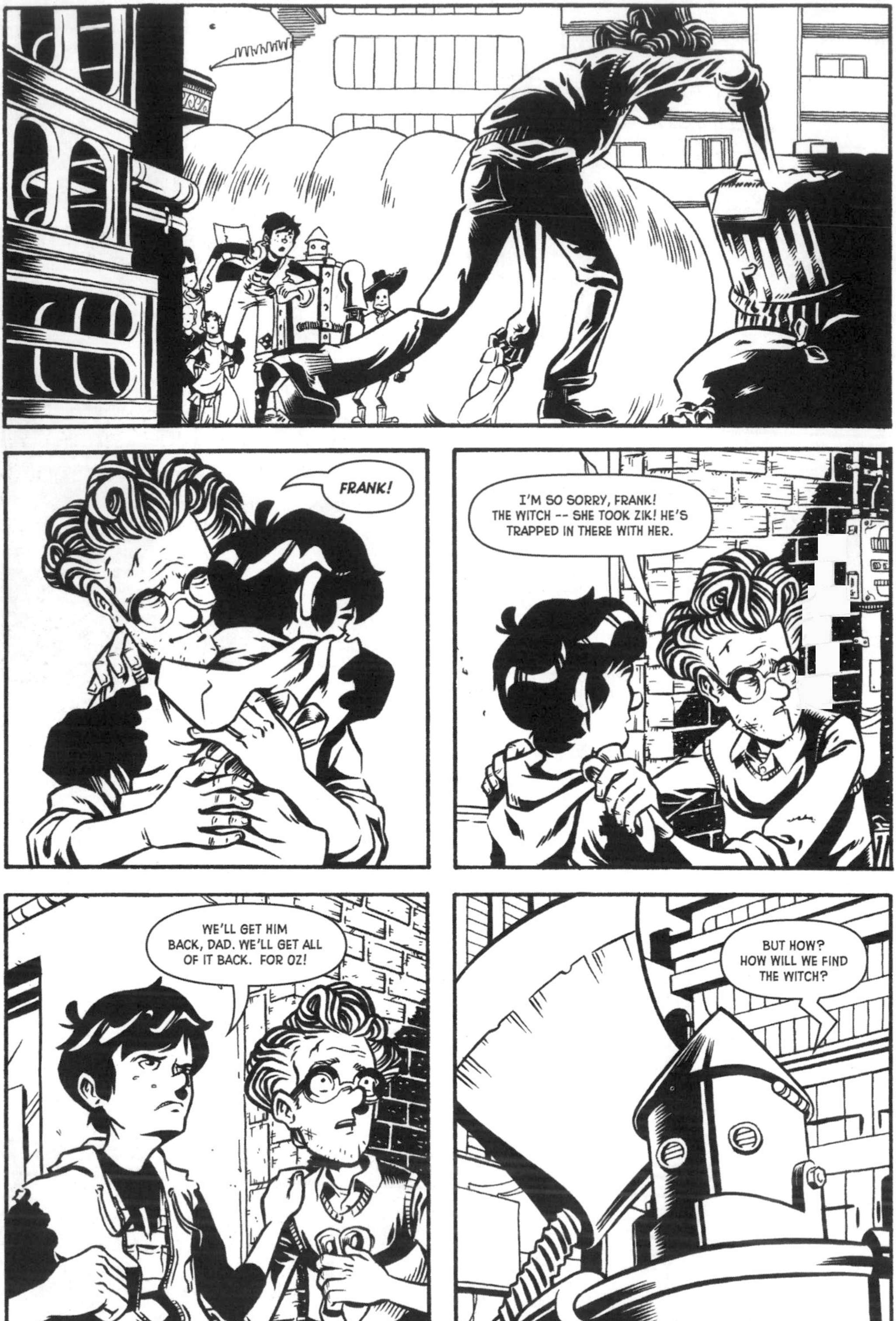
FRANK!
I'M SO SORRY, FRANK! THE WITCH -- SHE TOOK ZIK! HE'S TRAPPED IN THERE WITH HER.
WE'LL GET HIM BACK, DAD. WE'LL GET ALL OF IT BACK. FOR OZ!
BUT HOW? HOW WILL WE FIND THE WITCH?

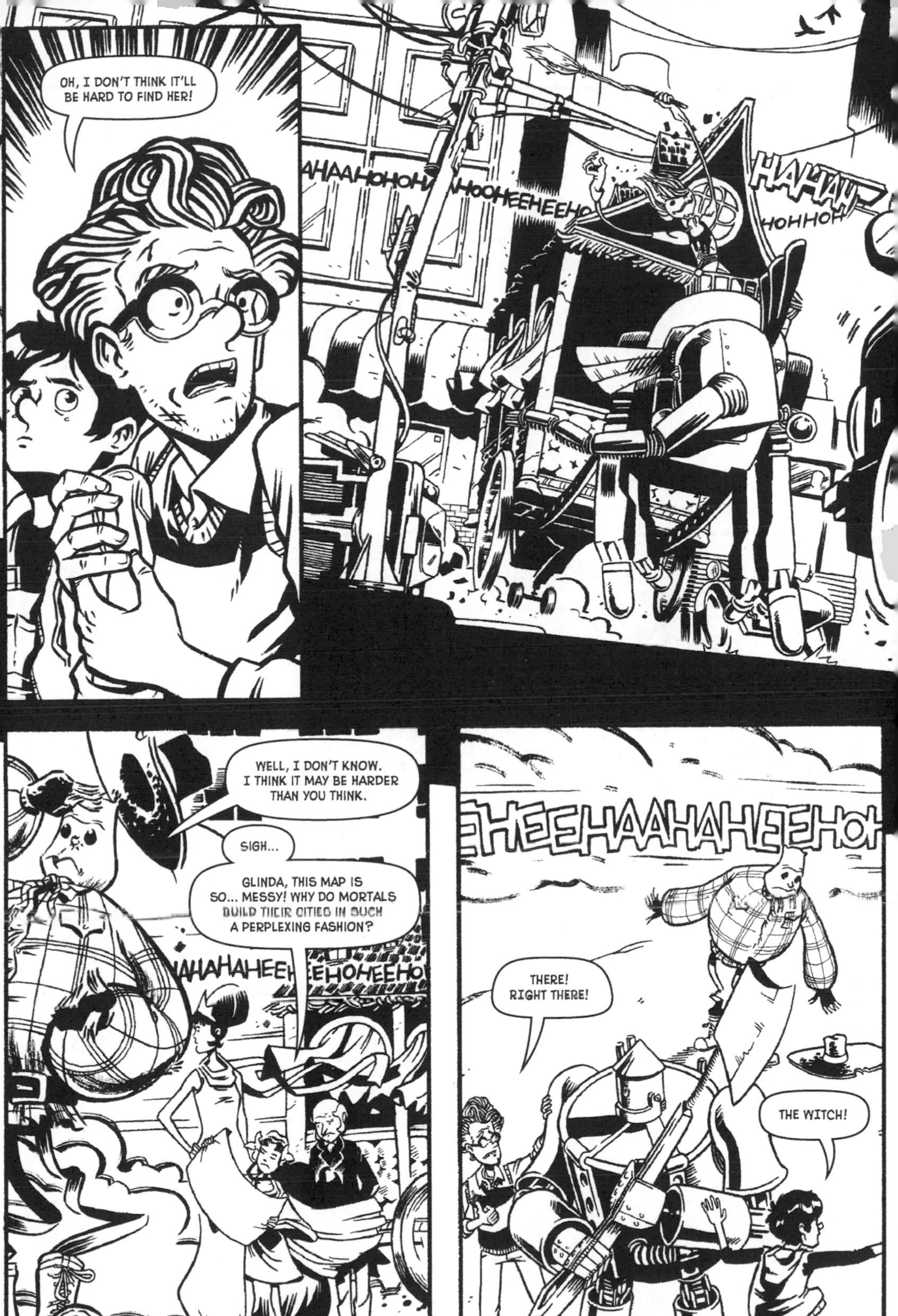
OH, I DON'T THINK IT'LL BE HARD TO FIND HER!
AHAAHOHOHAHOOHEEHEEHO
HAHAH
HOHHOH
WELL, I DON'T KNOW. I THINK IT MAY BE HARDER THAN YOU THINK.
SIGH...
GLINDA, THIS MAP IS SO... MESSY! WHY DO MORTALS BUILD THEIR CITIES IN SUCH A PERPLEXING FASHION?
AHAHAHEEHEEHOHEEHO
EHEEHAAHAHEEHOH
THERE! RIGHT THERE!
THE WITCH!

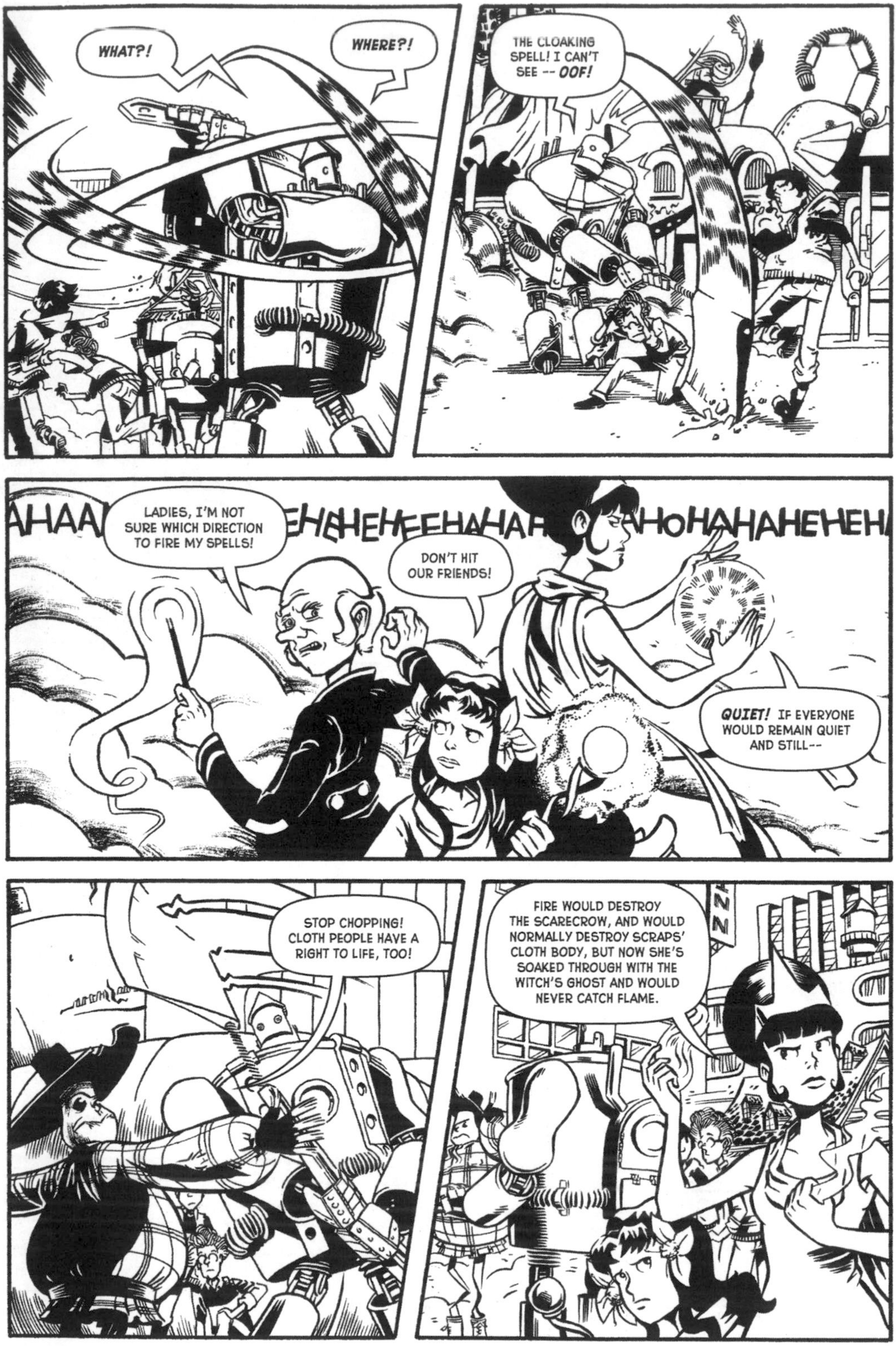
WHAT?!
WHERE?!
THE CLOAKING SPELL! I CAN'T SEE -- OOF!
LADIES, I'M NOT SURE WHICH DIRECTION TO FIRE MY SPELLS!
DON'T HIT OUR FRIENDS!
QUIET! IF EVERYONE WOULD REMAIN QUIET AND STILL--
STOP CHOPPING! CLOTH PEOPLE HAVE A RIGHT TO LIFE, TOO!
FIRE WOULD DESTROY THE SCARECROW, AND WOULD NORMALLY DESTROY SCRAPS' CLOTH BODY, BUT NOW SHE'S SOAKED THROUGH WITH THE WITCH'S GHOST AND WOULD NEVER CATCH FLAME.

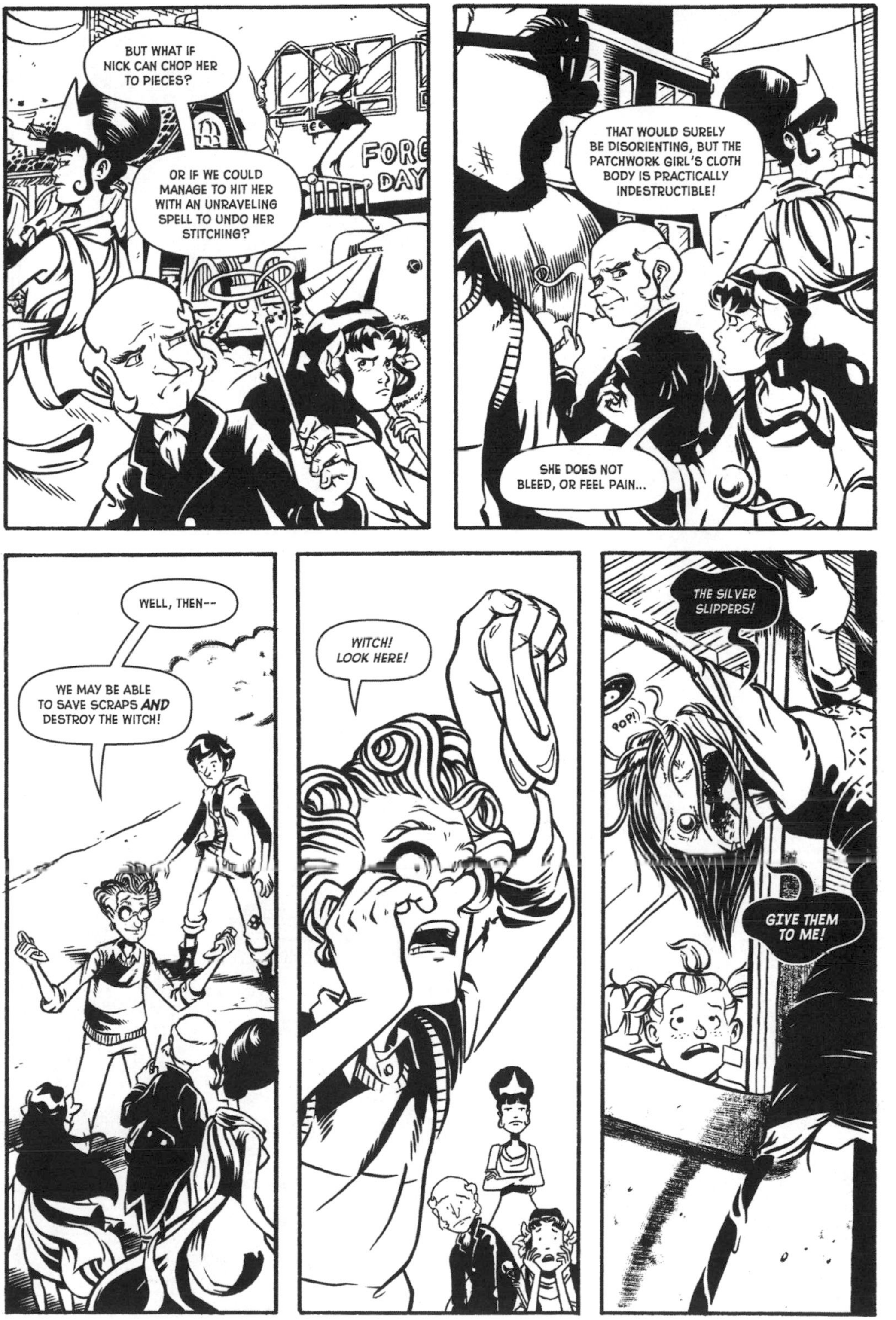
BUT WHAT IF NICK CAN CHOP HER TO PIECES?
OR IF WE COULD MANAGE TO HIT HER WITH AN UNRAVELING SPELL TO UNDO HER STITCHING?
THAT WOULD SURELY BE DISORIENTING, BUT THE PATCHWORK GIRL'S CLOTH BODY IS PRACTICALLY INDESTRUCTIBLE!
SHE DOES NOT BLEED, OR FEEL PAIN...
WELL, THEN--
WE MAY BE ABLE TO SAVE SCRAPS **AND** DESTROY THE WITCH!
WITCH! LOOK HERE!
THE SILVER SLIPPERS!
POP!
GIVE THEM TO ME!

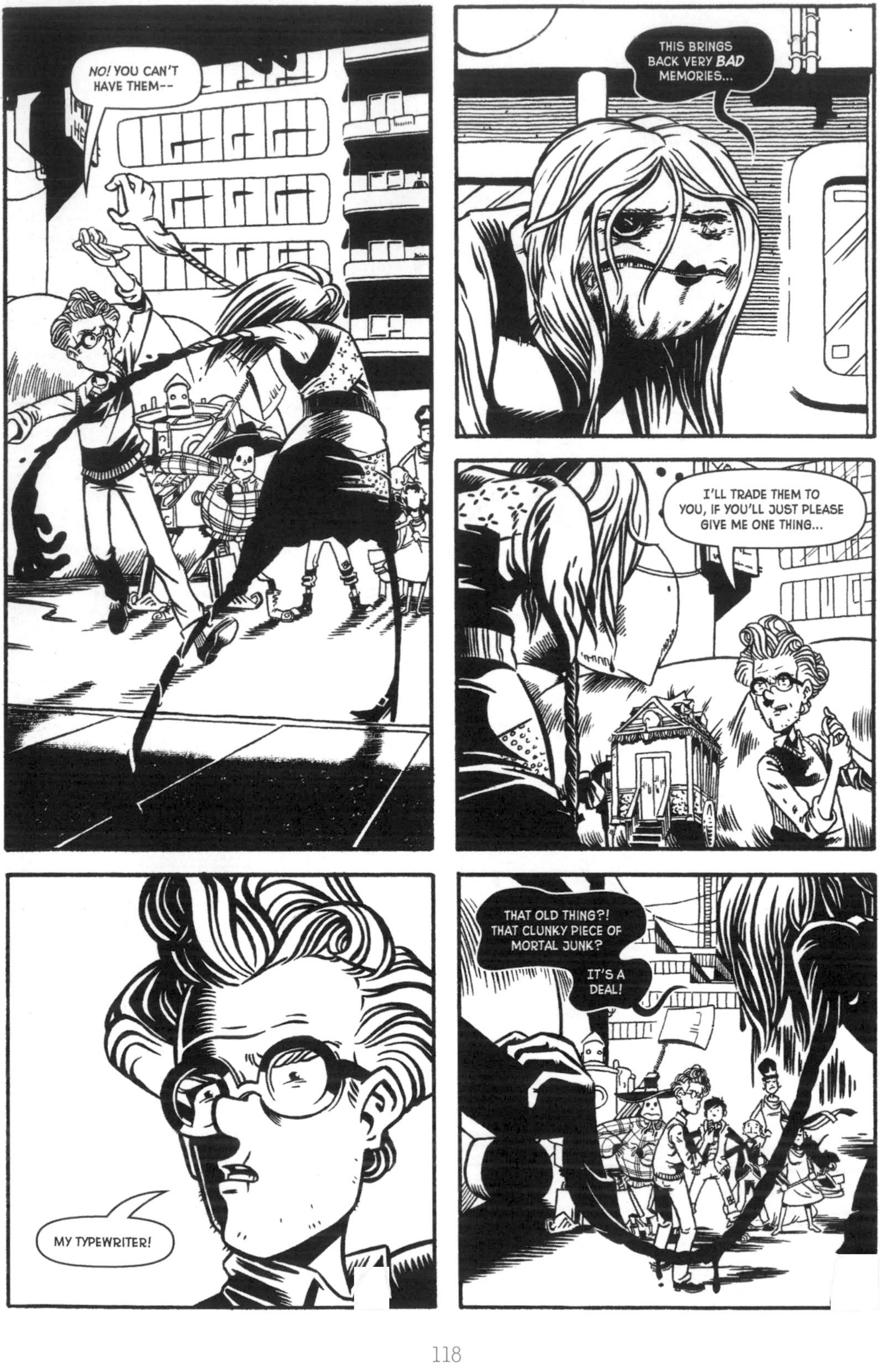

NO! YOU CAN'T HAVE THEM--
THIS BRINGS BACK VERY ***BAD*** MEMORIES...
I'LL TRADE THEM TO YOU, IF YOU'LL JUST PLEASE GIVE ME ONE THING...
MY TYPEWRITER!
THAT OLD THING?! THAT CLUNKY PIECE OF MORTAL JUNK?
IT'S A DEAL!

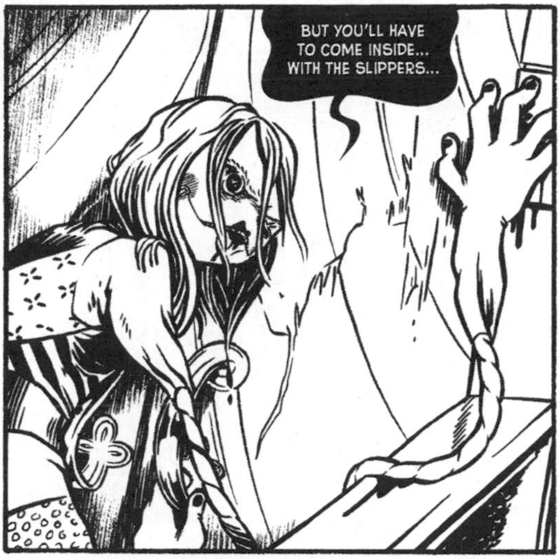
BUT YOU'LL HAVE TO COME INSIDE... WITH THE SLIPPERS...
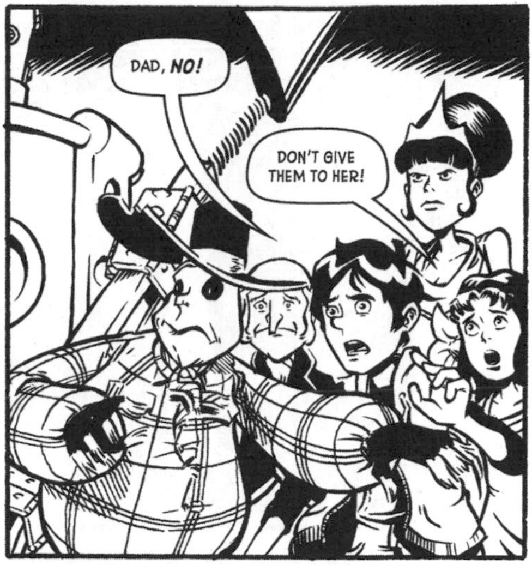
DAD, NO!
DON'T GIVE THEM TO HER!
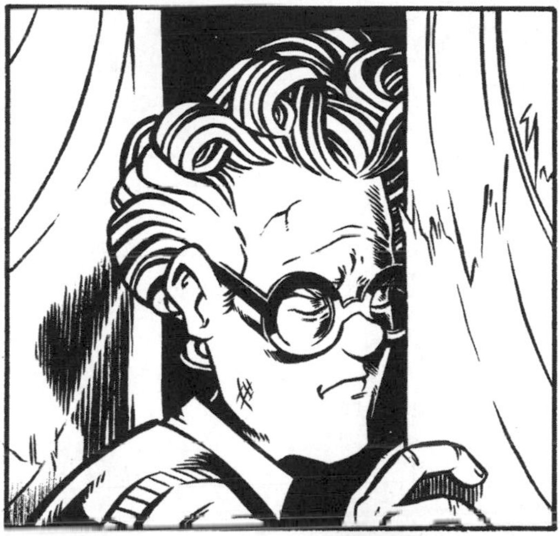
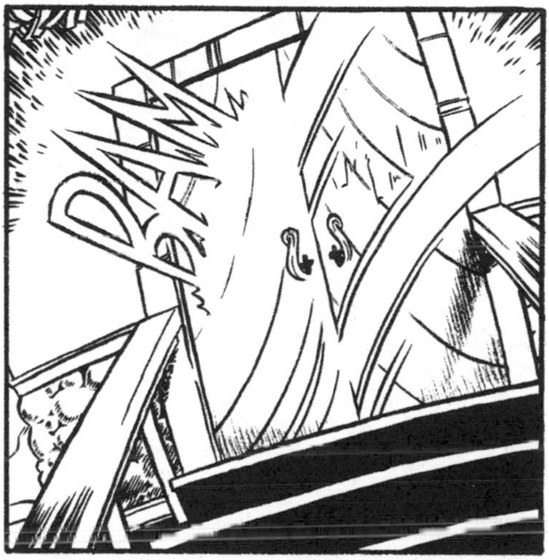
BLAM!
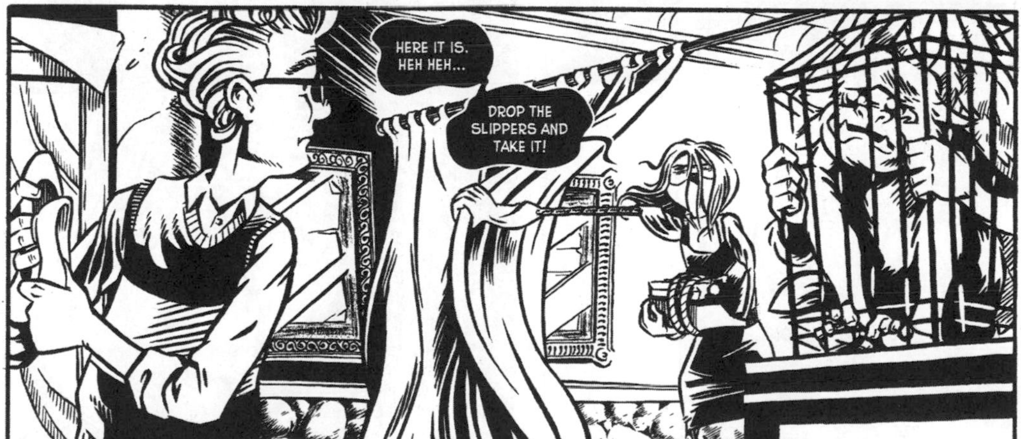
HERE IT IS. HEH HEH...
DROP THE SLIPPERS AND TAKE IT!

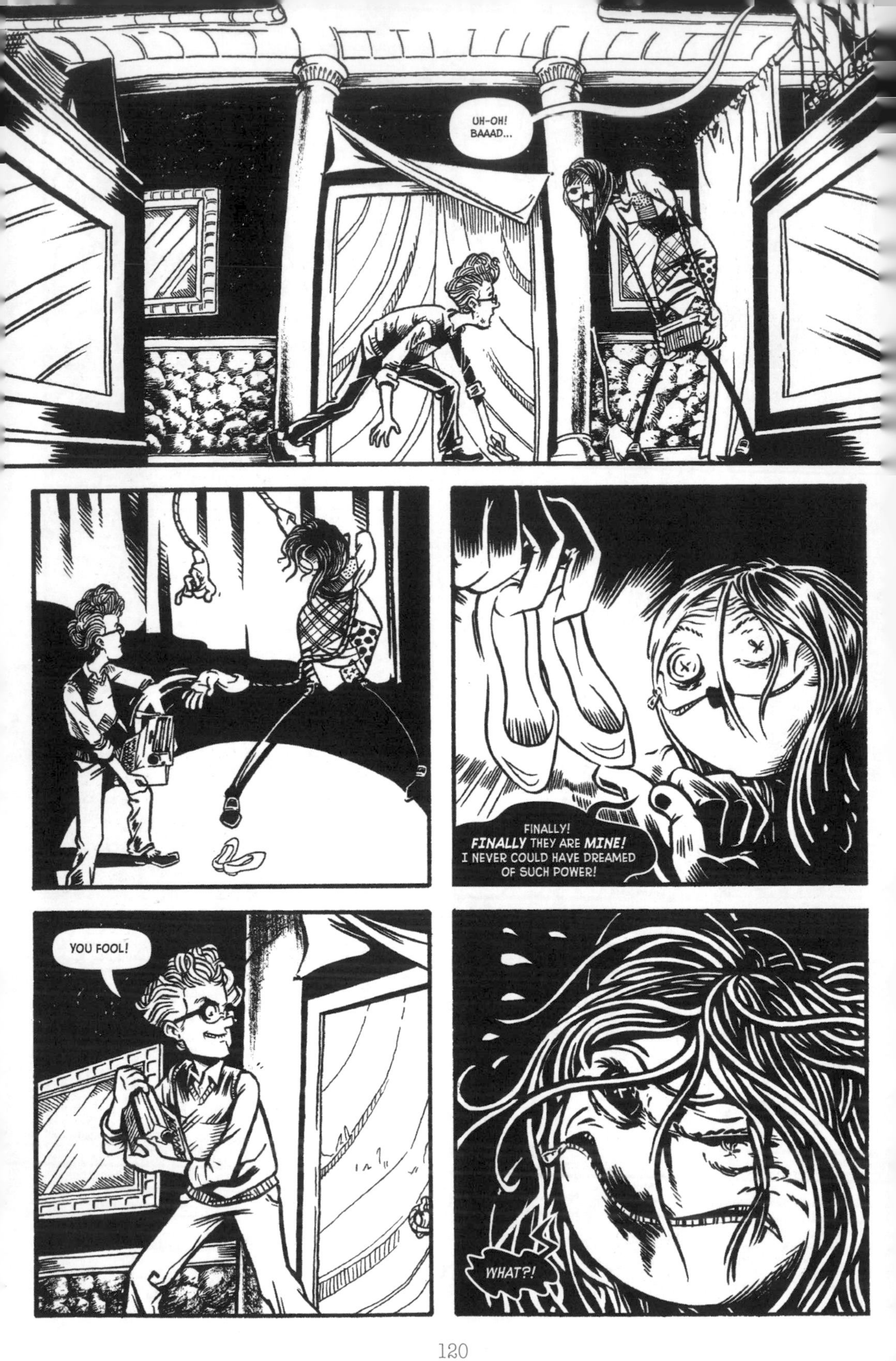
UH-OH! BAAAD...
FINALLY! FINALLY THEY ARE MINE! I NEVER COULD HAVE DREAMED OF SUCH POWER!
YOU FOOL!
WHAT?!

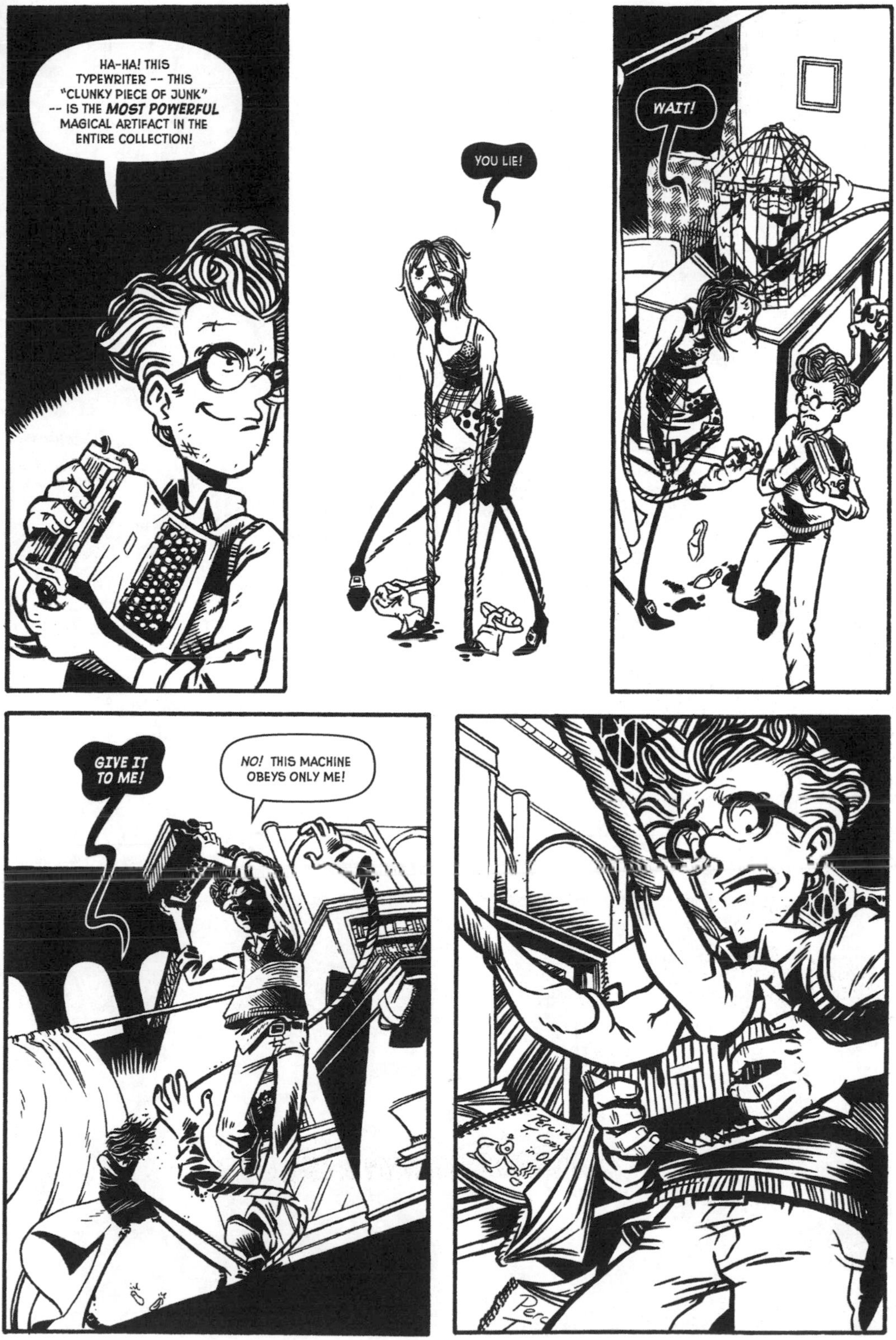
HA-HA! THIS TYPEWRITER -- THIS "CLUNKY PIECE OF JUNK" -- IS THE ***MOST POWERFUL*** MAGICAL ARTIFACT IN THE ENTIRE COLLECTION!
YOU LIE!
WAIT!
GIVE IT TO ME!
NO! THIS MACHINE OBEYS ONLY ME!

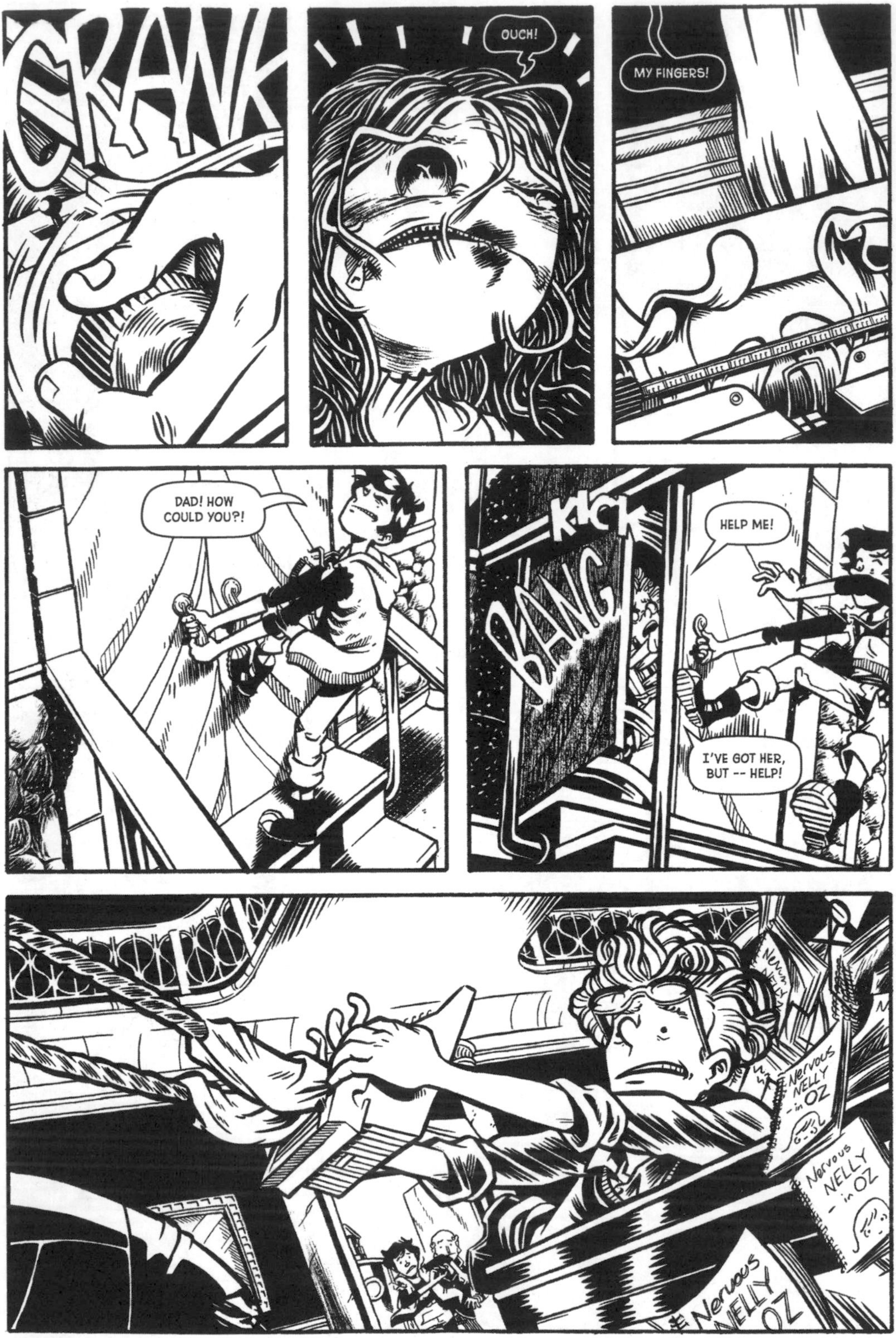
CRANK
OUCH!
MY FINGERS!
DAD! HOW COULD YOU?!
KICK
BANG
HELP ME!
I'VE GOT HER, BUT -- HELP!
Nervous NELLY
Nervous NELLY - in OZ
Nervous NELLY - in OZ
Nervous NELLY OZ

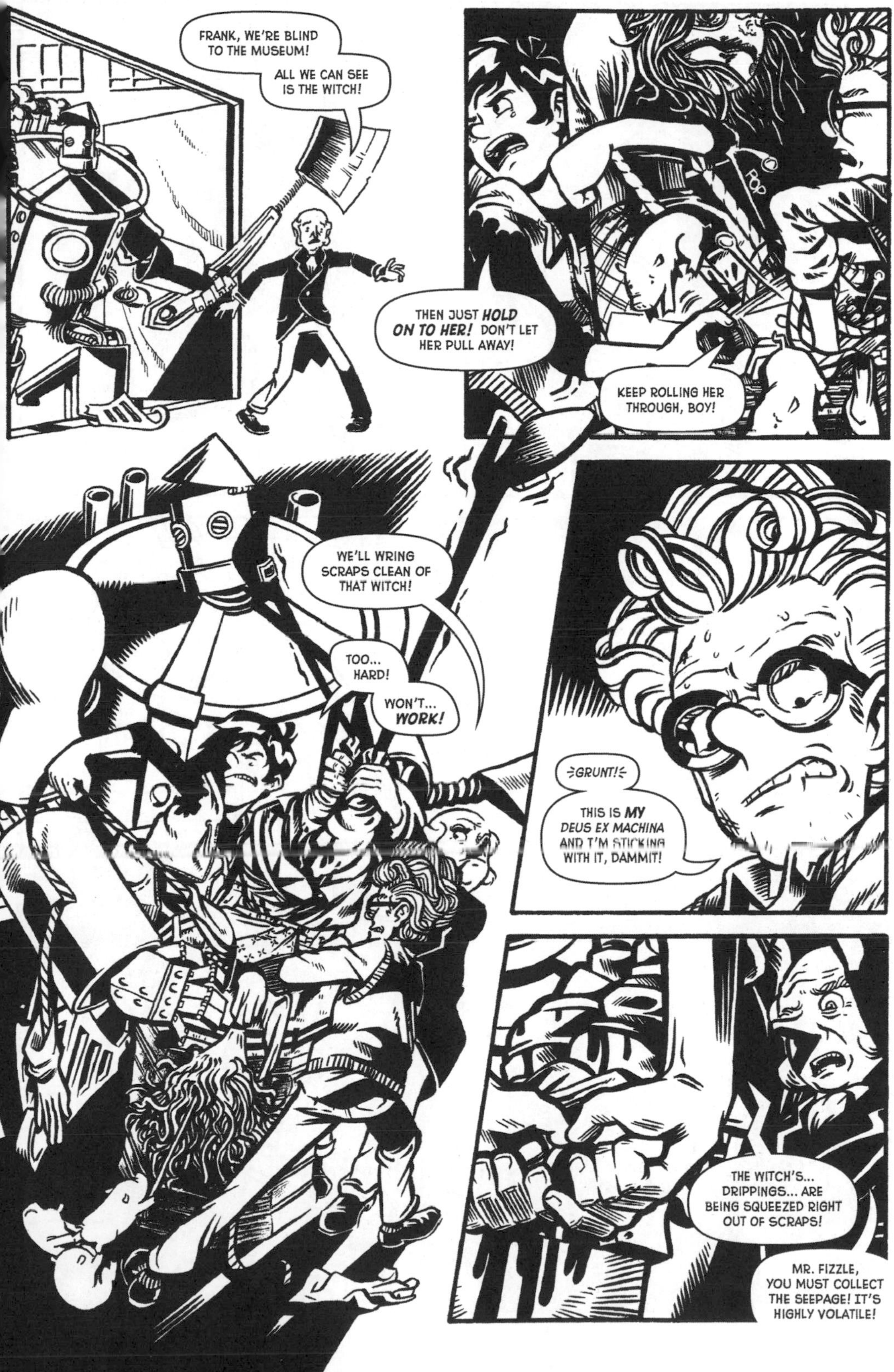
FRANK, WE'RE BLIND TO THE MUSEUM!
ALL WE CAN SEE IS THE WITCH!
POP
THEN JUST **HOLD ON TO HER!** DON'T LET HER PULL AWAY!
KEEP ROLLING HER THROUGH, BOY!
WE'LL WRING SCRAPS CLEAN OF THAT WITCH!
TOO... HARD!
WON'T... **WORK!**
GRUNT!
THIS IS **MY** *DEUS EX MACHINA* AND I'M STICKING WITH IT, DAMMIT!
THE WITCH'S... DRIPPINGS... ARE BEING SQUEEZED RIGHT OUT OF SCRAPS!
MR. FIZZLE, YOU MUST COLLECT THE SEEPAGE! IT'S HIGHLY VOLATILE!

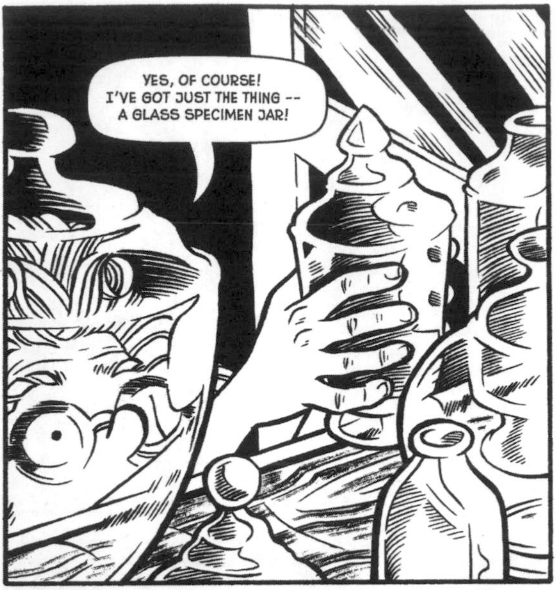
YES, OF COURSE! I'VE GOT JUST THE THING -- A GLASS SPECIMEN JAR!

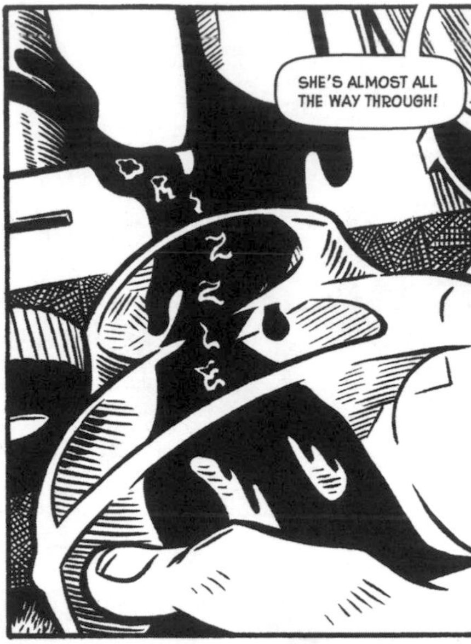
SHE'S ALMOST ALL THE WAY THROUGH!
DRIZZLE

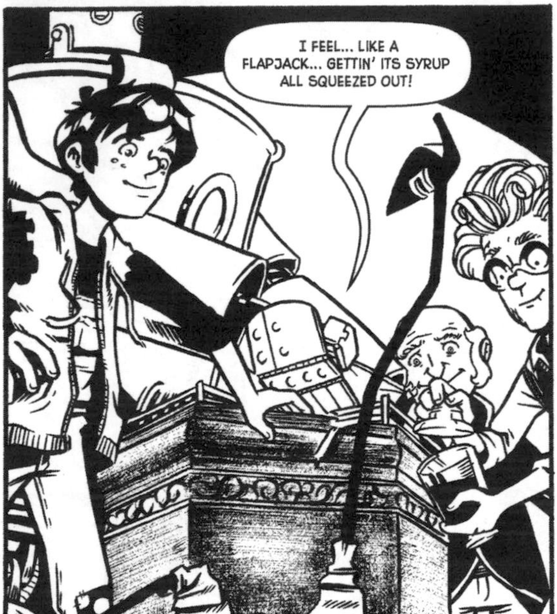
I FEEL... LIKE A FLAPJACK... GETTIN' ITS SYRUP ALL SQUEEZED OUT!

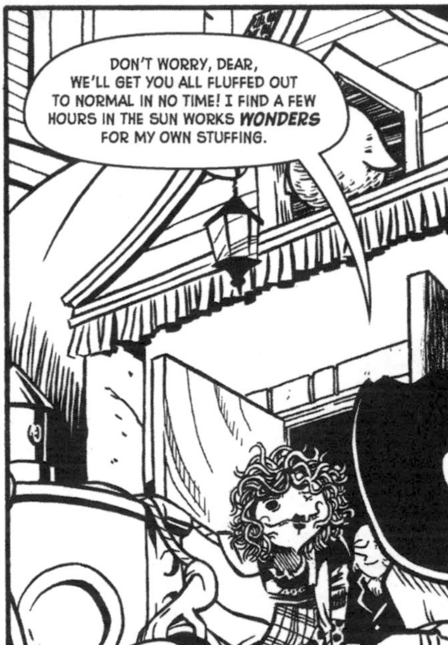
DON'T WORRY, DEAR, WE'LL GET YOU ALL FLUFFED OUT TO NORMAL IN NO TIME! I FIND A FEW HOURS IN THE SUN WORKS WONDERS FOR MY OWN STUFFING.

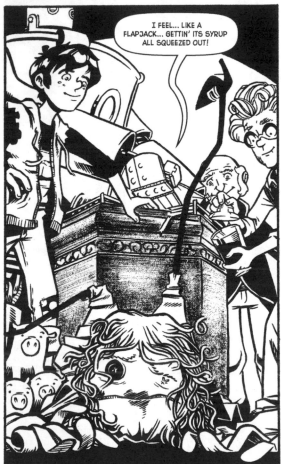

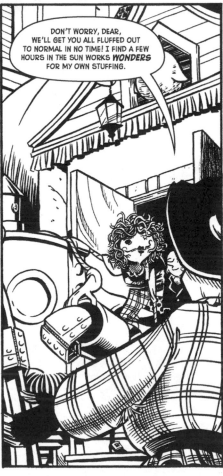

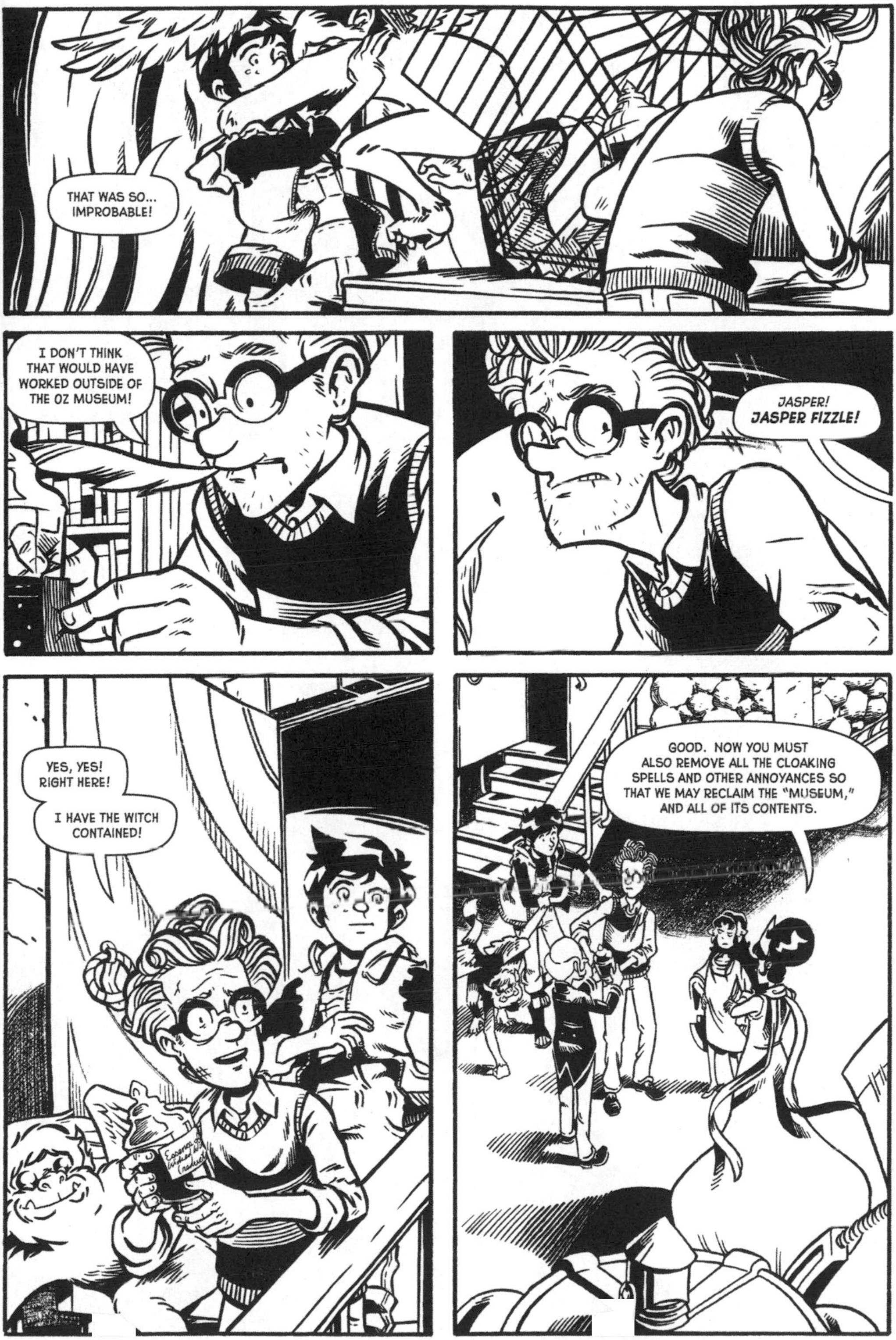
THAT WAS SO... IMPROBABLE!
I DON'T THINK THAT WOULD HAVE WORKED OUTSIDE OF THE OZ MUSEUM!
JASPER! **JASPER FIZZLE!**
YES, YES! RIGHT HERE!
I HAVE THE WITCH CONTAINED!
GOOD. NOW YOU MUST ALSO REMOVE ALL THE CLOAKING SPELLS AND OTHER ANNOYANCES SO THAT WE MAY RECLAIM THE "MUSEUM," AND ALL OF ITS CONTENTS.

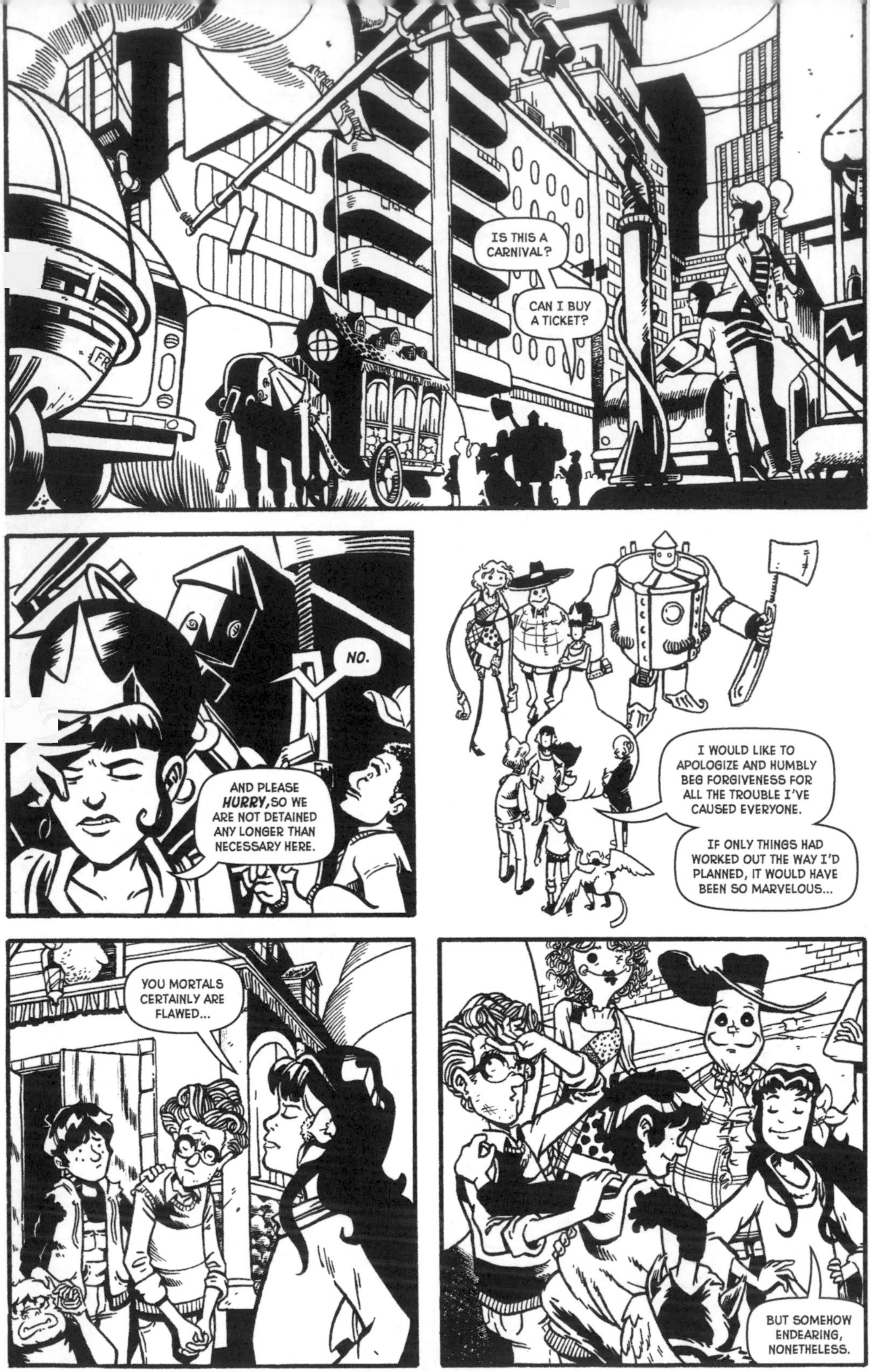
IS THIS A CARNIVAL?
CAN I BUY A TICKET?
NO.
AND PLEASE HURRY, SO WE ARE NOT DETAINED ANY LONGER THAN NECESSARY HERE.
I WOULD LIKE TO APOLOGIZE AND HUMBLY BEG FORGIVENESS FOR ALL THE TROUBLE I'VE CAUSED EVERYONE.
IF ONLY THINGS HAD WORKED OUT THE WAY I'D PLANNED, IT WOULD HAVE BEEN SO MARVELOUS...
YOU MORTALS CERTAINLY ARE FLAWED...
BUT SOMEHOW ENDEARING, NONETHELESS.

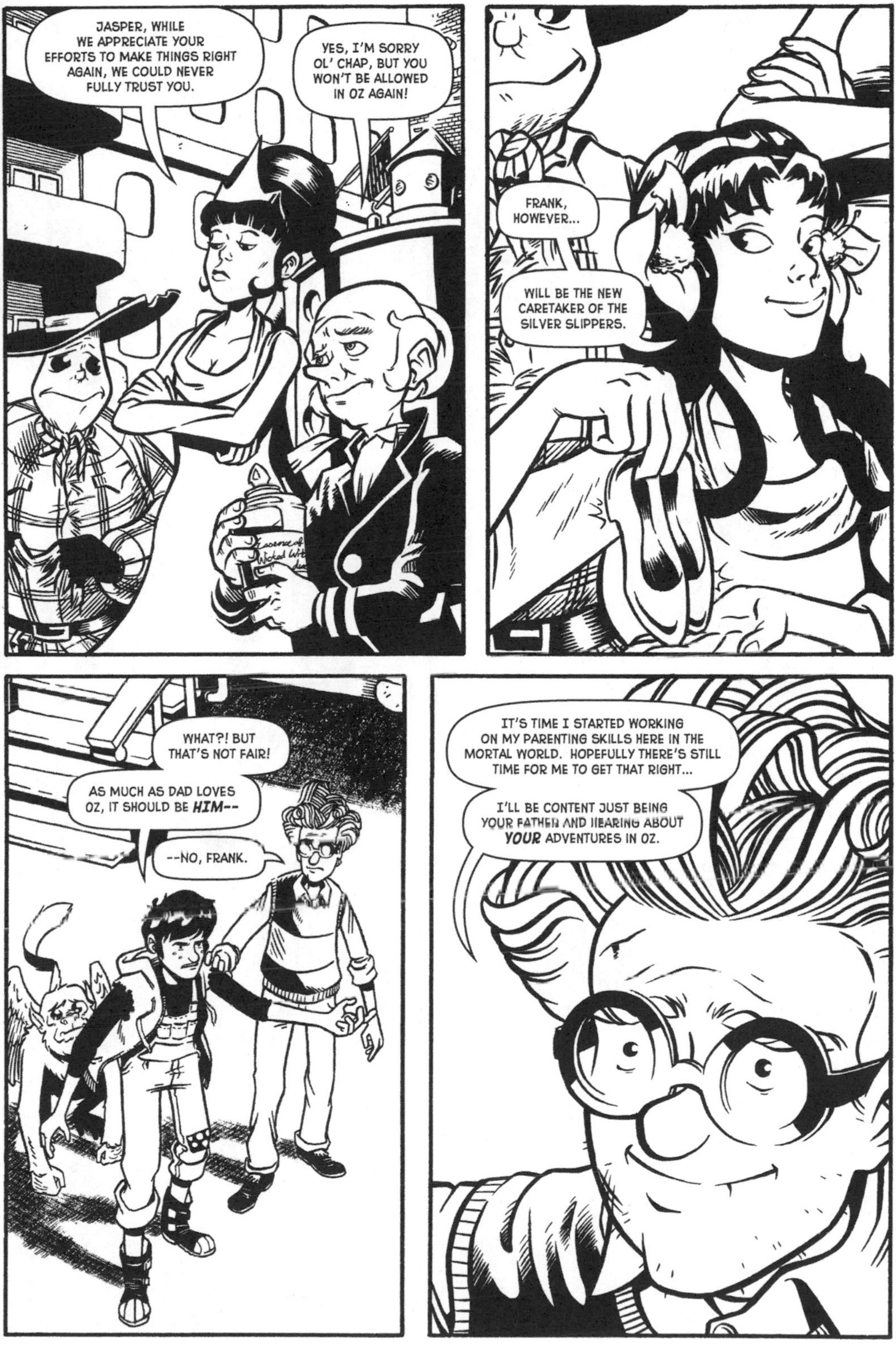
JASPER, WHILE WE APPRECIATE YOUR EFFORTS TO MAKE THINGS RIGHT AGAIN, WE COULD NEVER FULLY TRUST YOU.
YES, I'M SORRY OL' CHAP, BUT YOU WON'T BE ALLOWED IN OZ AGAIN!
FRANK, HOWEVER...
WILL BE THE NEW CARETAKER OF THE SILVER SLIPPERS.
WHAT?! BUT THAT'S NOT FAIR!
AS MUCH AS DAD LOVES OZ, IT SHOULD BE ***HIM--***
--NO, FRANK.
IT'S TIME I STARTED WORKING ON MY PARENTING SKILLS HERE IN THE MORTAL WORLD. HOPEFULLY THERE'S STILL TIME FOR ME TO GET THAT RIGHT...
I'LL BE CONTENT JUST BEING YOUR FATHER AND HEARING ABOUT ***YOUR*** ADVENTURES IN OZ.

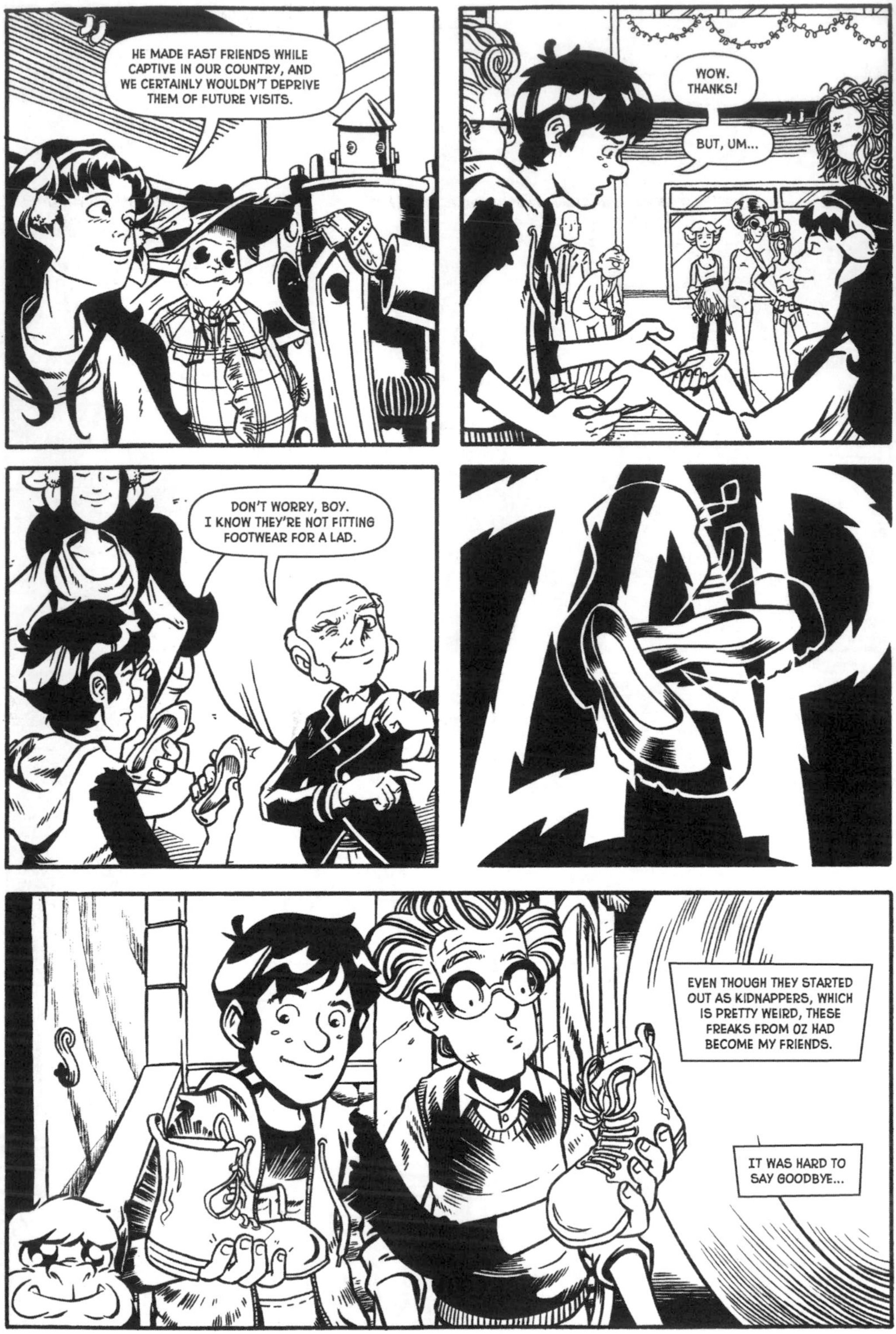
HE MADE FAST FRIENDS WHILE CAPTIVE IN OUR COUNTRY, AND WE CERTAINLY WOULDN'T DEPRIVE THEM OF FUTURE VISITS.
WOW. THANKS!
BUT, UM...
DON'T WORRY, BOY. I KNOW THEY'RE NOT FITTING FOOTWEAR FOR A LAD.
EVEN THOUGH THEY STARTED OUT AS KIDNAPPERS, WHICH IS PRETTY WEIRD, THESE FREAKS FROM OZ HAD BECOME MY FRIENDS.
IT WAS HARD TO SAY GOODBYE...

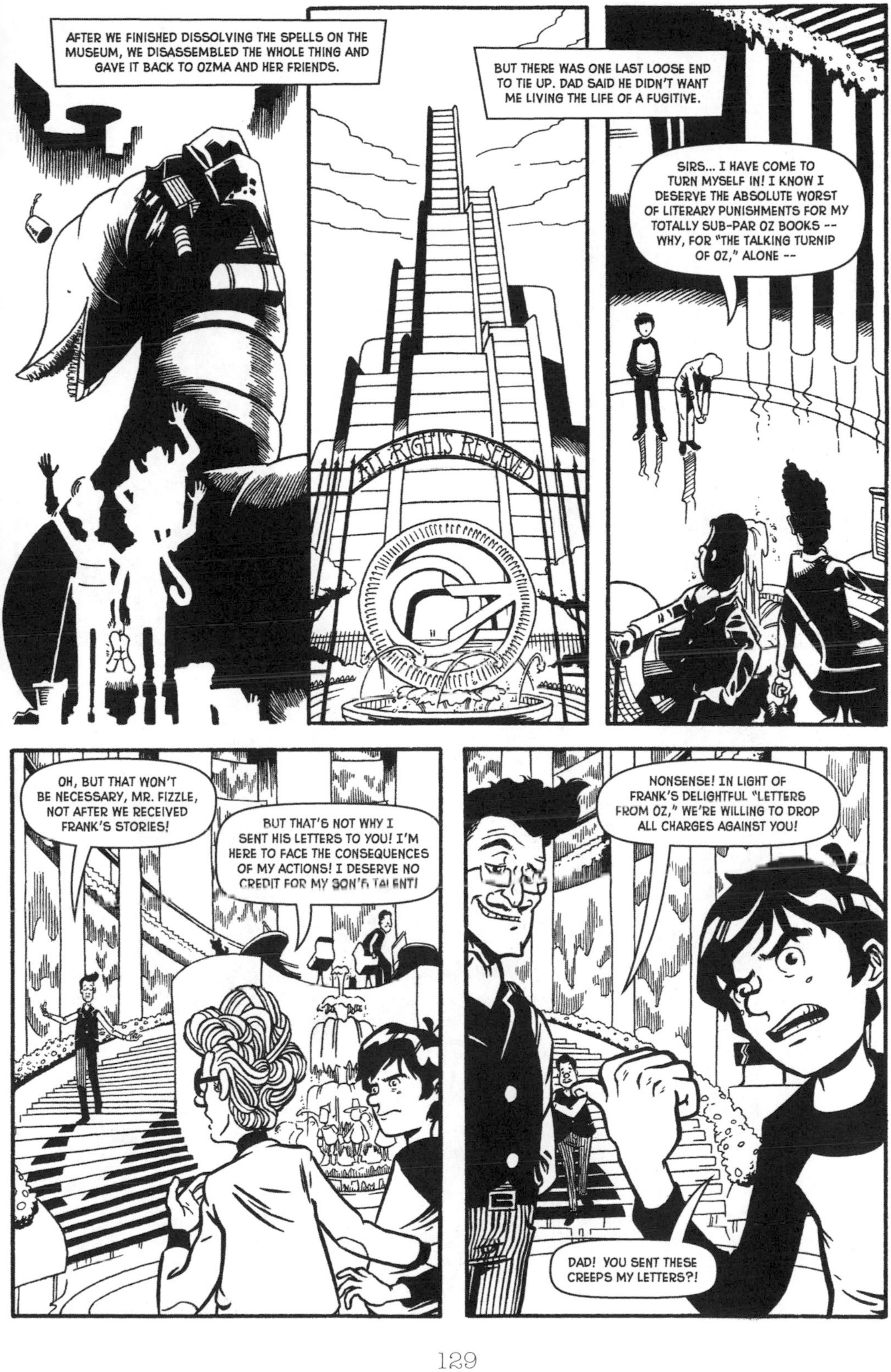
AFTER WE FINISHED DISSOLVING THE SPELLS ON THE MUSEUM, WE DISASSEMBLED THE WHOLE THING AND GAVE IT BACK TO OZMA AND HER FRIENDS.
BUT THERE WAS ONE LAST LOOSE END TO TIE UP. DAD SAID HE DIDN'T WANT ME LIVING THE LIFE OF A FUGITIVE.
ALL RIGHTS RESERVED
SIRS... I HAVE COME TO TURN MYSELF IN! I KNOW I DESERVE THE ABSOLUTE WORST OF LITERARY PUNISHMENTS FOR MY TOTALLY SUB-PAR OZ BOOKS -- WHY, FOR "THE TALKING TURNIP OF OZ," ALONE --
OH, BUT THAT WON'T BE NECESSARY, MR. FIZZLE, NOT AFTER WE RECEIVED FRANK'S STORIES!
BUT THAT'S NOT WHY I SENT HIS LETTERS TO YOU! I'M HERE TO FACE THE CONSEQUENCES OF MY ACTIONS! I DESERVE NO CREDIT FOR MY SON'S TALENT!
NONSENSE! IN LIGHT OF FRANK'S DELIGHTFUL "LETTERS FROM OZ," WE'RE WILLING TO DROP ALL CHARGES AGAINST YOU!
DAD! YOU SENT THESE CREEPS MY LETTERS?!

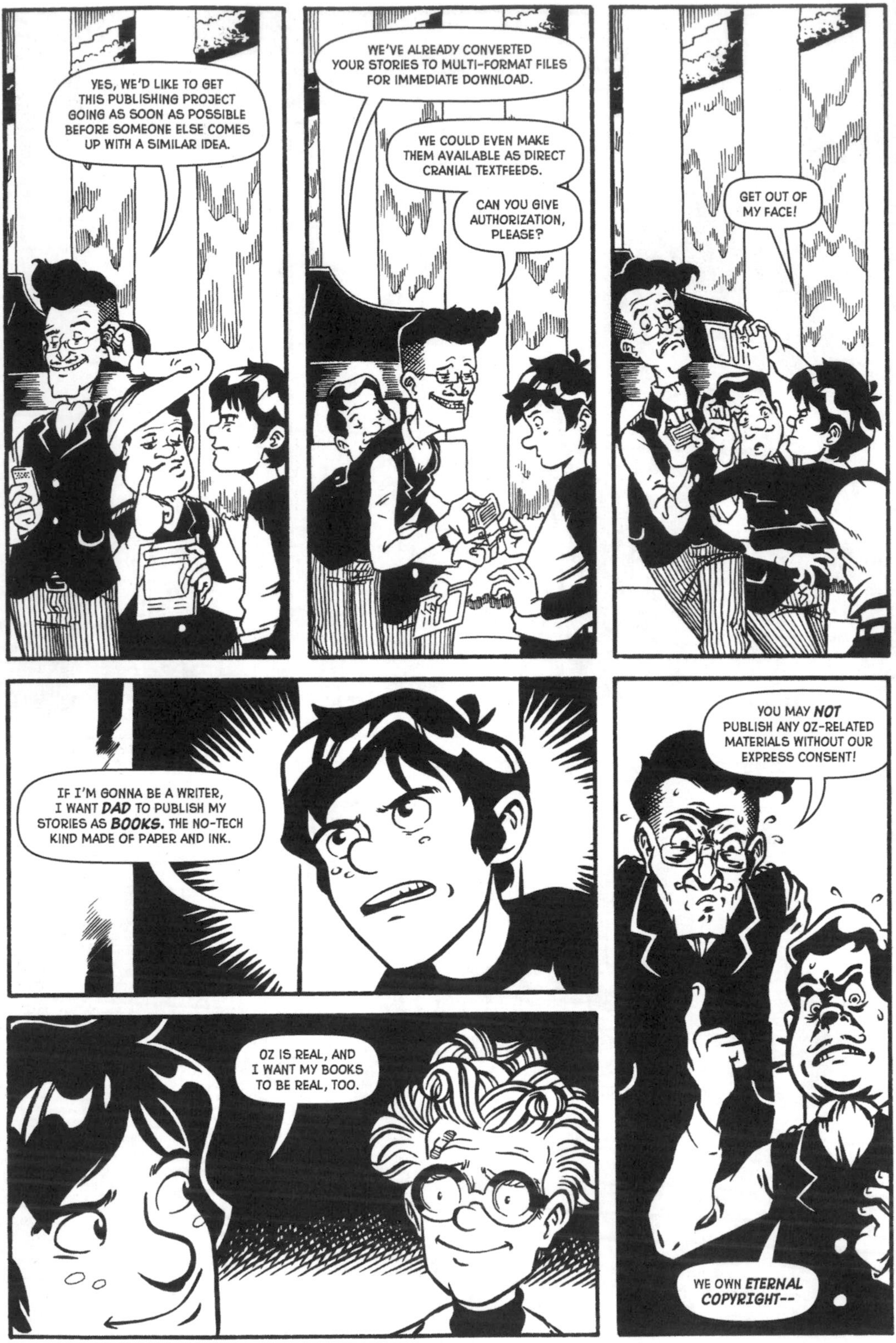
YES, WE'D LIKE TO GET THIS PUBLISHING PROJECT GOING AS SOON AS POSSIBLE BEFORE SOMEONE ELSE COMES UP WITH A SIMILAR IDEA.
WE'VE ALREADY CONVERTED YOUR STORIES TO MULTI-FORMAT FILES FOR IMMEDIATE DOWNLOAD.
WE COULD EVEN MAKE THEM AVAILABLE AS DIRECT CRANIAL TEXTFEEDS.
CAN YOU GIVE AUTHORIZATION, PLEASE?
GET OUT OF MY FACE!
IF I'M GONNA BE A WRITER, I WANT **DAD** TO PUBLISH MY STORIES AS **BOOKS.** THE NO-TECH KIND MADE OF PAPER AND INK.
OZ IS REAL, AND I WANT MY BOOKS TO BE REAL, TOO.
YOU MAY **NOT** PUBLISH ANY OZ-RELATED MATERIALS WITHOUT OUR EXPRESS CONSENT!
WE OWN **ETERNAL COPYRIGHT--**

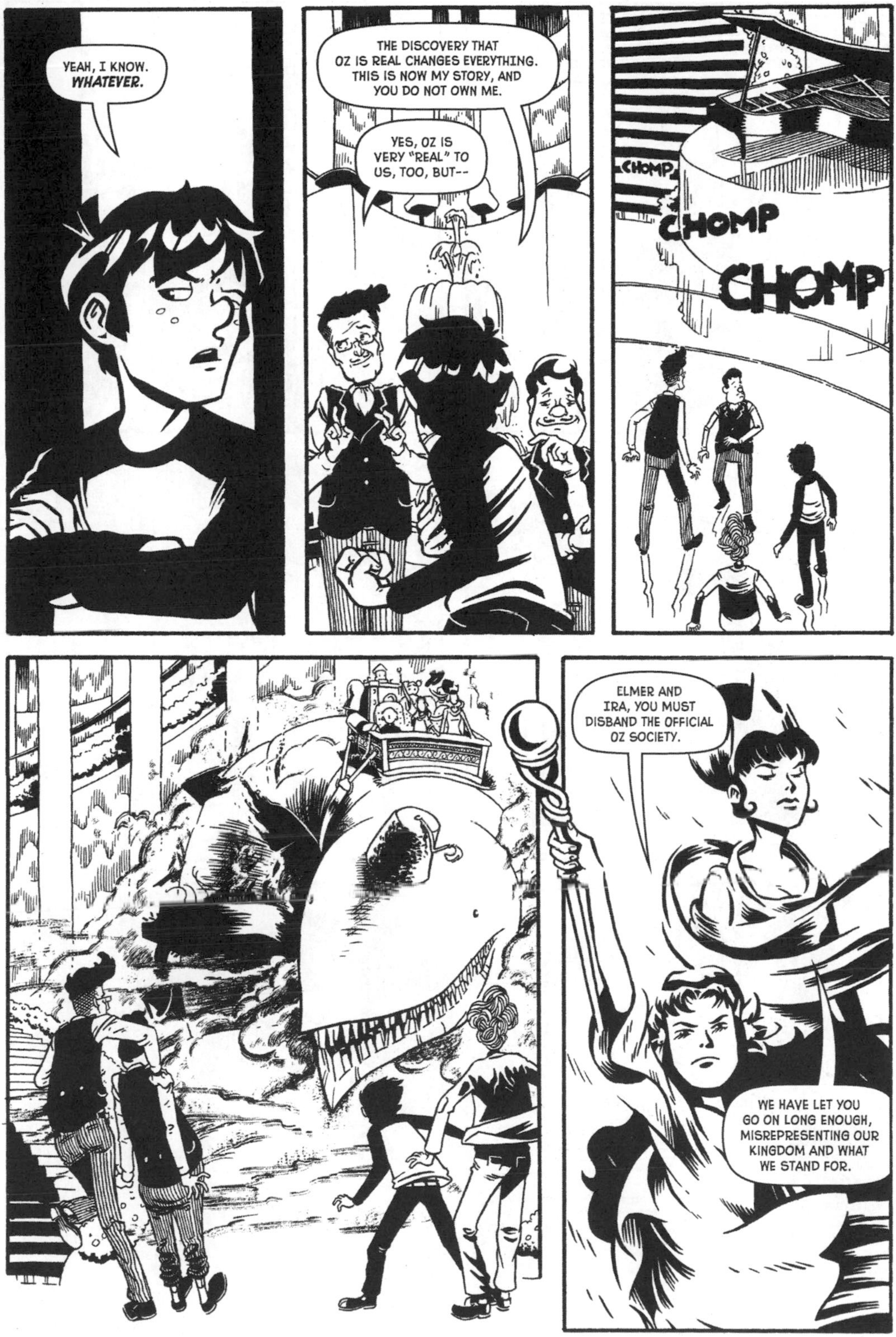
YEAH, I KNOW. WHATEVER.
THE DISCOVERY THAT OZ IS REAL CHANGES EVERYTHING. THIS IS NOW MY STORY, AND YOU DO NOT OWN ME.
YES, OZ IS VERY "REAL" TO US, TOO, BUT--
CHOMP
CHOMP
CHOMP
ELMER AND IRA, YOU MUST DISBAND THE OFFICIAL OZ SOCIETY.
WE HAVE LET YOU GO ON LONG ENOUGH, MISREPRESENTING OUR KINGDOM AND WHAT WE STAND FOR.

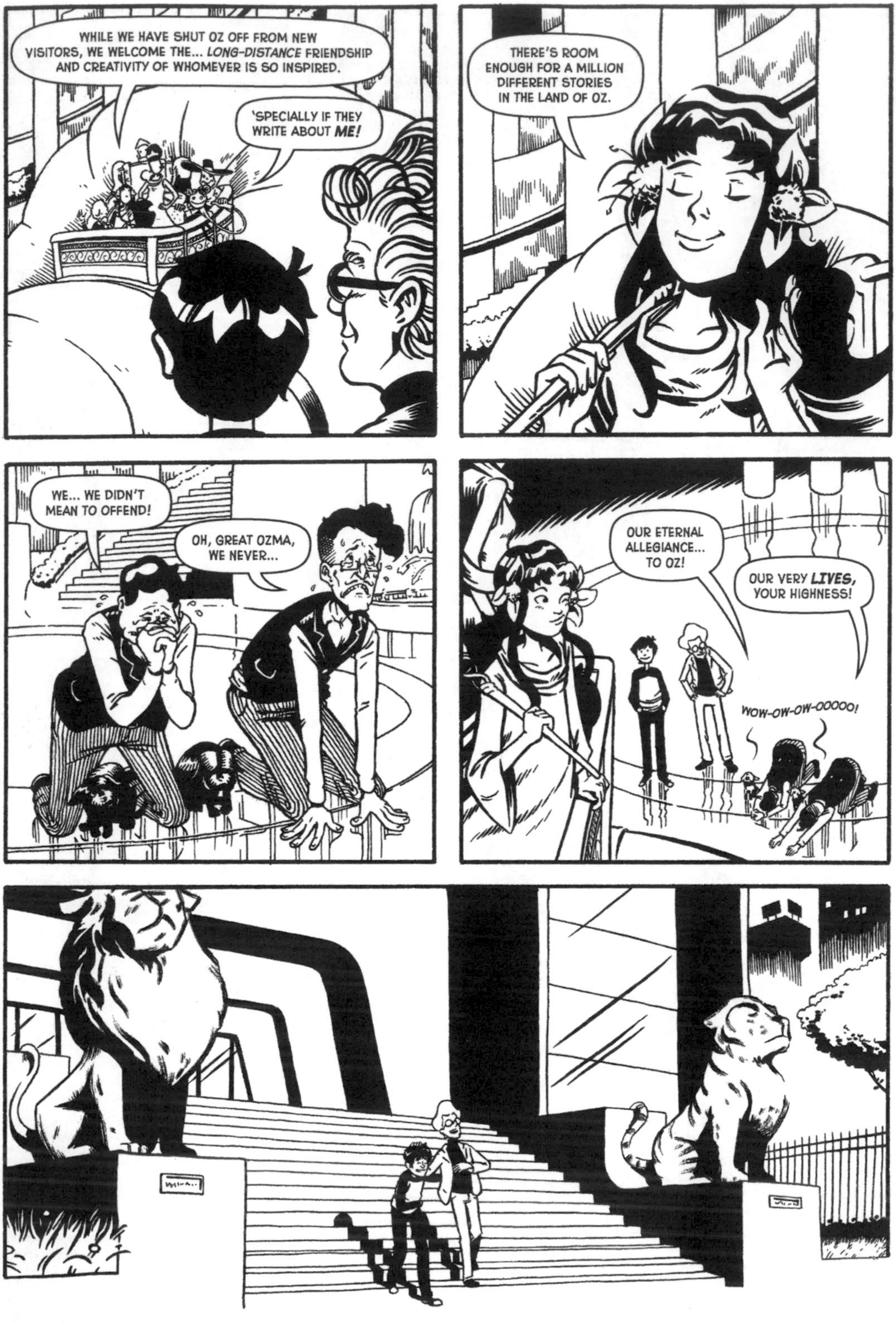
WHILE WE HAVE SHUT OZ OFF FROM NEW VISITORS, WE WELCOME THE... *LONG-DISTANCE* FRIENDSHIP AND CREATIVITY OF WHOMEVER IS SO INSPIRED.
'SPECIALLY IF THEY WRITE ABOUT ***ME!***
THERE'S ROOM ENOUGH FOR A MILLION DIFFERENT STORIES IN THE LAND OF OZ.
WE... WE DIDN'T MEAN TO OFFEND!
OH, GREAT OZMA, WE NEVER...
OUR ETERNAL ALLEGIANCE... TO OZ!
OUR VERY ***LIVES,*** YOUR HIGHNESS!
WOW-OW-OW-OOOOO!

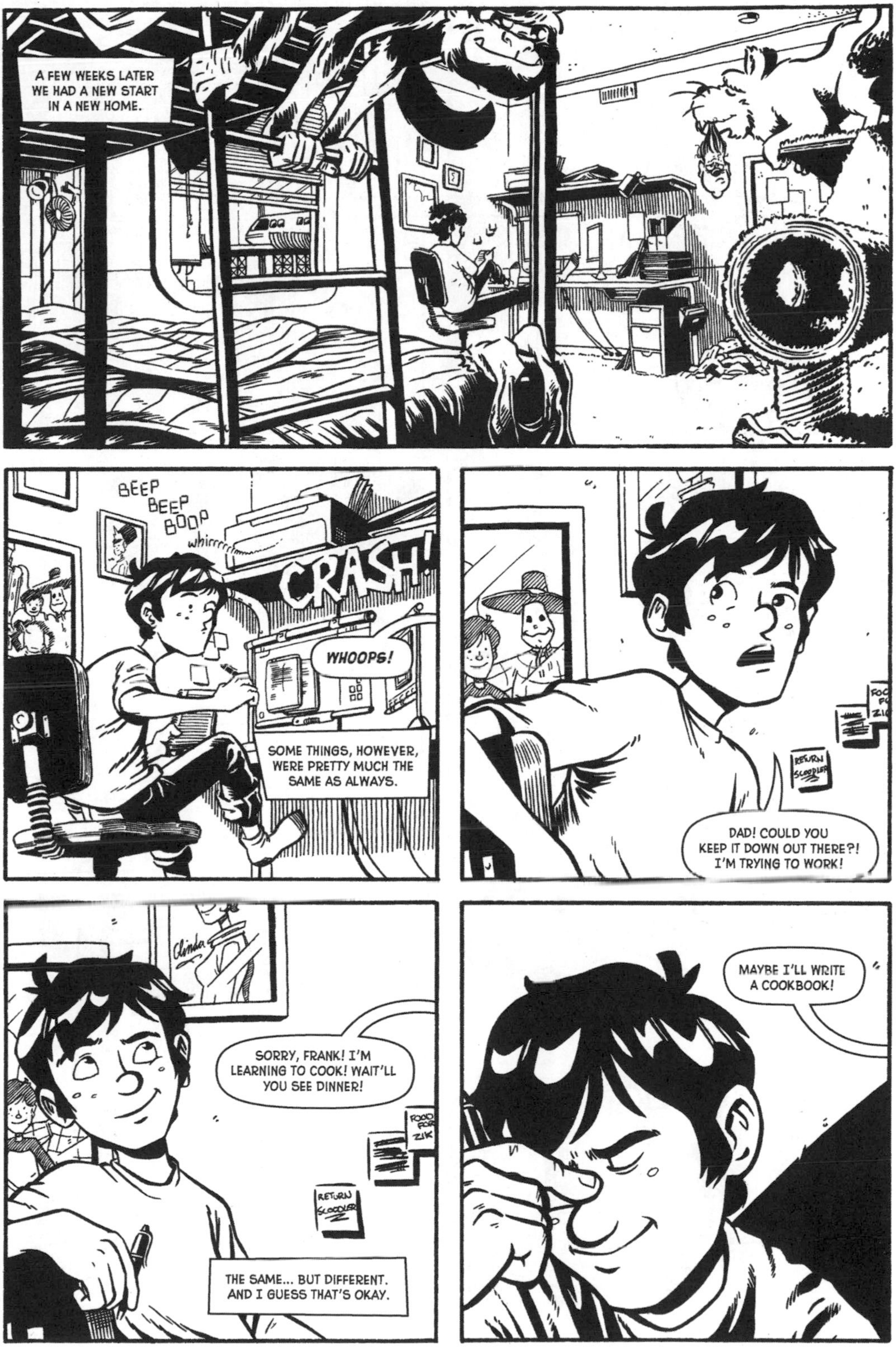
A FEW WEEKS LATER WE HAD A NEW START IN A NEW HOME.
BEEP BEEP BOOP
whirrrrr
CRASH!
WHOOPS!
SOME THINGS, HOWEVER, WERE PRETTY MUCH THE SAME AS ALWAYS.
RETURN SCOODLER
DAD! COULD YOU KEEP IT DOWN OUT THERE?! I'M TRYING TO WORK!
Clinda
SORRY, FRANK! I'M LEARNING TO COOK! WAIT'LL YOU SEE DINNER!
FOOD FOR ZIK
RETURN SCOODLER
THE SAME... BUT DIFFERENT. AND I GUESS THAT'S OKAY.
MAYBE I'LL WRITE A COOKBOOK!

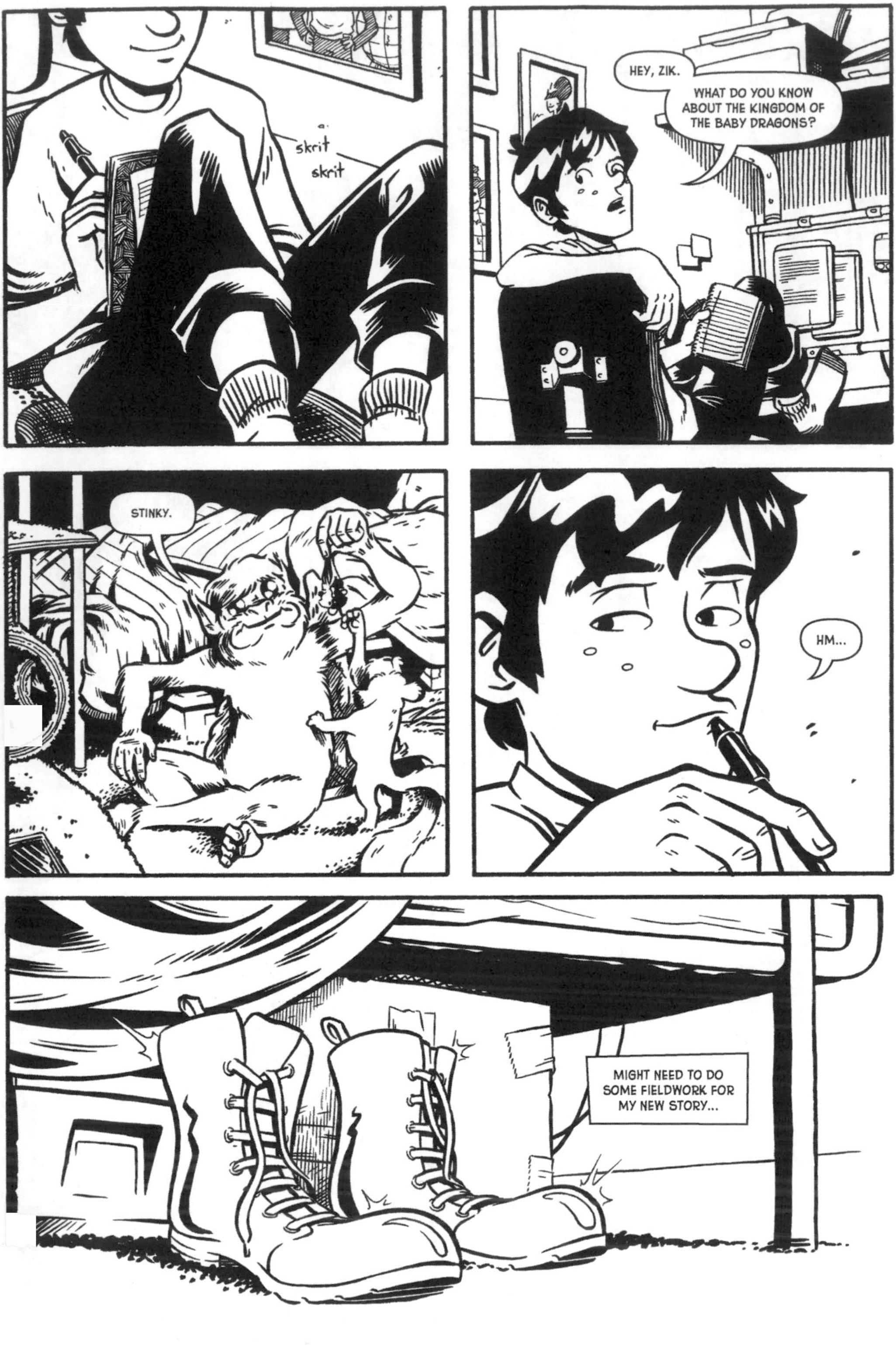
skrit
skrit
HEY, ZIK.
WHAT DO YOU KNOW ABOUT THE KINGDOM OF THE BABY DRAGONS?
STINKY.
HM...
MIGHT NEED TO DO SOME FIELDWORK FOR MY NEW STORY...

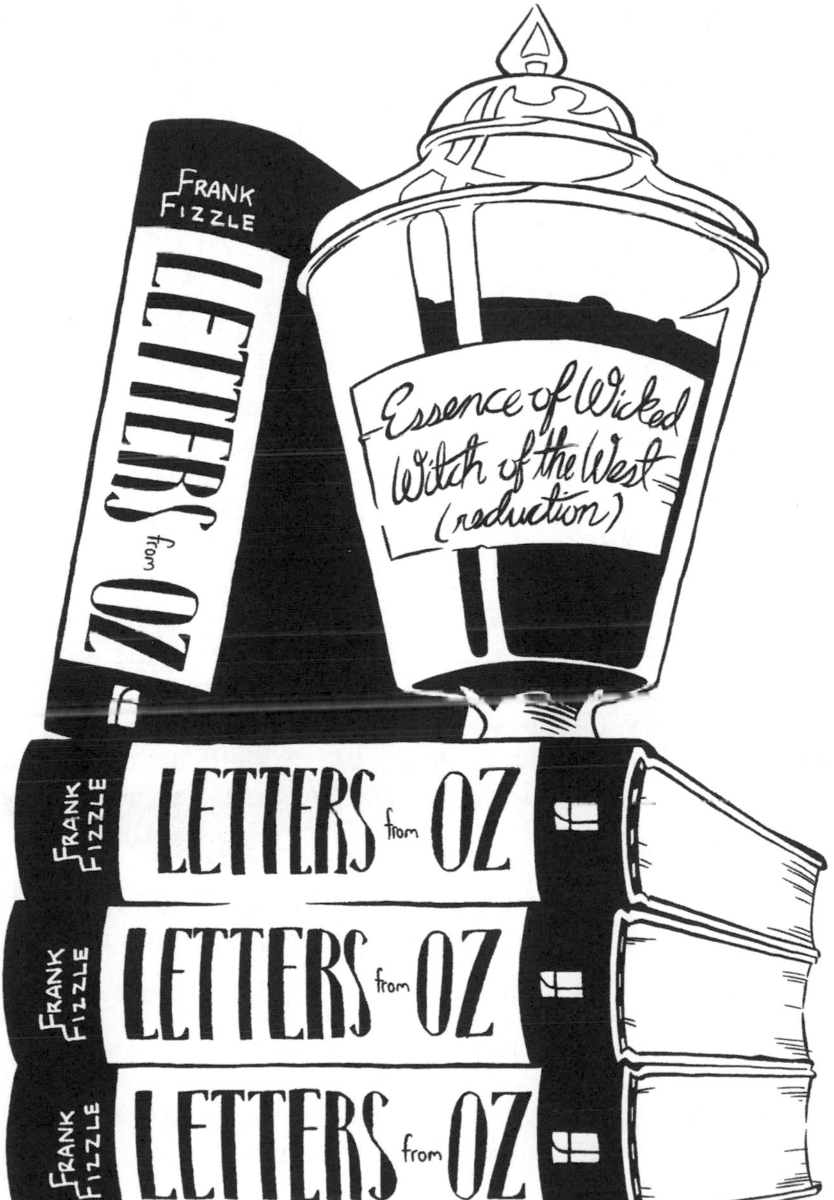
FRANK FIZZLE
LETTERS from OZ
Essence of Wicked Witch of the West (reduction)
FRANK FIZZLE
LETTERS from OZ
FRANK FIZZLE
LETTERS from OZ
FRANK FIZZLE
LETTERS from OZ

The following is
an excerpt from
Nervous Nelly in Oz,
by Jasper Fizzle.

In her richly-decorated apartments within the Emerald City, Ozma sat on a velvet couch, surrounded by her friends. The fairy ruler's dainty slippers peeked out from beneath her gauzy dress, which billowed and sparkled like mist.

She raised a slender hand and bade Nervous Nelly come closer.

Nelly's jittery feet clattered in her humble peasant shoes as she drew closer to Ozma, causing trills of good-humored laughter to cascade from the others present.

Ozma gestured gracefully to her friends, saying to Nelly, "My friends laugh WITH you, my dear, not AT your clumsiness. No one is ever cruel or mean-spirited in the Emerald City."

"Gosh, Nelly, I never seen anyone so nervous as you!" laughed Dorothy, placing an encouraging hand on Nelly's trembling arm. The plucky Kansas girl smiled gaily into Nelly's grim and homely face. "Why, we've tried just 'bout EVERYTHING I could think of to calm you down, but nothing seems t' work!"

"Even my soothing purr just startles and frightens you!" groused Eureka, the little pink kitten, scamping about on the mirrored floor.

"Yes," agreed Ozma, frowning prettily. "Even Percival T. Cozy's magical Fairy-Blossom Tea has had no effect upon poor Nelly's condition."

Percival whistled sadly through his frowning spout, his voluminous garment with its many fine ribbons and bows puffing out and sighing in defeat.

"Oh, Ozma dearest," whined the nervous maid in her faltering falsetto, "You've taken me so kindly to your bosom, but I fear I am too much a burden on you and your faithful friends."

Ozma clasped Nelly's hands in her own and replied, "Sweet Nelly, can you not be comforted to know that no-one may ever die or be truly harmed in the Land of Oz? Surely there is no reason to fret so."

"But I'm so dreadfully nervous that the new Prince of the Popinjays will not find me winsome enough to gain his favor, and I so want to be a joy to others. Especially the new Prince!"

"Ozma!" rasped the Talking Turnip in its funny little voice. "Nervous Nelly must find the Tranquili-Tree of Oz, and taste of its calming fruit!"

Ozma smiled upon the turnip, her perfect little teeth like gleaming pearls, her lips like silken bows. "Why, you are a most intelligent tuber."

The turnip blushed a dark purple and shuffled its feet.

STEP-BY-STEP BREAKDOWN
Script and Sketch

ISSUE 1, PAGE 17

PAGE 17 PANEL 1

FRANK (Desperate to find a rational explanation): I don't know where you found that monkey thing, but it's probably just a genetic experiment. Or maybe a genetic "anomaly." I was just reading about third nipples, and people born with tails, and--

JASPER (Taking Frank by the hand, and leading him out the back door): It's much more than just Zik, here. Come with me, Frank...

PAGE 17 PANEL 2

Jasper leads Frank into the back yard, which is small, and bordered by high walls and chain link fence. A very urban, crowded back yard. In the middle of it, filling the small space, is a colorful vehicle that looks like a cross between a gypsy caravan and a museum on wheels. It looks fantastical and improbable, with stone columns and high windows. A shiny copper clockwork beast of burden is harnessed to it.

(NOTE: The clockwork beast can be anything you want, but should vaguely resemble Tik-Tok the Clockwork Man, who first appears in "Ozma of Oz." The same manufacturer who built Tik-Tok also built this beast of burden.)

JASPER: Come and see what I've brought back!

FRANK (eyes bugged out at the clockwork beast): What the...?!

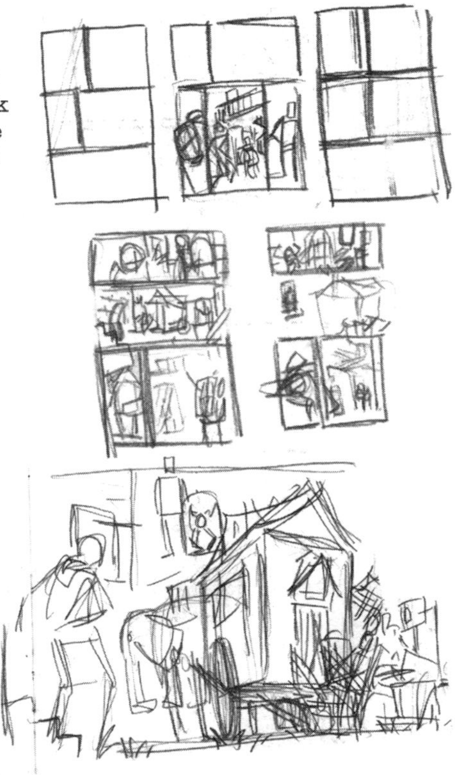

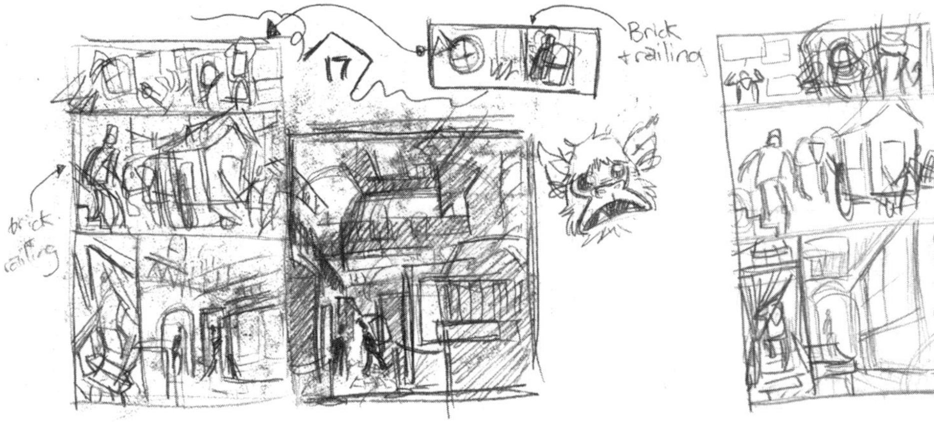
17
Brick railing
brick railing

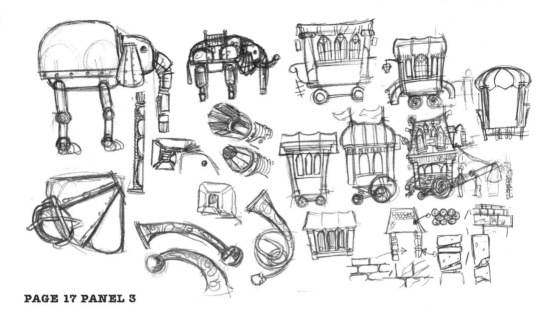

PAGE 17 PANEL 3

As they enter through the door of the caravan, Frank is amazed to see that on the inside it appears to be much larger than on the outside. From the inside, it looks like an old-fashioned Victorian cabinet of curiosities, with rows of live animals in cages, and glass-fronted cabinets full of potions in labeled jars and bottles, and tall shelves of books, and niches in the walls with displays of strange artifacts.

    FRANK: How... How is it so much larger inside than out?

    JASPER: It's an enchantment! I bartered it from a Winkie Wizard.

PAGE 17 PANEL 4

    FRANK (Overwhelmed, having a hard time processing it): Oh.

        (NOTE TO LETTERER: Frank's "Oh" should be smaller, to indicate a small, overwhelmed voice.)

    JASPER: Oz exists, Frank! It's not just a dream, or a dusty old book, it's an un-corrupted paradise! It's been sitting there all this time, waiting for someone like ME to bring new stories to our world.

PAGE 17 PANEL 5

    JASPER: You see, I've already started interviewing some of these creatures. I've been working with Zik to get the history of the Winged Monkeys down. Baum only got things half-right. I could write a book just about the Winged Monkeys and their struggles. People are always trying to use the poor creatures.

    ZIK (In the background, Jasper has set the cage down and is now ignoring Zik): Don't like cage!

STEP-BY-STEP BREAKDOWN
Rough Draft

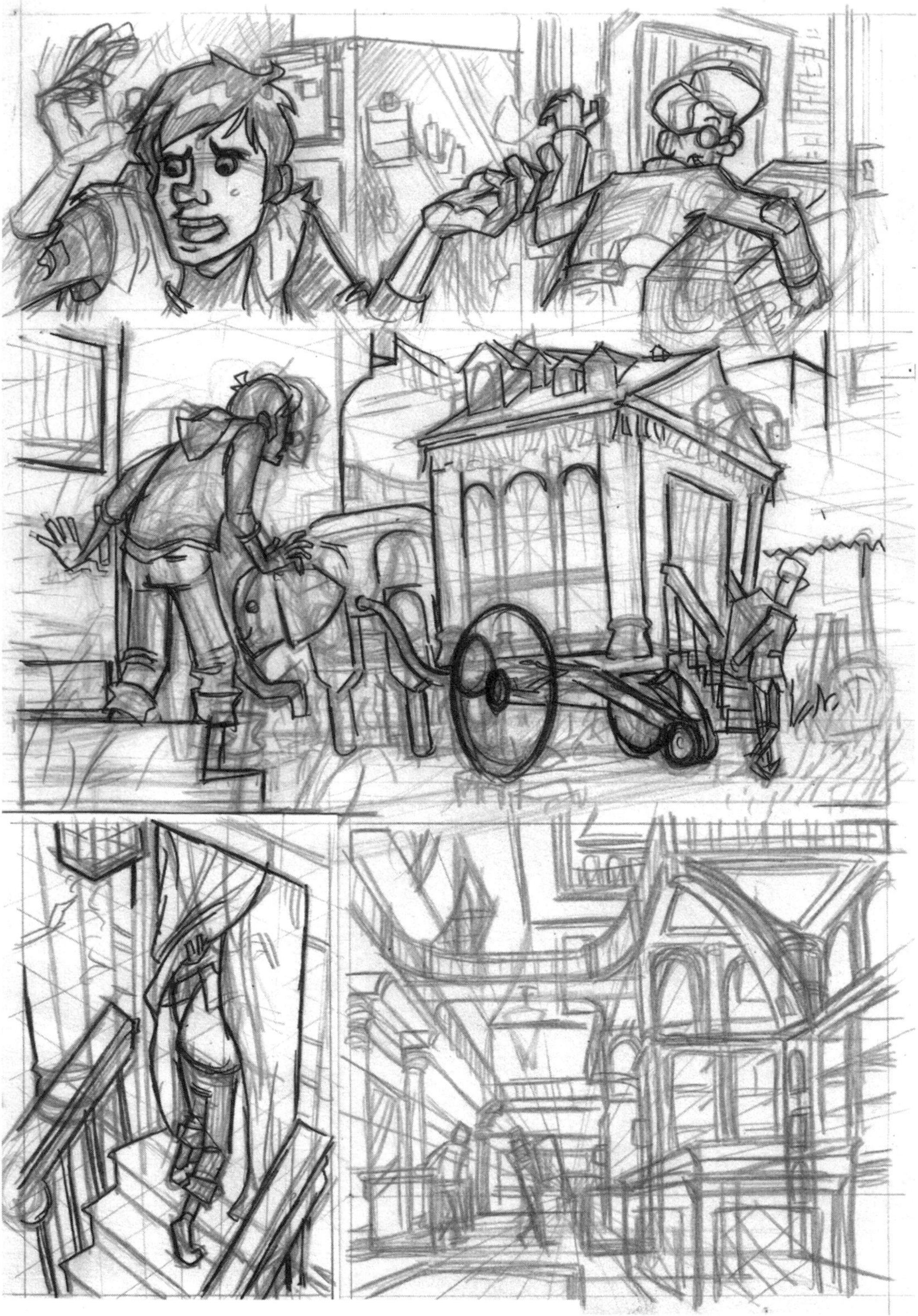

STEP-BY-STEP BREAKDOWN
Pencils

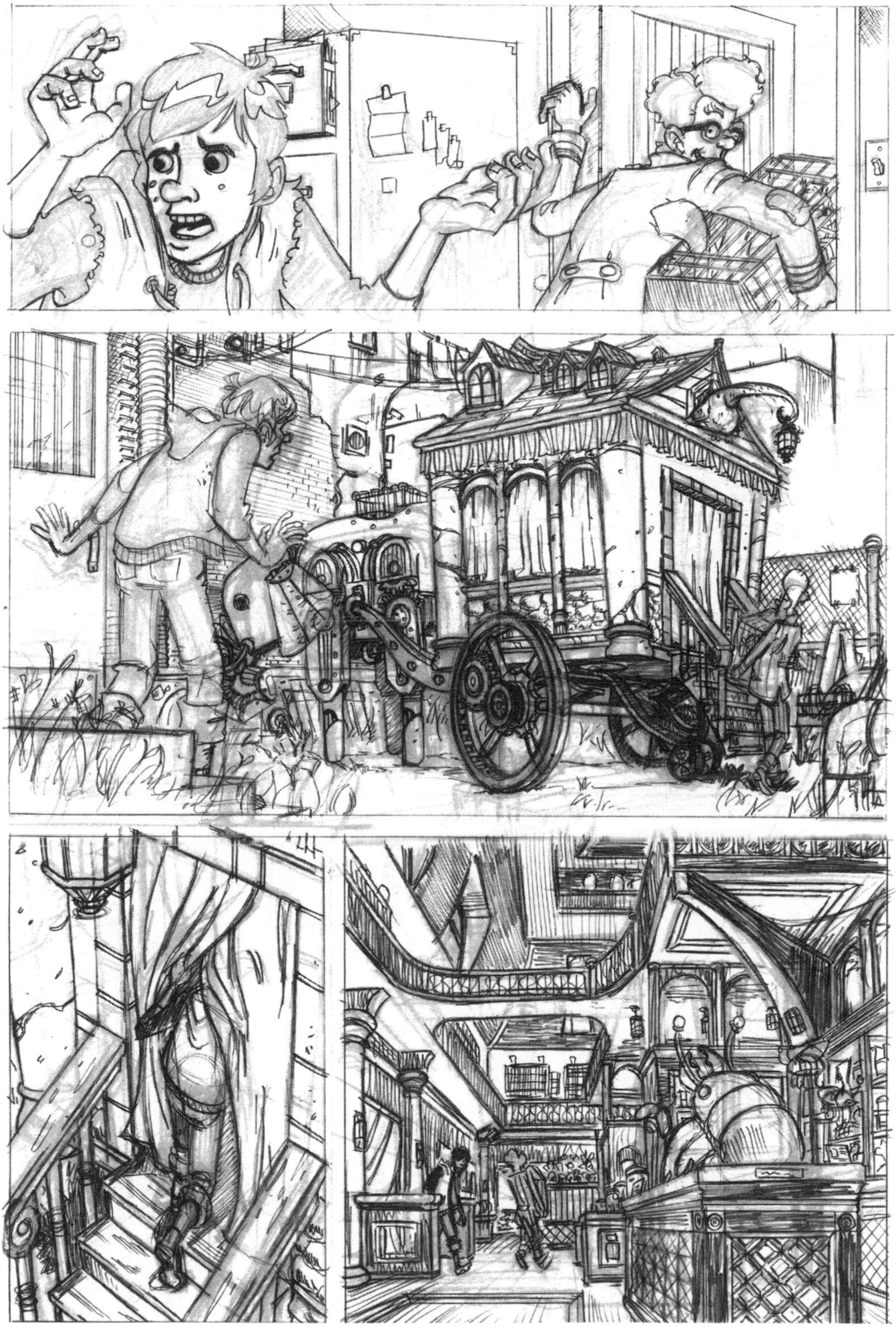

STEP-BY-STEP BREAKDOWN
Inks

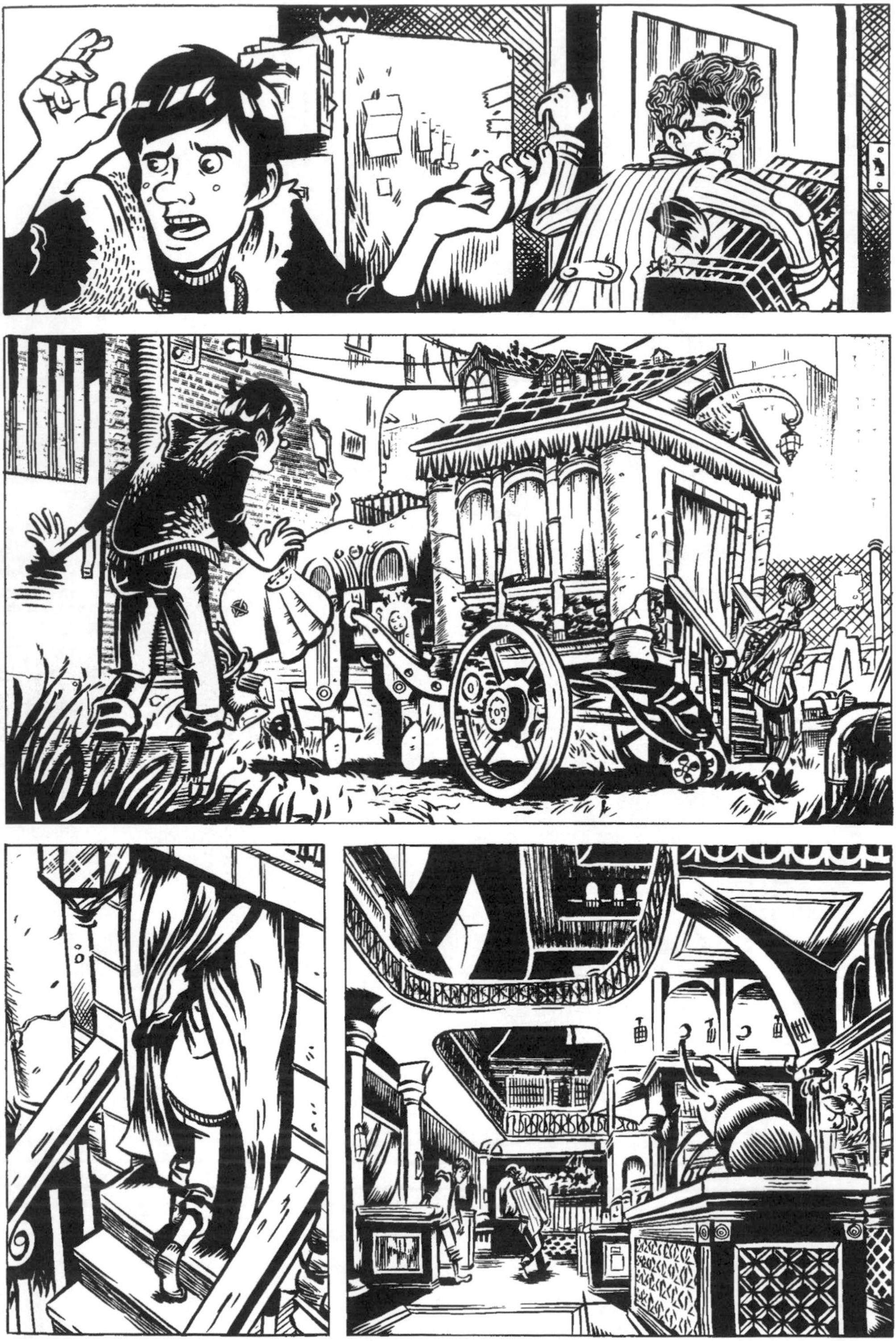

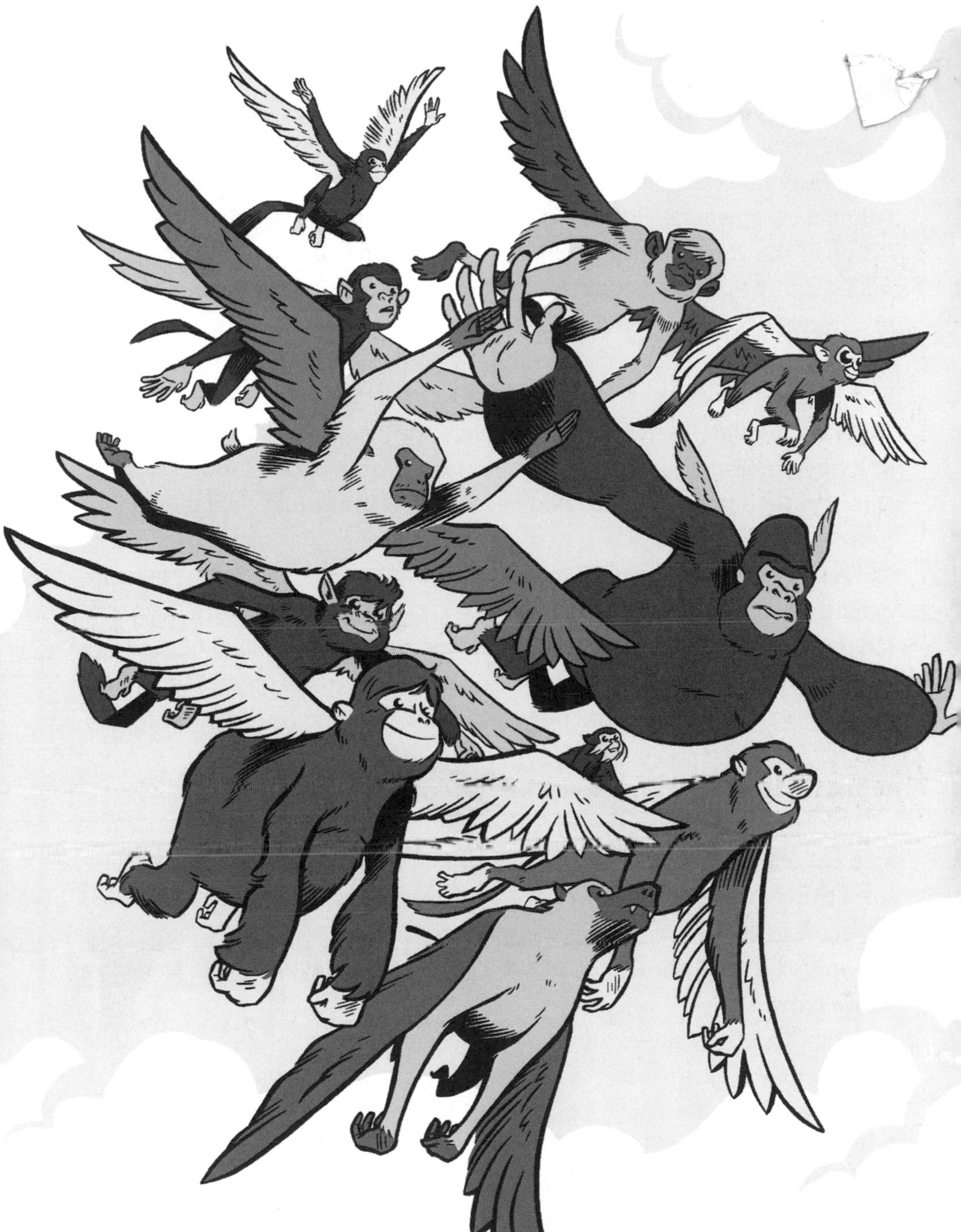

Interview with Tommy Kovac

conducted by David Maxine of Hungry Tiger Press
for the 2011 Winkie Convention

How were you introduced to Oz and Baum? Earliest Oz related memories?

As a child I was instantly infatuated by the MGM movie because of its colorful escapism and Margaret Hamilton's thrillingly terrifying Wicked Witch of the West. It felt like Christmas morning when that movie came on TV and I was spellbound every time. Then when I was about eight, I ordered the book from one of those mail-order classroom book clubs. As soon as it arrived, I devoured it like it was the gospel. It was perplexing and strange because of the antiquated phrasing, and different in tone from the movie. I loved it. I knew that the book was the REAL story, and any differences in the movie were just plain WRONG. I found Baum's Dorothy Gale to be resilient and confident, unlike Judy Garland's blubbering, warbly portrayal.

As I continued to gobble up all the rest of Baum's Oz books, I became certain that John R. Neill knew how Oz and its characters REALLY looked, even though Denslow had illustrated the first book. I turned my back forever on the brunette and braided Dorothy, and embraced wholeheartedly Neill's sassier and more fashionable blond Dorothy.

What is most appealing to you about Oz?

Oz provides a perfect escape into a safe and colorful world where fantastical friends are waiting. What could be better than that? Especially for a timid and socially awkward gay boy like me.

So how did ROYAL HISTORIAN come about? Where did the idea come from?

Dan Vado, president of SLG Publishing (who I've been with since 1999!) proposed the idea to me of doing an Oz comic about four summers ago. Dan's concept was to do an Oz book that was geared toward boys, and he particularly wanted to see the Tin Man looking really cool and intimidating with a big axe.

At first I was a little reticent to do an Oz book, partly because I had just finished writing "Wonderland," and wasn't sure if I wanted to continue working with other people's pre-existing creative properties. All of my pre-"Wonderland" comics ("Stitch," "Skelebunnies," and "Autumn") were creator-owned original properties. I was wary of being pigeon-holed as yet another fairy tale reinterpretation writer. The other thing that made me reticent was that so many Oz-related things already existed. It seemed like everything had already been done to and about Oz.

What made me accept the assignment was that I knew I couldn't let anyone ELSE at SLG do an Oz comic. I would have raged with jealousy and criticism. I love Oz, and if anyone is going to screw around with it, it should be ME. Or Eric Shanower. Or Gregory Maguire. That is my current short-list of Oz creators I approve of.

So what prompted the ideas for the Official Oz Society? As far as I know you haven't had a lot of contact with the International Wizard of Oz Club. Did you get any flack from Oz club members or GLBT folk for the presentation of the gay couple and their little dog, Toto? Since I myself have been a part of a high profile gay Oz couple (with a well-known Ozzy dog) I sorta HAVE to ask.

When I first wrote Frank's snarky quip about the Official Oz Society being "just a bunch of gay old men with dogs named Toto," and had Andy draw them as being prissy and foppish, I did wonder if some people might take it the wrong way. But I feel it's important as a creator NOT to second-guess yourself based on what you fear some people might think. Frank is a fifteen-year-old boy, and I've worked with teenagers in the public school system (as a library technician) for about seventeen years now. I can assure you, Frank's comment is EXACTLY how they talk, even if they're very gay-friendly. Plus, there's obviously a bit of me in Frank's character, and I'm irreverent about everything, including (and especially) myself.

I know there was some negative reader reaction initially, particularly from people who didn't realize that I myself am gay. I've had a few people tell me they were put off at first, not sure how to take the snarky comments, but then the series won them over and now they really like it. That's exactly what I like to hear. I certainly understand what it's like to be sensitive about certain issues, but you shouldn't take yourself so seriously that you lose your sense of humor.

Like you and I talked about before, it might have eased people's reactions to those bits of dialogue if SLG had included some biographical info about the creators, namely that I'm a married gay man who's been in a committed relationship for 21 years now. But I don't know if I like the idea of underestimating my readers and assuming they can't differentiate be-tween fictional characters and the real people who create them without having it spelled out for them. Plus I'm not sure if my being gay makes it any more or less acceptable for me to joke about gay issues and gender-role issues. I do know that what I wrote was genuine and felt right for the characters in that situation.

As far as the real International Wizard of Oz Club goes, I had never heard of them when I started writing "The Royal Historian of Oz"! My fic-tional "Official Oz Society" is mostly a reflection of my own intensely ter-ritorial feelings about Baum's work. Many years ago I tried reading some of Ruth Plumly Thompson's Oz books, but they are far too pun-oriented for me. The same with all the other post-Baum "royal historians." I do, howev-er, have a soft spot for Jack Snow's "The Shaggy Man of Oz," because it was the FIRST of the post-Baum Oz books that I ever stumbled across. I found it in my elementary school library and was shocked to find an Oz book I'd never heard of, that was not listed on any of my fourteen Baum-authored books at home. I have to admit the IDEA of Oz existing beyond Baum was a revelation.

When I discovered Eric Shanower's Oz comics, I was thrilled because I felt he got things "right." I can't help but be ridiculously judgmental when it comes to Oz creations. The world Baum created was a place I retreated to all throughout my childhood and even my teen years, whenever life seemed too scary and harsh. It became very real to me, but of course I realize that everyone internalizes Oz differently. What seems correctly "Ozzy" to one person might seem like Baum blasphemy to the next.

I was afraid of Baum blasphemy when Gregory Maguire's "Wicked" hit the mainstream so squarely. I refused to read it for a long time, in spite of (or because of) many people saying, "Hey, Tommy! You like the Wizard of Oz, right? You HAVE to read this book!" I'm a contrary person at heart, so an effusive recommendation is usually an absolute assurance that I will never read something.

I finally decided to read "Wicked" even though I kept thinking, "I will HATE this book," mainly so I could tell people in detail exactly what I hated about it. But to my surprise I was won over. It was nothing like what I was expecting, and such a completely different creature from the Oz I grew up with. I moved Maguire into the "approved" category.

In the past ten years there have been so many Oz-related comics - what

do you think is fueling the Oz comic tidal-wave?

Well, I'd like to say it's the enduring power of Baum's original fantastic vision, but I'm afraid it probably has more to do with the fact that the publishing industry, including comics, only wants safe bets. Whatever is already familiar and easily-digestible to the public.

You used to draw your comics as well as write. How did you end up just writing ROYAL HISTORIAN? Are you still drawing these days?

Well, I didn't make a million dollars and get to quit my day job during my first couple of years in comics. I like the idea of regular paychecks and good insurance, so I'm still working as a full-time library technician, thankfully something I enjoy doing. But the pressure of writing and illustrating my own comics on top of working full-time became overwhelming part-way through my series, "Autumn." I sort of crashed and burned and had to take a break, and let my publisher know that I really wanted to try writing for someone ELSE to illustrate, which hopefully would be a more manageable workload. That led to "Wonderland" illustrated by Sonny Liew, and now "Royal Historian" illustrated by Andy Hirsch. Andy is awesomely talented and awesome to work with. I still draw all the time, just for fun. Doodles, sketches, etc. I do lots of original artwork for the library I work in, which ends up on the bulletin boards and bookmarks and stuff. The kids dig it.

What books did you love best as a kid? As an adult?

When I was a wee one, my favorites were the Oz books of course, plus "Alice's Adventures in Wonderland" and "Through the Looking-Glass," the Narnia books, the "Chronicles of Prydain" by Lloyd Alexander, the Raggedy Ann & Andy books by Johnny Gruelle, the "Dark Is Rising" series by Susan Cooper, and the Moomintroll books by Tove Jansson.

As an adult my favorite genres are fantasy, sci-fi, and horror. Anne Rice, Clive Barker, Dan Simmons, Robert R. McCammon, Tad Williams, Poppy Z. Brite, Caitlin R. Kiernan, Gregory Keyes, Tanith Lee, George R. R. Martin. I also like thrillers. I'm totally addicted to the "Pendergast" books by Preston & Child. I go through periods where I read nothing but fantasy, then I'll switch to horror and glut myself on that for a while. As an adult my tastes run pretty dark! Recently one of the students I work with recommended a book to me by saying, "I really think you'd like it, Mr. Kovac. Somebody gets murdered gruesomely in the first 10 pages!" (She knows that's usually my prerequisite.)

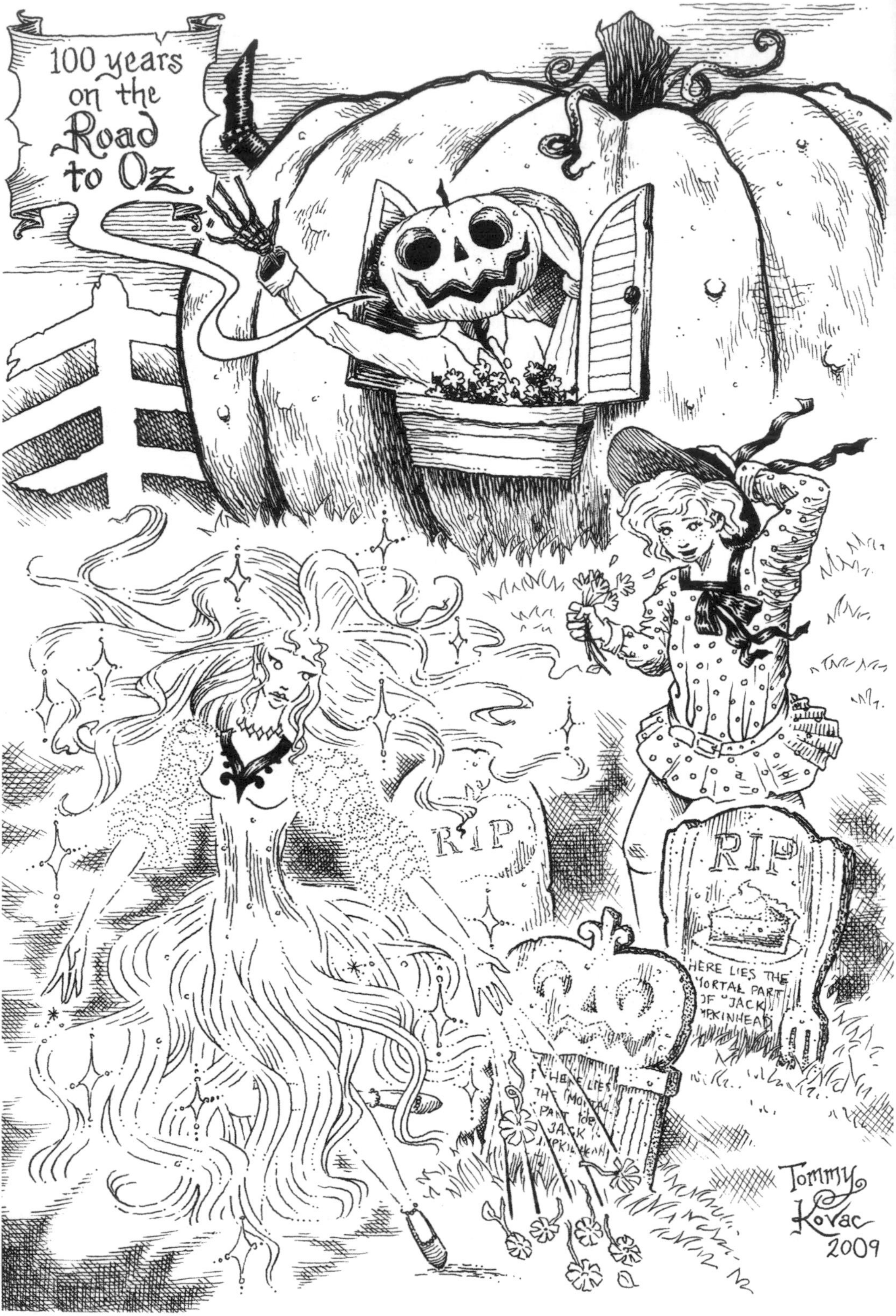
100 years on the Road to Oz
RIP
RIP
HERE LIES THE
Tommy Kovac 2009

POLYCHROME AND DOROTHY BRINGING FLOWERS TO
JACK PUMPKINHEAD'S GRAVEYARD OF ROTTED HEADS

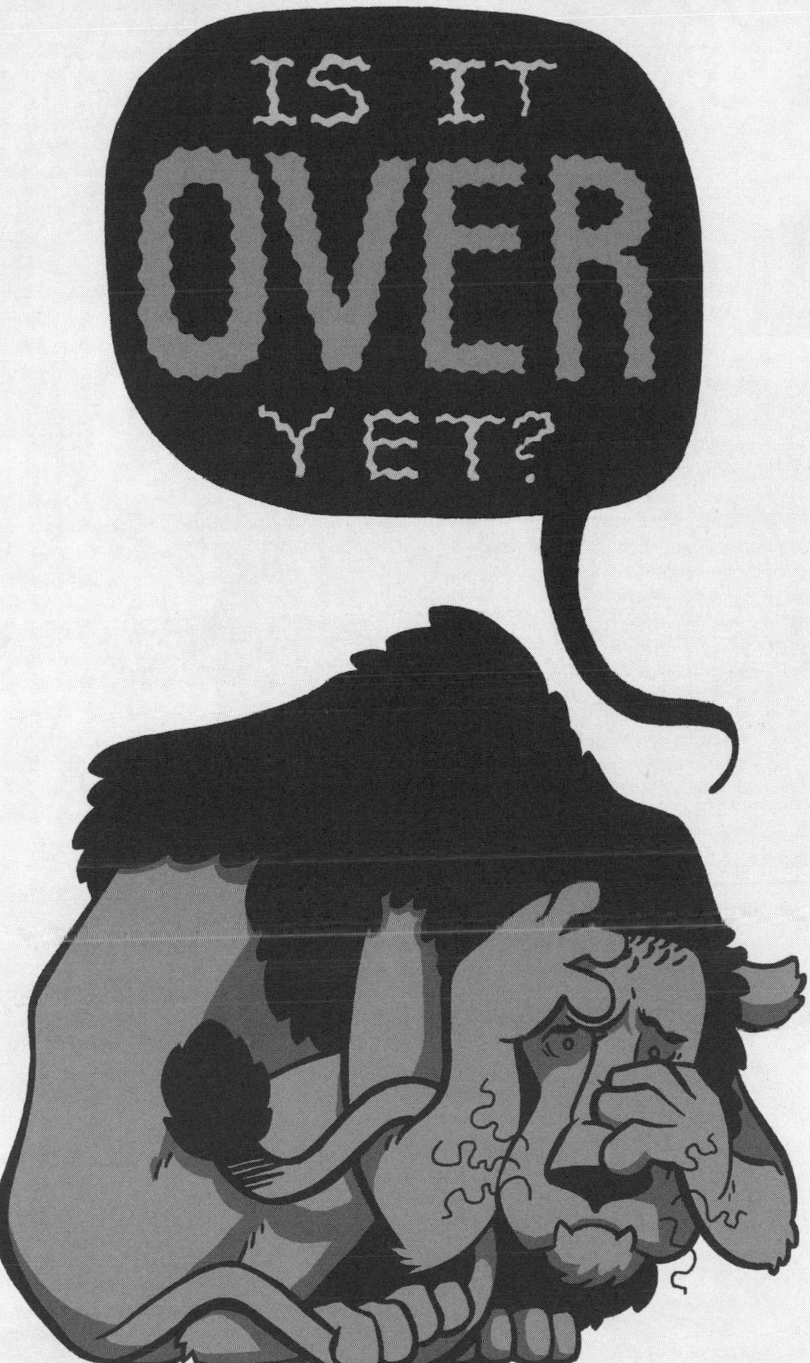
IS IT
OVER
YET?

Tommy Kovac grew up with the Oz books by L. Frank Baum, thanks to parents who encouraged reading. He highly recommends you read all 14 original Oz books.*

Kovac began writing and illustrating comics in 1999. He wrote & illustrated the original series, "Stitch," "Skelebunnies," and "Autumn," through SLG Publishing. He also wrote "Wonderland" (illustrated by Sonny Liew) for SLG/Disney. It was selected for the American Library Association's "Great Graphic Novels For Teens" list for 2010.

Kovac belongs to the Society of Children's Book Writers & Illustrators, as well as a writer's critique group. He currently works full-time as a Library technician for a 7th-12th grade college prep academy, and resides in California, with his husband, Anthony. They've been together since 1990, and although they don't have 2 little dogs named Toto, they do have one little dog named Esther. She has no opinion whatsoever about Oz or L. Frank Baum.

Kovac would like to add a special thanks to the supportive and enthusiastic International Oz Club (ozclub.org) and its members, some of whom actually enjoyed being cast as villains in our book.

Though born in 1987, Andy Hirsch's childhood reading leaned more towards boys' adventure fare from decades before, especially Dad's old "Tom Swift, Jr." collection. There were also cowdogs, warrior mice, and a whole bunch more of whatever the local libraries had on hand.

Andy has been drawing since he could pick up a crayon and, thanks to an encouraging family, has rarely stopped since. He would read every comic in the paper, even the soaps, but didn't begin drawing his own until getting a "Calvin and Hobbes" book from the school's mail-order book club. In high school, he began making his own minicomics and trying his hand at the occassional webcomic. He went on to study sequential art at the Savannah College of Art and Design and graduated in 2010. "The Royal Historian of Oz" is his first published work.

Andy currently resides in the untamed suburbs of Texas with his special lady and favorite dog. They are a very good girl and boy respectively, though only one of them has a fuzzy belly.

He would like to extend his heartfelt thanks to his parents for their endless encouragement and support of an unlikely career path.

***RECOMMENDED READING: (all by L. Frank Baum)**
The Wizard of Oz · The Land of Oz · Ozma of Oz · Dorothy and the Wizard in Oz
The Road to Oz · The Emerald City of Oz · The Patchwork Girl of Oz
Tik-Tok of Oz · The Scarecrow of Oz · Rinkitink in Oz
The Lost Princess of Oz · The Tin Woodman of Oz
The Magic of Oz · Glinda of Oz

BE OFFICIAL

Show your loyalty to all things Oz and get your Official Oz Society T-Shirt today! Show your allegiance to one of the greatest secret organizations since

REDACTED

Order from
WWW.SLGCOMIC.COM/OZSHOP